# THE ESSAYS AND PUBLIC LECTURES OF JOHN CARRICK

# THE ESSAYS *and* PUBLIC LECTURES *of* JOHN CARRICK

John Carrick

WIPF & STOCK · Eugene, Oregon

THE ESSAYS AND PUBLIC LECTURES OF JOHN CARRICK



Wipf & Stock
An Imprint of Wipf and Stock Publishers
199 W. 8th Ave., Suite 3
Eugene, OR 97401

www.wipfandstock.com

PAPERBACK ISBN: 978-1-6667-7628-7
HARDCOVER ISBN: 978-1-6667-7629-4
EBOOK ISBN: 978-1-6667-7630-0

07/22/24

The author gratefully acknowledges permission to present a revised version of "Jonathan Edwards and the Deists," which first appeared in *Banner of Truth* (Aug.–Sept. 1988) 22–34.

TO

LOUISE, JONNY, AVI, & DAVID

# CONTENTS

# ACKNOWLEDGMENTS

I WOULD like to express my deep gratitude to my friend, Bill Ryan, who from the beginning has taken a kindly interest in this work and who has been very generous with his time in helping me with technological/formatting issues.

I would also like to thank my student friend, Sean Edwards, for his kind help in this project. Sean has been a kind of research assistant to me on numerous occasions in the writing of this book, and I am deeply grateful to him.

Last, but not least, I would like to express my gratitude to my wife, Linda, for her patience and support with regard to this project. Without her care and help, this book would not have been possible.

# EDWARDS IN THE HANDS OF ENGLISH PROFESSORS[1]

WRITING in 2005, Philip F. Gura, William S. Newman Distinguished Professor of American Literature and Culture at the University of North Carolina, Chapel Hill, lamented "the fact that the Yale edition has only two scholars from a literature department on the board, thus implicitly delivering Edwards to the historians and seminarians, putting out of the loop the kinds of professors of literature who, thirty years earlier, had kept him prominent in their journal articles and books. Let us recall, too, that in the 1950s Miller himself, an English professor, headed this project."[2] I do not share Gura's lament. I acknowledge readily the fact that the remarkable renaissance of interest in Jonathan Edwards in the last seventy years or so owes a great deal to professors of literature such as Perry Miller (1905–63), Cabot Professor of American Literature at Harvard University; M. X. Lesser, Professor Emeritus of English at Northeastern University; and Wilson H. Kimnach, formerly professor of English and now Presidential Professor in the Humanities at the University of Bridgeport. But I do not regard the influence of these English professors as an unmitigated blessing. Indeed, I regard their influence within the Yale project as a whole as inordinate. This influence is particularly strong in the area of the sermonic material. Of the twenty-seven projected volumes in the Yale series, six are devoted to Edwards' sermons. It is a significant fact that at least 50 percent of this sermonic material has been entrusted to English professors—volumes 10, 19, and 25. Volume 19 was edited by M. X. Lesser, and volumes 10 and 25 have been edited by Wilson H. Kimnach. Kimnach is also responsible for the "General Introduction to the Sermons: Jonathan Edwards' Art of

1. This lecture was given at the national conference of the Evangelical Theological Society, Washington, DC, Nov. 16, 2006.

2. Gura, "Lost and Found," 92.

Prophesying." This is a very significant essay on Edwards' preaching, and it essentially sets the tone for Yale's approach to his sermons.

It is impossible to ignore both the general significance and the specific views of Perry Miller in the recent rehabilitation of Jonathan Edwards. There can be no doubt that Miller was the major driving force behind the Yale edition initiated in 1957. His admiration of and his enthusiasm for Edwards are unquestionable; but some of his views on Edwards are very much open to question. Indeed, in some areas they are wildly eccentric. I do not deny that there are flashes of brilliance in Miller's influential biography *Jonathan Edwards* (1949). Particularly impressive is Miller's ability to evoke something of the atmosphere of eighteenth-century New England. The eccentricity of Miller's position emerges, however, in his views concerning what he regards as "the cryptic element in Edwards' writing":[3]

> Edwards' writing is an immense cryptogram, the passionate oratory of the revival no less than the hard reasoning of the treatise on the will. The way he delivered his sermons is enough to confirm the suspicion that there was an occult secret in them: no display, no inflection, no consideration of the audience. . . . His writings are almost a hoax, not to be read but to be seen through.[4]

The problem here lies in Miller's central thesis, which interprets Edwards almost exclusively in terms of the influence of Locke and Newton. As far as Miller is concerned, Edwards' writings—his sermons included—require an esoteric deciphering; and the double key that unlocks this cipher is, according to the Harvard scholar, that of John Locke and Sir Isaac Newton. This thesis is, I believe, massively flawed. It should be noted that it is one thing to assert that Edwards was, as a young man, significantly influenced by "the new philosophy" and "the new science" which were introduced into the curriculum at Yale ca. 1718 as a result of the Dummer gift of books; it is quite another thing to suggest that Locke and Newton constitute the keys that unlock the "immense cryptogram" of Edwards' writings. Indeed, it is difficult to avoid the conclusion that Miller was virtually obsessed with the idea that the major formative influences upon Edwards were Locke and Newton. This fact is demonstrated by specific reference to both the philosopher and the scientist on page after page of Miller's intellectual biography. Edwards' finest biographer, George M. Marsden, offers the following justifiable criticisms of

3. Miller, *Jonathan Edwards*, 50.

4. Miller, *Jonathan Edwards*, 51. Miller further insists: "The Freedom of the Will is an immense cipher" (262).

Miller's biography: "Miller's portrait is . . . a triumph of the imagination."[5] "Miller . . . let his creativity get the best of him in his biography of Edwards."[6] Marsden describes Miller's biography as "influential, brilliant, and often misleading."[7] It must, therefore, be insisted upon, *contra* Miller, that Edwards' style is not cryptic, but plain; it is not esoteric, but transparent.[8] The principal influences upon Edwards were, moreover, not Newton and Locke, but the Bible and the great heritage of the Reformers and the Puritans; and the "occult secret" that, according to Miller, lay behind the sermons and their undramatic delivery was, I contend, none other than the invisible power of the sovereign Spirit of God.

It is important to note that, to his credit, Wilson H. Kimnach rejects Miller's views with regard to Edwards' preaching:

> Ever since Perry Miller insisted throughout his critical biography, *Jonathan Edwards* . . . , that JE was habitually secretive and verbally cryptic or gnomic in his pulpit utterances, composing statements that are "almost a hoax, not to be read but to be seen through" . . . , scholars have tended to treat sermons as if they were less the "essential Edwards" than notebook entries or learned treatises. However, sustained comparison of all three categories of writing reveals no disinclination on JE's part to reveal his deepest thoughts and values to any congregation, even one composed of frontiersmen and Indians. . . . His sermons were no hoaxes.[9]

Kimnach's assessment here is both correct and shrewd; and it should be emphasized that Kimnach's analysis of Edwards' preaching is the most thorough and incisive yet to appear. Kimnach has done much to restore the significance of Edwards' sermons in academic circles. He has, in his two volumes in the Yale edition, subjected Edwards' sermons to the most searching literary analysis. But that is both the strength and the weakness of Kimnach's work. His approach is essentially academic and literary. It is insufficiently spiritual and homiletical; and its tendency is continually that of reducing Edwards' preaching to rhetorical theory.

5. Marsden, *Jonathan Edwards*, 61.

6. Miller, *Jonathan Edwards*, 60–61.

7. Miller, *Jonathan Edwards*, xvii.

8. Wilson H. Kimnach deals with Miller's eccentric, although influential, views in this respect: "Edwards did not preach 'esoteric cryptograms' over the heads of his people" (in Edwards, *Sermons and Discourses, 1743–1758*, 25:81).

9. Edwards, *Sermons and Discourses, 1743–1758*, 25:81n46.

The homiletical weakness of the various English professors significantly involved in Edwardsean scholarship emerges, I believe, in the following areas:

## 1) THE ISSUE OF THE SERMON FORM

Wilson H. Kimnach alleges that the period 1743–58 is characterized by "a long diminuendo in homiletical emphasis."[10] He observes "the notable decline in sermon composition in the 1740s and 1750s"[11] and "the virtual end of sustained effort in the composition of sermons"[12] during this period. Indeed, Kimnach detects what he describes as the ultimate *deterioration*, *fragmentation*, *disintegration*, and *marginalization* of the sermon in Edwards' hands:[13]

> The evidence of the sermon manuscripts of the forties indicates that, even before 1744, Edwards was giving several things priority over the sermons, whether in materials or effort in production. As the decade wears on, . . . the sermon booklets look more and more like bundles of waste paper and the outlines grow more and more like bare lists.[14]

> Thus in his last years Edwards seems to have continued to concern himself primarily with his studies, his publications, his role in the international clerical and intellectual community, and with such important practical matters as preserving his mission and defending his hapless Indians against the vicious depredations of frontier entrepreneurs. As a result, his career as a preacher faded away into a few scrawled lines on old notebook leaves.[15]

It should be noted that the major line of evidence for Kimnach's conclusion here is the undeniable transition on Edwards' part away from the full manuscript to the outline. This transition has now been irrefutably established by the Yale series. The transition itself is, of course, inextricably connected with a movement towards extemporaneousness in delivery. But does the evidence adduced by Kimnach support his conclusion? It is, surely,

10. Edwards, *Sermons and Discourses, 1743–1758*, 25:83.

11. Edwards, *Sermons and Discourses, 1720–1723*, 10:73.

12. Edwards, *Sermons and Discourses, 1720–1723*, 10:115.

13. See Edwards, *Sermons and Discourses, 1720–1723*, 10:36.

14. Edwards, *Sermons and Discourses, 1743–1758*, 25:23.

15. Edwards, *Sermons and Discourses, 1720–1723*, 10:127.

a *non sequitur* to assume, on the basis of an otherwise increasingly outlinish approach to sermon preparation, that Edwards' attitude to his preaching was necessarily perfunctory and his performance necessarily disappointing. The basic problem with Kimnach's position is that it fails to distinguish between *the sermon form* and *the act of preaching*. It is surely quite wrong to regard the sermon as some sort of unalterable, inviolable art form. Preachers develop; and as they develop, so the sermon form itself evolves. Indeed, both homiletical wisdom and homiletical experience indicate that (to use an Edwardsean mode of expression) "these two opposite principles" of meticulous writing and reading on the one hand and extemporaneous utterance on the other "should rise and fall, like the two opposite scales of a balance; when one rises the other sinks."[16] Thus it is absolutely certain that, as Edwards wrote less, so he extemporized more; but it is also theoretically quite possible that the diminution in writing and the increase in extemporizing indicate, not a fading, but a flowering of his career as a preacher. It is theoretically quite possible that what Edwards gained by extemporizing surpassed, or at least balanced, what he lost.

Kimnach notes that, while the Indian sermon manuscripts are "generally skimpy to skeletal,"[17] there is, in Stockbridge, "a strange Indian Summer of the sermon for three brief weeks"[18] in January 1751. But the very fact that Kimnach adverts to this "strange Indian Summer of the sermon" demonstrates that the Yale editor thinks instinctively in terms of the full manuscript. Kimnach's tacit assumption here appears to be that the full manuscript betokens maximal care and maximal performance, whereas the brief outline betokens less than maximal care and less than maximal performance. But this is a gratuitous assumption, and it tends to confuse *methodology* on the one hand with both *motivation* and *performance* on the other. Kimnach might be correct in his hypothesis, at least to some extent and in some respects; but the evidence he adduces does not establish his conclusion. So much depends, in extemporaneous preaching, upon the degree of reflection, meditation, indeed rumination upon the matter of the sermon. Mere outlines can be very deceptive.

Moreover, the tenuousness of Kimnach's line of reasoning at this point can be easily demonstrated by means of a historical analogy. It is a fact that during the first ten years of his ministry, in South Wales (1927–38), D. Martyn Lloyd-Jones wrote out one sermon each week. He did this, he

16. The allusion here is to a mode of expression utilized in Edwards, *Works* (Hickman), 1:259.

17. Edwards, *Sermons and Discourses, 1743–1758*, 25:56n31.

18. Edwards, *Sermons and Discourses, 1720–1723*, 10:125.

himself informs us, not in order to read the sermon from the pulpit, but essentially as a homiletical discipline. It is also a fact that he did not continue this particular discipline subsequent to his becoming the minister of Westminster Chapel in London. His practice throughout his ministry of thirty years in London (1938–68) was that of preaching extemporaneously from an outline, sometimes written out on the back of an envelope. A superficial comparison of his method in Wales and that in London might lead one to conclude that there was a deterioration or disintegration of the sermon form in Lloyd-Jones' hands. But this were fatally to confuse the sermon form with the act of preaching. It is utterly impossible to glean from one of Lloyd-Jones' sermon outlines either the richness of the content or the drama of the delivery. The sermon outline represents but the bare bones; it was only in the preaching of the sermon that those bare bones came to life with such energy and power. I do not pretend that the New England minister was a preacher of the calibre of the minister of Westminster Chapel. Lloyd-Jones was an orator; Edwards was not. But the analogy demonstrates the need for caution. It should never be forgotten that there is a mysterious, elusive, intangible, spiritual element in preaching that can never be fully captured merely by the scholarly examination of manuscripts.

## 2) THE ISSUE OF THE USE OF IMAGERY

It is interesting to note that, just as "Sinners in the Hands of an Angry God" has been incorporated into anthologies of American literature and has been read, as a piece of literature, by countless American students, so too this sermon has, in the last seventy years or so, been analyzed by a number of significant literary critics. In an influential article published in 1949 and entitled "The Artistry of Jonathan Edwards," Edwin H. Cady, Andrew W. Mellon Professor of English at Duke University, argued that the springs of the success of "Sinners in the Hands of an Angry God" lie in the fact that "it is in the widest sense a work of literary art.[19] . . . By all the ordinary tests, 'Sinners in the Hands of an Angry God' is a genuine work of literary art and testifies to Jonathan Edwards' right to the name of artist."[20] More precisely, Cady pinpoints the preacher's imagery as lying at the heart of this artistry: "Although thought, form, and imagery in the sermon are one, the great emotional power of the discourse comes primarily from the rich and versatile imagery."[21] Cady insists that "the secret of the effectiveness, then and since,

19. Cady, "Artistry of Jonathan Edwards," 61.
20. Cady, "Artistry of Jonathan Edwards," 72.
21. Cady, "Artistry of Jonathan Edwards," 63.

of 'Sinners in the Hands of an Angry God' resides first in the organic oneness of theme, image, and 'application.' More directly, the emotional force of the sermon springs from the imagery itself, especially from the freshly imaginative, native figures which burned into the minds of his audience Edwards' vision of the horrible predicament of the sinner without grace."[22] Cady is somewhat dismissive of what he regards as the more outworn, conventional, biblical images employed by the visiting preacher at Enfield; conversely, he emphasizes the "surprisingly homely and immediate"[23] character of what he regards as the most striking images utilized in the sermon, namely, the image of slipping—"a condition then as now realizable every New England winter"[24]—and also "the climactic figure of the entire sermon,"[25] that of the spider held over the fire—an image which would have been familiar "to a people who lived long months by the hearth."[26] In similar vein J. A. Leo Lemay, Henry Francis du Pont Winterthur Professor of English at the University of Delaware, has more recently observed that "the images add to the suspense because they are, almost invariably, suspenseful: walking on air, the waters dammed up, the drawn bow and pointed arrow, the spider images, and the falling, slipping, sliding images. The most tension-filled images are found in the Application."[27] Lemay insists that it is *inter alia* "because of its suspenseful and archetypal imagery" that "Sinners in the Hands of an Angry God" is "a masterpiece of rhetorical strategies."[28] The same tendency to view Edwards' preaching almost entirely from a *literary* or *rhetorical* standpoint also emerges in Kimnach's analysis of the source of the power of the Enfield sermon: "Probably it was the striking amalgam of colloquial immediacy and archetypal authority in the organic texture of *Sinners*, rather than a single category of tropes, that 'burned into the minds' of the people of Enfield."[29]

In response to such evaluations of "Sinners in the Hands of an Angry God" I would emphasize that I have no wish to deny Edwards' considerable literary or rhetorical skills. Indeed, I believe that these skills can be demonstrated from a wide range of his sermons. There is indeed an artistry about Edwards' greatest sermons and there is indeed an artistry about this

22. Cady, "Artistry of Jonathan Edwards," 71.
23. Cady, "Artistry of Jonathan Edwards," 66.
24. Cady, "Artistry of Jonathan Edwards," 66.
25. Cady, "Artistry of Jonathan Edwards," 67.
26. Cady, "Artistry of Jonathan Edwards," 67.
27. Lemay, "Rhetorical Strategies," 190.
28. Lemay, "Rhetorical Strategies," 191.
29. Edwards, *Sermons and Discourses, 1720–1723*, 10:210–11.

particular sermon. But the consistent tendency here—indeed, the frequent tendency of modern Edwardsean scholarship—is that of interpreting the astonishing effectiveness of "Sinners in the Hands of an Angry God," in terms of (as Harry S. Stout and Nathan O. Hatch express it) "Edwards' rhetorical genius in using verbal imagery."[30] Indeed, the evidence suggests that the history professors have been influenced in their assessment by the English professors at this point.[31] In short, the approach of these scholars tends to be *reductionistic* rather than *nuanced*; its tendency is *naturalistic* rather than *supernaturalistic*. This interpretation does not, in principle, exclude the implication that any skillful literary artist or homiletician could, almost at will, reproduce such effects as those displayed at Enfield, provided that he accumulate a sufficient number of powerful rhetorical metaphors.

## 3) THE ISSUE OF THE SPIRIT OF GOD

The problem is that rhetorical theory is utterly unable to account for Enfield, and it always will be unable to account for it. More precisely, the basic problem with the evaluations of Cady, Lemay, Kimnach, Stout, and Hatch is that, in a manner that is regrettably characteristic of this school of thought, there is, on their part, little or no overt recognition of the Spirit of God; there is little or no overt recognition either of his existence, his sovereignty, or his power. Certainly, it is important to acknowledge that the editors of the Yale series have contributed much that is both scholarly and valuable in their definitive and critical edition of Edwards' works. But the basic problem with the approach of the Yale editors of the *Sermons and Discourses* is that they tend to view Edwards' preaching almost entirely from a *literary* rather than from a *spiritual* and *homiletical* standpoint. Perry Miller, the first general editor of the Yale series, set the trend in this respect in his influential biography. "The truth is," Miller insisted, "Edwards was infinitely more than a theologian. He was one of America's five or six major artists, who happened to work with ideas instead of with poems or novels."[32] This tendency to view Edwards as an artist reemerges repeatedly in Kimnach's "General Introduction to the Sermons." Edwards is viewed by Kimnach essentially as

30. Edwards, *Sermons and Discourses, 1739–1742*, 22:401.

31. See Edwards, *Sermons and Discourses, 1739–1742*, 22:400–402.

32. Miller, *Jonathan Edwards*, xxxi. "It is this Edwards, the artist and the writer, that my volume seeks to expound" (xxxiii).

"a homiletical author"[33] or as "a homiletical artist,"[34] while the sermon itself is viewed essentially as a literary art form:

> An essay, a play, a poem, indeed any work of literature, is ultimately the product of that mysterious mental activity known as the "creative process." The making of a sermon is likewise a truly artistic process, requiring of an effective preacher a degree of imaginative power and artistic discipline at least comparable to that of a poet.[35]

I do not deny that there is an element of truth in Miller's and Kimnach's position here. There is indeed a "creative process" involved in the preparation of sermons and there is indeed a certain artistry. In the very nature of the case this process involves significant mental activity. Indeed, I lament the lack of artistry and the rhetorical impoverishment characteristic of much modern preaching. But the problem with Kimnach's assertion, however, is that, characteristically, it emphasizes the *literary* aspects of sermon preparation rather than the *spiritual* aspects. It must be insisted upon that there is something quite unique about the sermon that sets it apart from "an essay, a play, a poem, indeed any work of literature." It is essentially *a spiritual genre*; and, as such, it is essentially different in kind.

Speaking more generally of the power of Edwards' preaching, Kimnach makes this observation:

> If the proof comes from authority, whence the power? Again, it seems that the logical structure is peripheral to the source of literary power in Edwards' sermons. Though the subtle persuasion which results from a carefully structured argument is important, the prime source of power lies in Edwards' use of certain literary devices such as imagery, metaphor, repetition, and allusion.[36]

It will be noted that, while lip service is paid here to the authority of the Scriptures, no acknowledgment whatsoever is made of the Spirit of God. Kimnach insists that "the prime source of power lies in Edwards' use of certain literary devices such as imagery, metaphor, repetition, and allusion." It must surely be obvious to the Yale editors themselves that no-one would have disagreed more with this assessment than the New England preacher himself. Certainly, he would have acknowledged that such "literary devices" and "stylistic techniques" are not unimportant in the preaching of God's

33. Edwards, *Sermons and Discourses, 1720–1723*, 10:xii.
34. Edwards, *Sermons and Discourses, 1743–1758*, 25:258.
35. Edwards, *Sermons and Discourses, 1720–1723*, 10:42.
36. Edwards, *Sermons and Discourses, 1720–1723*, 10:197.

word. It is crucial to note that Edwards did not neglect language; he did not, as a preacher, despise rhetoric or neglect the use of means. Indeed, his use of means is very considerable and his rhetorical skills have been, historically, much neglected. But the crucial question is this: Can "imagery, metaphor, repetition, and allusion" raise sinners from the dead? Can such things sanctify the people of God? Can they revive God's work in the midst of the years? Are "literary devices," "stylistic techniques," and "colloquial immediacy" sufficient to accomplish such things? The very posing of the question reveals the answer. Thus the Yale editors often betray a largely naturalistic interpretation of the phenomena witnessed under Edwards' preaching ministry. Michael J. McClymond is, I believe, correct when he alleges that modern Edwardsean scholarship is often characterized by a decontextualizing and a detheologizing of Edwards' ideas: "Following Miller's lead, much of the recent scholarship on Edwards tends toward a secularizing and naturalizing interpretation of his ideas." Thus Edwards' preaching is often reduced, McClymond contends, to "rhetorical theory."[37]

I would further contend that there is such a thing as a homiletical mind; and I would contend that this homiletical mind can only be truly possessed by those that have significant experience in preaching. Preaching is an art and it is a sacred, complex, mysterious art. By definition and of necessity, I believe, this homiletical mind will not be found in those that do not preach; it will not be found in men that are English professors, and not preachers, however high their academic qualifications and however rigorous their research may be. In the very nature of the case English professors have little or no experience of that most arduous and sacred act—that of preaching the word of God week after week to sinners and saints. Indeed, they are non-practitioners of the very art that they are seeking to analyze. Such experience is surely indispensable in assessing and evaluating the more complex and even esoteric aspects of preaching. The validity of this position can be easily demonstrated, I believe, by asking this question: Would Yale University Press entrust a definitive critical edition of the works of William Shakespeare into the hands of preachers and homileticians? It was, surely, antecedently predictable that the committing of the assessment and evaluation of Edwards' sermons into the hands of English professors would result in the reduction of the sermon to a mere literary genre and the reduction of his preaching to rhetorical theory. Thus if "atheists for Edwards" need to be reminded of the ancient Anselmian adage *credo ut intelligam* (I believe in order that I may understand), is it not the case that literary critics need to be reminded of the principle (if I might coin a phrase in the homiletical

37. McClymond, *Encounters with God*, 4.

realm) *ago ut intelligam* (I practice in order that I may understand)? If *faith* is an essential prerequisite to understanding in the area of theology, then is not *practice* also an essential prerequisite to understanding in the area of preaching? *Credenda; agenda! There are things that must be believed; there are things that must be practiced!* This double gerundive is, I feel, of crucial significance with regard to a proper understanding and interpretation of the preaching of Jonathan Edwards.

# EVANGELICALS AND THE OXFORD MOVEMENT[1]

"FROM beginnings so small, from elements of thought so fortuitous, with prospects so unpromising, the Anglo-Catholic party suddenly became a power in the National Church, and an object of alarm to her rulers and friends. . . . In a very few years a school of opinion was formed, fixed in its principles, indefinite and progressive in their range; and it extended itself into every part of the country."[2] It was thus that the presiding genius of the Oxford Movement, John Henry Newman, described in later years the drama that had convulsed the religious world over a period of some twelve years, from 1833 to 1845. Variously known as Tractarianism or Puseyism, the drama of the Oxford Movement involved a remarkable rise in the fortunes and influence of the Anglo-Catholic party within our shores and beyond, the repercussions and reverberations of which are still with us today, 150 years later.

## THE POLITICAL CLIMATE

What, then, were the circumstances under which the Oxford Movement arose? Well, it was in fact a political impetus, even a political crisis—"a revolution in the relations between Church and State"[3]—which gave opportunity to the rise of the Oxford Movement and which provided its occasion. The era was one of reform, and the times were those of agitation and change. The Catholic Emancipation of 1829, for instance, now allowed Roman Catholics to sit in the Parliament at Westminster. Again, in the following year, 1830,

1. This lecture was an Annual Evangelical Library lecture and was given at Westminster Chapel, London, July 4, 1983.

2. Newman, *Apologia pro Vita Sua*, 51.

3. Chadwick, *Mind of Oxford Movement*, 14.

the Liberal Whigs came to power after a long period of Tory ascendancy, while two years later, in 1832, the triumph of the Reform Bill further weakened the Tory traditions upon which, in the minds of High Churchmen, the authority of the Church seemed to rest politically. Furthermore, the Irish Church of 1833, with its suppression of ten out of twenty-two Irish bishoprics—and that in defiance of the opinion of the established church—was the final confirmation in the minds of certain High Churchmen that this was the hour of peril for the English Church. Thus, when on Sunday, July 14, 1833, John Keble, professor of poetry at the University of Oxford, preached the assize sermon in the university pulpit, he took as his theme the alarmist one of "National Apostasy." "If it be true anywhere," said Keble, "that such enactments are forced on the Legislature by public opinion, is APOSTASY too hard a word to describe the temper of that nation?"[4] To Keble and other High Churchmen it was "the grossest Erastianism,"[5] it was "Erastian sacrilege,"[6] that a civil government—and a Whig government at that!—should seek to lay hands on the established church. Moreover, this sacrilegious invasion of the rights of the church aroused the fears of Tory High Churchmen that the new Liberal-Whig Government might engage in further intrusion and further high-handed changes with regard to the established church. Thus Keble and his friends felt that it was now time to assert that even if the church were disestablished, even if there were a complete separation between church and state, and even if the state followed the example of the United States of America and became outwardly and constitutionally indifferent to religion, the Church of England still retains a claim upon the allegiance of Englishmen precisely because this church teaches Catholic truth, and as such manifests itself to be the authorized and commissioned agent of Christ and his apostles to the people of this country. Thus John Keble, in his sermon of July 14, 1833, issued a call for devotion to "the cause of the Apostolical Church in these realms."[7] For Keble and his fellow High Churchmen, the authority of the church did not rest upon the authority of the state; the church possessed a divine authority whatever the state may do, and that divine authority lay for them in the doctrine of the apostolic succession.

John Keble's assize sermon of July 14, 1833, marks, then, the commencement of the Oxford Movement. John Henry Newman, for his part, informs us in his *Apologia* that he "ever considered and kept the day, as the

4. Keble, *National Apostasy*, 16.
5. Cited in Vidler, *Age of Revolution*, 50.
6. Vidler, *Age of Revolution*, 49.
7. Keble, *National Apostasy*, 26.

start of the religious movement of 1833."[8] In the course of the next eight years some ninety "tracts" were published, issuing in the main from the pens of John Henry Newman, Edward Bouverie Pusey, John Keble, Richard Hurrell Froude, Charles Marriott, and Isaac Williams, all of whom, significantly (with the one exception of Isaac Williams), were fellows of Oriel College, Oxford. The first of these Tracts was published by Newman on September 9, 1833, and in this tract Newman reiterated Keble's emphasis upon the apostolic succession. "I fear we have neglected," he wrote, "the real ground on which our authority is built—OUR APOSTOLICAL DESCENT."[9] Bishops, he asserted, were the "SUCCESSORS OF THE APOSTLES," and ministers of the Church of England were appointed the "assistants, and in some sense representatives" of the bishops by the laying on of hands.[10] There was, Newman contended, this unbroken historic succession, this lineal descent from the apostles themselves which gave authentic standing to the Church of England within Christendom.

This, then, was the Tractarians' initial counterblast against what they perceived to be Liberal aggression and the scourge of Erastianism—a scourge which Newman described as "that *double usurpation*, the interference of the Church in temporals, of the State in spirituals."[11] Moreover, the Tractarian mind tended to perceive a connection between Erastianism and Liberalism. "With Froude," wrote Newman, "Erastianism,—that is the union of Church and State,—was the parent, or if not the parent, the serviceable and sufficient tool, of liberalism. Till that union was snapped, Christian doctrine never could be safe."[12]

The Tractarian mind of 1833 was, then, strongly anti-Erastian. Indeed, Newman himself asserted some thirty years later that "those anti-Erastian views of Church polity . . . were one of the most prominent features of the Tractarian movement."[13] However, there were other factors involved besides the political situation in England. July 1830, for instance, had witnessed the downfall of the Restoration monarchy in France—a new revolution, this, which appeared to be directed against the church as well as against the throne, and which sent a shudder of alarm through conservative circles everywhere. "The French," wrote Newman to Hurrell Froude, "are an awful people. . . . This revolution seems to me the triumph of irreligion. . . . The

8. Newman, *Apologia pro Vita Sua*, 23.

9. Vidler, *Age of Revolution*, 50.

10. Cited in Reardon, *Religious Thought in Reformation*, 97.

11. Cited in Newman, *Apologia pro Vita Sua*, 8.

12. Newman, *Apologia pro Vita Sua*, 25–26.

13. Newman, *Apologia pro Vita Sua*, 8.

effect of this miserable French affair will be great in England."[14] Its effect on Newman himself was certainly considerable, for he himself tells us that when in Algiers during his Mediterranean journey of 1832–33, he could not bring himself to look at the tricolor on a French vessel there, and that when he was passing through Paris, he kept indoors for the whole period of twenty-four hours, such was his evident sensitivity to the pollution of Liberalism.

## LIBERALISM

However, it was not merely the politics of France which concerned the Tractarians; it was also the theology of Germany. For if the age was one of political reform and revolution in England and France, then it was equally one of theological innovation and reconstruction in Germany. Friedrich Schleiermacher, the man widely regarded as "the father of modern theology," had founded a whole new era in theology. It was an era of theological reinterpretation and reconstruction; the era of liberal theology had already begun, and Schleiermacher himself was now at his life's end.

Thus, as conservatives both in their politics and in their theology, the Tractarians were opposed to Liberalism in all its forms. As conservatives they feared the undermining of authority and tradition, they feared the destruction of consensus. New ideas were being propagated and filled the air; there was this "licence of opinion"[15] abroad, this "false liberty of thought";[16] there was this "free market in opinions."[17] Political Liberalism and religious Liberalism were thus identified in their minds, even confused, and were regarded as utterly anti-Christian. "The more serious thinkers among us," wrote Newman, "are used . . . to regard the spirit of Liberalism as the characteristic of the destined Antichrist."[18] Newman's battle, then, was with Liberalism; he felt that a stand had to be made against the liberal menace; and the essence of that menace lay in "the anti-dogmatic principle."[19] "The vital question was," wrote Newman, "how were we to keep the Church from being liberalized?"[20] A countermovement was clearly needed, he felt, and

14. Vidler, *Age of Revolution*, 45.
15. Newman, *Apologia pro Vita Sua*, 193.
16. Newman, *Apologia pro Vita Sua*, 193.
17. Chadwick, *Secularization of European Mind*, 27.
18. Newman, *Apologia pro Vita Sua*, 129.
19. Newman, *Apologia pro Vita Sua*, 191.
20. Newman, *Apologia pro Vita Sua*, 20.

the fundamental principle of that countermovement would be "the principle of dogma."[21] The Tractarians would take refuge in the dogmas of the ancient and undivided church.

Why was it, however, that the leaders of the Oxford Movement did not take refuge in the evangelical principle of "Scripture alone"? Why did they not, as a counterblast to theological Liberalism, reassert the divine authority of the Holy Scriptures alone, the great *sola scriptura* principle of the Reformation? For Newman the answer to this question lay in the connection which he perceived between the Reformation and Liberalism itself. "The spirit of lawlessness," he wrote, "came in with the Reformation, and Liberalism is its offspring."[22] "Rationalism," asserted Newman, "is the great evil of the day. . . . I am more certain that the Protestant [spirit], which I oppose, leads to infidelity, than that which I recommend, leads to Rome."[23] Newman was in fact tragically wrong on both scores here. On the one hand he overstates his case considerably when he asserts that the Protestant spirit leads to infidelity and that Liberalism is the offspring of the Reformation. For while Evangelicals are prepared to concede that both political and theological liberalism were ultimate by-products of the liberating spirit of the Reformation, they emphasize that theological Liberalism or Rationalism, for its part, was a corruption, and not a legitimate development, of the principles of the Reformation; they are under no obligation historically to posit anything more than this indirect connection between them. On the other hand, Newman's own secession to Rome in 1845 proves that the pathway of Catholic dogma does lead irresistibly in the direction of Rome.

In Newman's mind there, was, however, this strange identification between the spirit of Evangelicalism and the spirit of Liberalism. "I thought little of the Evangelicals as a class," Newman wrote. "I thought they played into the hands of the Liberals."[24] The connecting link in his mind was the principle or right of private judgment—a principle or right claimed both by Evangelicals and Liberals. Here again, however, Newman is guilty of failing to distinguish between things that differ; for the principle of private judgment as exercised by the Bereans, who "searched the scriptures daily, whether those things were so" (Acts 17:11) is quite different from the principle of private judgment as exercised by Friedrich Schleiermacher, who searched the scriptures regularly and sifted out those things that offended. In the former case the right of private judgment was exercised by men under

21. Newman, *Apologia pro Vita Sua*, 80.

22. Newman, *Apologia pro Vita Sua*, 129.

23. Newman, *Apologia pro Vita Sua*, 91.

24. Newman, *Apologia pro Vita Sua*, 21.

authority; in the latter case it was exercised by a man who had cut loose from external authority. Newman, however, failed to make this vital distinction, and as a result he tended to speak of Evangelicals and Evangelicalism in a very dismissive way, as if Evangelicalism were directly responsible for Liberalism! Thus it was not a return to evangelical doctrine which Newman and his fellow Tractarians urged; it was a return to the dogmas of the early centuries, the dogmas of the "church catholic and apostolic."

## THE ROMANTIC SPIRIT

There was, however, one further crucial factor in the rise of the Oxford Movement, and that was the spirit of the age. Newman himself concedes this when in his *Apologia*, he speaks of "a spirit afloat": "It was not so much a movement," he contended, "as a 'spirit afloat'"; it was within us, 'rising up in hearts where it was least suspected.'"[25] There was a particular climate, a particular atmosphere that prevailed—it was the Romantic environment of the day. Indeed, in his *Apologia*, Newman specifically mentions four of the great literary figures of the time—Sir Walter Scott, Robert Southey, William Wordsworth, and Samuel Taylor Coleridge. It was these men, Newman asserted, who prepared the imagination of the nation for the reception of Catholic truth. "Walter Scott," he wrote, ". . . turned men's minds in the direction of the middle ages."[26] Scott stimulated an interest in the medieval and the Gothic, an interest in antiquarianism. The Romantic mind, living in the Railway age, the age of the Industrial Revolution, felt at odds with the present, and felt this nostalgia for the past, the remote, and was greatly attracted by Scott's enchantment with the Middle Ages. The longing for "a deeper philosophy," "a higher philosophy,"[27] was part of the spirit of the age, so that the spirit of Tractarianism was, in Newman's words, "an adversary in the air, . . . unapproachable and incapable of being grasped, as being the result of causes far deeper than political or other visible agencies, the spiritual awakening of spiritual wants."[28]

What, then, was the essence of the Romantic spirit? Feeling, emotion, the cult of sensibility, sincerity, intensity, freedom, spontaneity, self-expression, instinct, impulse, intuition, mystery, depth, imagination, fantasy, vision, wonder, reverence, and awe—these are the notes which are of the essence of Romanticism. A dramatic reaction against the Enlightenment

25. Newman, *Apologia pro Vita Sua*, 66.
26. Newman, *Apologia pro Vita Sua*, 65.
27. Newman, *Apologia pro Vita Sua*, 65.
28. Newman, *Apologia pro Vita Sua*, 66.

of the nineteenth century had set in, and the Romantic movement was a vital part of that great swing of opinion against reason—the cold and barren concept of reason as taught by John Locke and accepted by the age of the Enlightenment. Throughout Europe there had been this great revolt against reason, logic, philosophy, and the empiricism of science. It was a "flight from Reason," a protest against rationalism in both art and life, an "almost universal turning from the head towards the heart."[29] Listen, for instance, to these lines from Wordsworth's poem "The Tables Turned":

> One impulse from a vernal wood
> May teach you more of man,
> Of moral evil and of good,
> Than all the sages can.[30]

Wordsworth is critical of "our meddling intellect," he is critical of "books," and instead he idealizes "spontaneous wisdom" and nature as our teacher.[31] The influence of Wordsworth upon the spirit of the age during the first three decades of the eighteenth century had been considerable, and by the 1830s the stars of both Wordsworth and Coleridge in Cambridge were in the ascendant. The Romantic movement reached its apogee in this decade.

Now, it is most significant that the leading Tractarians were in fact poets. John Keble was, of course, professor of poetry at Oxford from 1831 to 1841. Isaac Williams would almost certainly have been Keble's successor as professor of poetry in 1841 but for the controversy caused by his tracts on "reserve." Edward Pusey was regarded as the *doctor mysticus* of the movement, while John Henry Newman's remarkable gift for writing haunting prose was that of a genius. Listen to Newman's views on poetry: "Poetry," he writes,

> does not address the reason, but the imagination and affections; it leads to admiration, enthusiasm, devotion, love. The vague, the uncertain, the irregular, the sudden, are among its attributes and sources. Hence it is that a child's mind is so full of poetry because he knows so little; and an old man of the world so devoid of poetry, because his experience of facts is so wide.[32]

There is this typically Romantic trait—the idealization of a childlike or primitive view of the world—a view which is essentially poetic. "Alas!"

29. Chadwick, *Mind of Oxford Movement*, 55.
30. Wordsworth, "Tables Turned," stanza 6.
31. Wordsworth, "Tables Turned," stanzas 7, 3, 5.
32. Cited in Newsome, *Two Classes of Men*, 33.

wrote Newman on another occasion, "what are we doing all through life . . . but unlearning the world's poetry, and attaining to its prose!"[33] It is this wistful idealization of poetry and of the poetical that is so striking and so significant here on Newman's part, for it is the wistful idealization of an essentially Romantic mind.

Furthermore, the Romantic mind felt that the poet enjoyed a particular insight into reality, an intuitive perception of truth, even powers of divination. It was the imagination of the poet that enabled him to lift the veil upon reality. Listen for instance to William Blake:

> One Power alone makes a Poet:
> Imagination, The Divine Vision.[34]

The Romantic poet thus saw himself as a visionary—a visionary who, in his yearning for the infinite, was able by force of imagination to penetrate the veiled mysteries of the universe. All things, Coleridge once wrote, "counterfeit infinity,"[35] and if all things "counterfeit infinity," then everything can be taken as symbolical, as a type or a shadow of another world. Listen again to Coleridge:

> For all that meets the bodily sense I deem
> Symbolical, one mighty alphabet
> For infant minds; and we in this low world
> Placed with our back to bright Reality,
> That we may learn with young unwounded ken
> The substance from its shadow.[36]

Now there can be no doubt but that Coleridge's influence upon Newman was considerable, despite their differences. Newman himself wrote on one occasion: "Material phenomena are both the types and the instruments of real things unseen."[37] The natural world is regarded as an emblem of the unseen, spiritual world. David Newsome is thus quite correct when he writes that "Newman's fellow-Romantics . . . saw in the finite world glimpses of infinity, through their power to read the symbolism or to exercise the poetic imagination."[38] It was this "sacramentalism of nature and the world"[39] which

33. Cited in Newsome, *Two Classes of Men*, 68.
34. Blake, *Complete Writings*, 782.
35. Cited in Newsome, *Two Classes of Men*, 22.
36. Cited in Newsome, *Two Classes of Men*, 36.
37. Newman, *Apologia pro Vita Sua*, 12.
38. Newsome, *Two Classes of Men*, 70.
39. Chadwick, *Mind of Oxford Movement*, 18.

the Tractarians imbibed from the Romantics, and which explains to a very significant degree the deepening theological sacramentalism of the Oxford Movement. It was thus, wrote Newman, that Coleridge "made trial of his age, and succeeded in interesting its genius in the cause of Catholic truth."[40]

There is, then, a natural coalescing between the spirit and ethos of Romanticism and the spirit and ethos of Catholicism. John Henry Newman himself virtually concedes this when he writes, "The Church of Rome . . . alone, amid all the errors and evils of her practical system, has given free scope to the feelings of awe, mystery, tenderness, reverence, devotedness, and other feelings which may be especially called Catholic,"[41] and a crucial part of this natural coalescing between the Romantic spirit and the Catholic spirit is the symbolic and sacramental worldview which unites them both. "This poetic strand," writes Professor Owen Chadwick, " . . . was part of that symbolic and sacramental consciousness which formed the deepest link . . . between Romanticism and Catholicism."[42] John Henry Newman, despite his evangelical background, became a Catholic, and ultimately a Roman Catholic, because he was by nature and by temperament a Romantic.

## THE TRACTARIAN RULE OF FAITH

We turn now, then, to the vital issue of the Tractarians' rule of faith. Their appeal was not exclusively to the Scriptures; it was also to "antiquity." Their great emphasis was avowedly and unashamedly upon antiquity, ancient religion, the Fathers, the creeds, apostolic tradition, the witness of the primitive church. It was here that authority lay for the Tractarian mind. There was in the Tractarians this distinct veneration and idealization of the past which harmonized well with the backward glance of the Romantics. Did not Newman himself, when describing the spirit of the age, speak of "the general need of something deeper and more attractive, than what had offered itself elsewhere"[43]? This, the Tractarians felt, was to be found in the Catholic heritage of the Fathers, and it is interesting and of significance to note that the deep Platonism of the Fathers harmonized well with the Neoplatonism of the Romantic mind. Thus while it is true to say that the threat of Liberalism drove the Tractarians back to the past by way of reaction, it is also true to say that the charm of Romanticism lured them back to the past by way of

40. Newman, *Apologia pro Vita Sua*, 65.

41. Newman, *Apologia pro Vita Sua*, 112.

42. Chadwick, *Mind of Oxford Movement*, 64.

43. Newman, *Apologia pro Vita Sua*, 65.

attraction. They took refuge in the teaching of the fathers, and clearly felt that they had found a principle of authority to which they could appeal.

The influence of Dr. Hawkins in this respect was considerable. Newman's predecessor in the pulpit of St Mary's, Dr. Hawkins was later to become the provost of Oriel College, and it was from Dr. Hawkins that Newman gained his doctrine of tradition. As an undergraduate Newman heard Dr. Hawkins preach his famous sermon on the subject of tradition, and it was a sermon which subsequently was to make a most serious impression upon him. "Dr Hawkins . . . ," wrote Newman,

> lays down a proposition, self-evident as soon as stated, to those who have at all examined the structure of Scripture, viz. that the sacred text was never intended to teach doctrine, but only to prove it, and that, if we would learn doctrine, we must have recourse to the formularies of the Church; for instance to the Catechism, and to the Creeds. He considers, that, after learning from them the doctrines of Christianity the inquirer must verify them by Scripture.[44]

Thus Newman adopted, unquestioningly it seems, this idea from Dr. Hawkins that it is the church that teaches doctrine, while the Scriptures simply prove and verify the doctrine thus taught. We have here from the leader of the Oxford Movement a prime example of what William Cunningham described as "that depreciation of the Scriptures, that denial of their fitness, because of their obscurity and alleged imperfection, to be a sufficient rule or standard of faith, which stamp so peculiar a guilt and infamy upon . . . Tractarianism."[45] The Scriptures are subordinated by the Tractarians into a position which is merely secondary, while the creeds are elevated into a position which is primary. "Whatever doctrine the primitive ages unanimously attest," wrote Newman, "whether by consent of the Fathers, or by Councils, or by the events of history, or by controversies . . . is to be received as coming from the Apostles.[46] . . . The fundamental or essential doctrines are those which are contained in the Creed."[47] Thus Newman and the other Tractarians emphasized what they regarded as "the original deposit" of Christian truth—a deposit which was to be found in the so-called "orthodox consensus" and in which, they contended, all branches of the church agreed.

44. Newman, *Apologia pro Vita Sua*, 6.
45. Cunningham, *Historical Theology*, 1:186.
46. Cited in Chadwick, *Mind of Oxford Movement*, 123.
47. Cited in Chadwick, *Mind of Oxford Movement*, 125.

Clearly, then, the Tractarian rule of faith involved an open denial of the great *sola scriptura* principle of the Protestant Reformation. Tradition was elevated by the Tractarians into a joint rule of faith. "God's unwritten word," "the primitive, unwritten system," demanded for them the same reverence as his written word. There was for them this double rule of faith—the Bible *and* tradition. John Keble, for his part, clothed this idea in his own poetic language: "Tradition and Scripture were at first two streams flowing down from the mountain of God, but their waters presently became blended, and it were but a vain and unpractical inquiry, to call upon every one who drinks of them to say, how much of the healing draught came from one source, and how much from the other"[48]—an example, this, of a poetic and unscriptural analogy, dangerous at once for its poetry and its analogical reasoning.

But how did the Tractarians endeavour to define "tradition" itself? Well, at this point they had recourse to the Rule of Vincentius of Lérins, formulated in AD 434—*Quod semper, quod ubique, quod ab omnibus* (That which has *always* been believed, that which has been believed *everywhere*, that which has been believed *by all men*). John Keble was expressing the same idea when he spoke of "Antiquity, Universality, Catholicity."[49] It was the idea of a universal consensus on dogma, the idea of "catholic consent"; it was the old idea, familiar in the early centuries, of an "orthodox consensus" which was regarded as normative; and it was via this consensus that the Tractarians felt that they would recover for the church the Catholic heritage which it had lost.

The vital question, however, remains, and it is this: How valid and how practicable was this appeal to the orthodox consensus of the Fathers? William Goode, the most able and incisive Anglican assailant of Tractarian doctrine, pointed out that while the *theory* of the Tractarians was that "catholic consent" only can be relied upon, that which they "*practically* rely upon to prove this consent is often the dictum of half a dozen Fathers."[50] In other words, there was this strong selective, indeed arbitrary, element in the Tractarian approach to the Fathers. Newman himself, during his years of personal crisis after 1841, came to acknowledge that "after all we must use private judgment upon Antiquity."[51] Moreover, William Goode pointed out quite correctly that "the witness of Patristical Tradition . . . is of a discordant kind, and that even in fundamental points." There are these mutual contradictions among the fathers in that one Father destroys what another seeks

48. Cited in Chadwick, *Mind of Oxford Movement*, 130

49. Cited in Chadwick, *Mind of Oxford Movement*, 127.

50. Cited in Toon, *Evangelical Theology*, 126; emphasis original.

51. Newman, *Apologia pro Vita Sua*, 76.

to establish. Goode therefore contended, rightly, that the whole notion of a consentient testimony was "a mere dream of the imagination."[52]

What becomes, then, of the Rule of Vincentius which is so fundamental to the "orthodox consensus" and the concept of "catholic consent"? Well, at this point the Achilles' heel of this particular rule lies upon its very surface. It is a rule which appears to be completely oblivious to the power and tenacity of heresy. Jaroslav Pelikan, in *The Emergence of the Catholic Tradition*, writes that "it was inconceivable to the exponents of the orthodox consensus that there could be any contradiction between Scripture properly interpreted and the tradition of the ancient fathers."[53] The mere possibility that heresy might be found lurking within the "orthodox consensus" is dismissed *a priori* as inconceivable. Such a position betokens both a naïve underestimation of the depravity of man's heart and mind, and a naïve overestimation of the providential preservation of pure doctrine. The result is that this Rule of Vincentius actually *fossilizes* any heresy that is widely accepted as truth. It is a rule which not only includes light and excludes darkness, it also includes darkness and excludes light. It sanctions, perpetuates, and fossilizes ancient heresy as well as ancient orthodoxy. The ultimate effect of this rule, so fundamental to the concept of tradition, is to *inject* the word of man into the word of God and thus, like the traditions of Pharisaism, to make the word of God of none effect. It is for this reason that Merle d'Aubigné, in the course of a lecture given in 1842 entitled "Geneva and Oxford," spoke of this whole concept of tradition as being "a species of rationalism." It is one of the tragic ironies of the rise of the Oxford Movement that in fleeing from the rationalism of Germany, the Tractarians did but flee into the arms of a different rationalism—a rationalism "which introduces into Christian doctrine, as a rule, not the human reason of the present time, but the human reason of times past."[54]

When we turn to the creeds, however, it is a more subtle deficiency that we observe, namely, the relative silence of the creeds on certain vital doctrines. For while the creeds are generally excellent as a summary of scriptural doctrine on the subjects of the Trinity and the Person of Christ, there is in them a comparative neglect with regard to the doctrines of anthropology and soteriology. The doctrines of grace are thrown into the background, and there is this great inadequacy and insufficiency with regard to the divine method of the justification of the sinner. As W. G. T. Shedd emphasizes,

52. Cited in Toon, *Evangelical Theology*, 126.

53. Pelikan, *Emergence of Catholic Tradition*, 336–37.

54. Aubigné, *Geneva and Oxford*, 22.

the creeds are "inferior as to comprehensiveness."[55] There are these ancient omissions, these ancient deficiencies about them which render any return to the "ancient religion" of the early centuries potentially dangerous since, as Dr. Shedd rightly contends, "there was no barrier, of a *theoretical* kind, to the entrance of . . . the legalistic theory of justification."[56] Evangelical Protestants, therefore, are quite entitled to point out that the very rise of the Oxford Movement within the bosom of the Church of England was in no small measure due to the defectiveness, inadequacy, and insufficiency of the very creeds to which the Tractarians so gladly appealed.

## THE DOCTRINE OF JUSTIFICATION

We turn now, then, to the subject of the divine method of the justification of the sinner—a subject of such vital importance that the apostle Paul, in his epistle to the Galatians, pronounces the double anathema of God upon those who would fain pervert the doctrine of justification by faith alone in Christ. This was the doctrine which Martin Luther reputedly described as "the article of the standing or the falling of the church"; and yet it is also a doctrine upon which the creeds of the early centuries are silent. Now it was to this biblical doctrine of justification by faith alone in the merits and the work of Jesus Christ that the Tractarians showed considerable opposition. In 1843 a writer in the *British Critic* wrote of "the soul-destroying heresy of Luther on the subject of Justification,"[57] while Newman, for his part, had come to reject the doctrine of imputed righteousness which, from his evangelical days, he appears to have held from 1816 until 1826. He, like other Tractarians, felt that Evangelicalism bred mere antinomianism, and that the doctrine of justification by faith alone was therefore immoral because of this alleged result. Clearly Newman felt disillusioned by the low level of personal sanctification among Evangelicals. His great admiration for the Evangelical Thomas Scott was based upon the latter's "bold unworldliness"[58] and upon "his resolute opposition to Antinomianism."[59] However, as far as Newman was concerned, Evangelicalism had lost the spirit of Thomas Scott and had succumbed both to worldliness and antinomianism. "The Evangelical party itself," wrote Newman, ". . . seemed to have lost that simplicity and

55. Shedd, *History of Christian Doctrine*, 2:440.
56. Shedd, *History of Christian Doctrine*, 2:440, 441–42; emphasis original.
57. Cited in Toon, *Evangelical Theology*, 141.
58. Newman, *Apologia pro Vita Sua*, 3.
59. Newman, *Apologia pro Vita Sua*, 4.

unworldliness which I admired so much in . . . Scott."[60] It was Newman's perception of defects among Evangelicals in this respect that constitutes one of the factors which drove him increasingly away from Evangelicalism and in the direction of Catholicism.

However, if Newman regarded the evangelical doctrine of justification as unsound and erroneous, it is also true to say that in the earlier years of the Oxford Movement he regarded the Roman Catholic doctrine of justification as defective. Thus in his *Lectures on Justification*, published in 1838, Newman sought to steer a middle course between the Protestant and Roman Catholic doctrines of justification. He sought to establish a *via media* doctrine of justification, an intermediate doctrine, a new synthesis which would, he felt, fuse into one new doctrine the primary aspects of both Protestantism and Roman Catholicism. These *Lectures* he therefore regarded as "an Irenicon";[61] they had an irenic, even ecumenical, aim and purpose. "Their drift," he wrote, "is to show that there is little difference but what is verbal in the various views on justification whether found among Catholic or Protestant divines."[62] "I wished to fill up a ditch, the work of man."[63]

Newman contended, therefore, in his *Lectures* that "Justification by faith" and "Justification by obedience" are not "opposite doctrines," but "separate" and "not at all inconsistent with each other." He urged, indeed, that they are "so compatible in themselves, that they may be held both at once, or indifferently, either the one or the other," as being "but two modes of stating the same truth." Again, he asserted that "Justification by faith" and "Justification by baptism" need not be opposed to one another, for "baptism may be considered the instrument on God's part, faith on ours." "Baptism makes faith justifying." Thus, whereas the method of the Scriptures on this vital doctrine is that of antithesis or contrast, Newman's method is that of synthesis. "Justification," he wrote, "comes *through* the Sacraments; is received *by* faith; *consists* in God's inward presence, and *lives* in obedience. . . . Whether we say we are justified by faith, or by works, or by Sacraments, all these but mean this one doctrine, that we are justified by grace, which is given through Sacraments, impetrated by faith, manifested in works."[64]

But what saith the Scripture? Well, clearly the Scriptures define the divine method of the justification of the sinner in both negative and positive

60. Newman, *Apologia pro Vita Sua*, 20.

61. Dessain, "Sources of Newman's Power," 111.

62. Dessain, "Sources of Newman's Power," 121.

63. Newman, *Apologia pro Vita Sua*, 48.

64. Cited in Cunningham, *Historical Theology*, 2:123; emphasis original.

terms. Indeed, it is crucial that a doctrine as vulnerable to heresy as that of the divine method of the sinner's justification should be safeguarded by the use of both negative and positive terms. The negative statements are just as important as the positive statements for the apostle Paul. "Knowing," he writes to the Galatian church, "that a man is not justified by the works of the law, but by the faith of Jesus Christ, even we have believed in Jesus Christ, that we might be justified by the faith of Christ, and not by the works of the law: for by the works of the law shall no flesh be justified" (Gal 2:16). The apostle Paul, with his remarkable emphases and repetition here, defines justification in terms of antithesis, and not in terms of synthesis. Justification by faith alone and justification by works are opposites, and cannot be reconciled. Any attempt, therefore, to fuse justification by faith alone and justification by works, will inevitably result in the destruction of the system of justification by faith alone. There is no possible *via media* between these two positions; they are utterly incompatible and totally irreconcilable. G. S. Faber was right, therefore, to underline the logical absurdity of a position in which, according to Newman,

> we are justified by faith; we are justified by obedience; we are justified by baptism; we are justified conjointly by the two sacraments of baptism and the Lord's Supper. Our Justification precedes our faith, and our faith precedes our Justification. The word Justification cannot bear two meanings, yet it clearly does bear two meanings, to wit, the *accounting* righteous, and the *making* righteous. There is but one act of Justification, nevertheless there are ten thousand Justifications.[65]

Faber was right to describe Newman's *Lectures* as "a tissue of contradictions and inconsistencies."[66] For it is manifest that although Newman had an extremely subtle and ingenious mind, he did not have a very logical mind; there is this element of irrationality in Newman. Genius though he was in many respects, his avowed antipathy to logic is his Achilles' heel. "Newman," writes Professor Owen Chadwick, "dismissed theological logic."[67] "He is always skimming," writes G. M. Young, "along the verge of a logical catastrophe."[68] Now this antipathy to logic is one of the most significant features of the Romantic mind. David Newsome, in his fascinating book entitled *Two Classes of Men*, has shown that the Romantics seized upon "the idea of the reconciliation of opposites as the universal law for which they

65. Cited in J. Buchanan, *Doctrine of Justification*, 229; emphasis original.

66. Cited in J. Buchanan, *Doctrine of Justification*, 229.

67. Chadwick, *Newman*, 12.

68. Cited in Newsome, *Two Classes of Men*, 72.

strength and subtlety of Romish theology—made the following cogent and incisive statement with regard to the "sacramental principle" of the Oxford Movement:

> If popery be Satan's masterpiece, the theory and practice of the sacraments may perhaps be regarded as the most finished and perfect department in this great work of his. And it is not in the least surprising, that when recently the great adversary set himself to check and overturn the scriptural and evangelical principles which were gaining a considerable influence in the Church of England, he should have chiefly made use of the sacramental principle for effecting his design,—that is, the principle that there is an invariable connection between participation in the sacraments and the enjoyment of spiritual blessings, and that the sacraments have an inherent power or virtue whereby they produce these appropriate effects. In no other way, and by no other process, could he have succeeded to such an extent as he has done, in leading men to disregard and despise all that Scripture teaches us concerning our helpless and ruined condition by nature; concerning the necessity of a regeneration of our moral nature by the power of the Holy Spirit; concerning the way and manner in which, according to the divine method of justification, pardon and acceptance have been procured and are bestowed; concerning the place and function of faith in the salvation of sinners; and concerning the true elements and distinguishing characteristics of all those things that accompany salvation,—and, finally, in no other way could he have succeeded to such an extent in leading men who have been ministers in a Protestant church to submit openly and unreservedly to that system of doctrine and practice which is immeasurably better fitted than any other to accomplish his purposes, by leading men to build wholly upon a false foundation, and to reject the counsel of God against themselves; while it is better fitted than any other to retain men in the most degrading, and, humanly speaking, the most hopeless bondage.[77]

For without ever formally denying the message of the cross, the "sacramental principle" tends by its very nature to throw the cross of Christ into the background and thus to neutralize its efficacy and power. It is this "sacramental principle" which constitutes the masterpiece within the masterpiece of Satan.

77. Cunningham, *Historical Theology*, 2:141–42.

## ATTITUDES TO THE REFORMATION

Clearly, then, the Oxford Movement, with its "sacramental principle," its doctrine of justification, and its excessive deference to the Fathers, involved a definite antagonism to the great principles of the Protestant Reformation, for it involved the attempted overthrow, by men within the Church of England, of those hallmarks of the Protestant faith—the *sola scriptura* principle, the *sola gratia* principle, and the principle of *sola fide*. Indeed, Tractarianism demonstrated itself increasingly to be anti-scriptural, anti-evangelical, and anti-Protestant; and if some Evangelicals were slow to realize or acknowledge this, then all remaining doubts on this score should have been removed by the publication in 1838 of the literary *Remains* of Newman's great friend, the deceased Richard Hurrell Froude. "Really I hate the Reformation and the Reformers more and more," Froude had written. "The Reformation was a limb badly set—it must be broken again in order to be righted."[78] Froude, a great admirer of medieval Catholicism, asserted that the Tractarian position was this: "We are Catholics without Popery, and Church of England men without Protestantism."[79] Thus, while it was true that, in the early stages at least, one of the avowed aims of the Oxford Movement was the principle of anti-Romanism, in actual fact the spirit of anti-Protestantism was a much more prominent feature of the movement, and this inevitably so, since Catholic principles and Catholic dogma are infinitely more anti-Protestant than anti-Romanist. There was this common desire among the Tractarians to undo the Reformation of the sixteenth century and to "unprotestantize" the national church.[80] Newman himself spoke of the need for "a second Reformation—a better reformation, for it would be a return not to the sixteenth century, but to the seventeenth."[81] It was a return to the theology of the Caroline divines and the nonjurors of the seventeenth century that Newman desired—a return to the High Church tradition of men such as Andrewes, Hammond, and Laud. It is not in the least surprising, therefore, that the Tractarians began to manifest an increasing indulgence of Rome, and indeed an increasing nostalgia for Rome. "Speak *gently* of thy sister's fall," John Keble had urged in his *Christian Year*.[82] Again, Hurrell Froude's dying exhortation against uncharitableness with regard to Rome had its impact upon Newman. "I learned," wrote Newman, "to have tender feelings

78. Cited in Chadwick, *Victorian Church*, 1:175.

79. Cited in Reardon, *Religious Thought in Victorian*, 95.

80. Aubigné, *Geneva and Oxford*, 8.

81. Newman, *Apologia pro Vita Sua*, 29.

82. Cited in Newman, *Apologia pro Vita Sua*, 35; emphasis original.

towards her'";[83] and by 1840 he had himself drawn up prayers for Christian unity. There was increasingly in John Henry Newman this same irenic, quasi-ecumenical spirit, and it is surely not at all without significance that the seeds of the ecumenical movement were sown in this poetic, Romantic, and sentimental climate of the Oxford Movement. It was in this climate that Christian love was elevated above Christian truth, and Christian truth was sacrificed to Christian unity; it was in this climate that men began to "put darkness for light, and light for darkness" and held up the great and glorious Protestant Reformation as the great scapegoat of the Christian church. It must never be forgotten, therefore, that the movement of 1833 which some historians hail as the "Anglican revival" of the nineteenth century was, in fact, essentially an Oxford Counter-Reformation.

## TRACT 90

As far as the Tractarians themselves were concerned, however, it was initially a *via media* or middle system that they sought to establish. This concept of the *via media* or "golden mean" was, of course, by no means new or original in the Church of England; Matthew Parker, the first Elizabethan Archbishop of Canterbury in the sixteenth century, had spoken of this "golden mean" which would, he felt, preserve within the fold of the one church both Protestants and Catholics. John Henry Newman, however, felt that the *via media* needed to be defined more closely—he wanted to draw it out into a definite shape and character. "It was not as yet objective and real," he wrote. "It was at present a paper religion."[84] Newman wanted to buttress and fortify this middle system; he wanted to prove that Anglo-Catholicism was in fact "a substantive religion."[85] It was, then, with this intention in mind that Newman published, in February 1841, Tract 90, the last and most famous of the Tracts, on the subject of the Thirty-Nine Articles. Essentially Tract 90 was, for Newman, an experiment—"a hazardous experiment,—like proving cannon,"[86] he said. He wanted to make "fair trial how much the English Church will bear,"[87] to inquire "how far the Articles were tolerant of a Catholic, or even a Roman interpretation."[88] Newman wanted to see

83. Newman, *Apologia pro Vita Sua*, 36.
84. Newman, *Apologia pro Vita Sua*, 46.
85. Newman, *Apologia pro Vita Sua*, 46.
86. Newman, *Apologia pro Vita Sua*, 90.
87. Newman, *Apologia pro Vita Sua*, 90.
88. Newman, *Apologia pro Vita Sua*, 58.

how great an infusion of Catholic truth the Church of England would bear before it burst, as it were, only to show that she was after all purely and essentially Protestant. It was his contention that the Thirty-Nine Articles were "ambiguous formularies,"[89] that they were characterized by "vagueness and indecisiveness,"[90] that there was an "elasticity"[91] about them, and that they were therefore "not uncatholic."[92] The first principle of all in Tract 90, Newman asserted, was "to take our reformed confessions in the most Catholic sense they will admit: we have no duties towards their framers."[93]

Newman's "hazardous experiment," however, failed. Tract 90 met with considerable opposition, and justifiably so, for there can be no doubt that Newman was overstating his case with regard to the alleged Catholic sense of the Thirty-Nine Articles. Evangelical Protestants are not afraid to concede, however, that Newman's case does have a certain plausibility, for it is undeniable that the Thirty-Nine Articles did provide Newman with a lever and a handle for his position. It is undeniable that there are weaknesses and deficiencies in the Thirty-Nine Articles which can be exploited by anyone who is bent on making the articles, rather than the Holy Scriptures, the judge and arbiter of truth. It cannot be denied, for instance, that article 27 is a very unsatisfactory statement on the subject of baptism and leaves the door open for a doctrine of baptismal regeneration when it asserts that "baptism is not only a sign of profession and mark of difference . . . but is also a sign of regeneration or new birth whereby, as by an instrument, they that receive Baptism rightly are grafted into the Church."[94] There is a confusion here between baptism as a sign of regeneration, and baptism as an instrument of regeneration, so that John Henry Newman would be quite entitled, in this case, to assert the "vagueness and indecisiveness," indeed the "elasticity," of this particular article. Article 27 is, indeed, in this respect, an "ambiguous formulary." Again, it cannot be denied that article 28, on the subject of the Lord's Supper, gives the Tractarians a lever and a handle for their doctrine of the real presence; for while the doctrine of transubstantiation is rejected as "repugnant to the plain words of Scripture," the door is left open for a doctrine of consubstantiation to be construed from the following statement: "The body of Christ is given, taken, and eaten, in the Supper, only after an heavenly and spiritual manner." These are words which harmonize

89. Newman, *Apologia pro Vita Sua*, 148.

90. Newman, *Apologia pro Vita Sua*, 57.

91. Newman, *Apologia pro Vita Sua*, 53.

92. Newman, "Remarks," para. 3.

93. Newman, *Apologia pro Vita Sua*, 87.

94. Protestant Episcopal Church, "Articles of Religion," art. 27.

well with Pusey's insistence upon a real, though spiritual and supernatural, presence of the body of Christ in the Lord's Supper, and may in that sense be described in Newman's words as "not uncatholic." Again, it cannot be denied that articles 32 and 36 contain some dangerous statements on the subject of "priests";[95] for in these two articles "priests" are tacitly accepted as part of the Anglican doctrine of the three orders of "Bishops, Priests, and Deacons."[96] Once again, it cannot be denied that the Church of England has never rid itself of the concept of a special priesthood; there is a Catholic undertone within the Thirty-Nine Articles.

However, it must be pointed out in response to Newman that the real issue with regard to the Thirty-Nine Articles is not in fact the degree of their "catholicity," but rather the degree of their scripturalness. The great question with regard to the articles should not be how far the articles are tolerant of a Catholic interpretation, but rather how far the articles reflect faithfully the doctrine of God's Holy Word. The great tragedy of John Henry Newman lies in his over-preoccupation, indeed his obsession, with the creeds and articles of men. It must never be forgotten that the latter are not infallible, and indeed that they are characterized by real inadequacies and deficiencies, and must themselves be ever brought to the bar of the infallible word of God. It is the Scriptures—not the articles—which "cannot be broken" (John 10:35).

For Newman, however, the opposition and hostility aroused by Tract 90 meant the demolition of the *via media* as a definite theory. Moreover, this collapse of the *via media* theory was hastened in Newman's mind by his study of the Arian controversy in the summer of 1841. Newman saw that in the Arian controversy there were three parties—the pure Arians, the semi-Arians, and Rome. The pure Arians, he contended, were the heretics; the semi-Arians represented the *via media* position; while the truth in the Arian controversy lay with the Church of Rome. Similarly in the nineteenth century, Newman asserted, Protestants are the heretics; Anglicans represent the *via media* position; while the truth lies with Rome. "The truth lay, not with the *Via Media*," Newman wrote, "but with what was called 'the extreme party.'"[97] "In the controversies of the early centuries," Newman contended, "the Roman Church was ever on the right side, which was of course a *prima facie* argument in favour of Rome and against Anglicanism now."[98] Newman's reasoning here is, of course, a classic *non sequitur*. It is a prime example of the danger of that reasoning by analogy in which he so delighted. It simply

95. Protestant Episcopal Church, "Articles of Religion," arts. 32, 36.

96. Protestant Episcopal Church, "Articles of Religion," art. 32.

97. Newman, *Apologia pro Vita Sua*, 93.

98. Newman, *Apologia pro Vita Sua*, 109.

does not follow that, because the Church of Rome was on the side of truth in the Arian controversy and in certain other controversies of the early centuries, she is necessarily on the side of truth in all other doctrines. Evangelical Protestants are ready to concede that the Church of Rome is orthodox in its doctrine of the Person of Christ and of the Trinity, just as they are ready to assert that the Church of Rome is heretical in its doctrine of the sacraments and of the justification of the sinner. Darkness and light are mixed together in the Church of Rome, and damnable heresies coexist together with certain truths. Questions of doctrine, therefore, are not settled en bloc by means of subtle, historical parallels; rather they are settled by bringing them, one by one, to the scrutiny of the Holy Word of God. Newman, however, had come by this route to the conclusion that the *via media* was "untenable," that it was "an impossible idea,"[99] that it was in fact merely "a paper system,"[100] and that the Church of England was merely a "paper Church."[101] By the end of 1841 Newman was on his "death-bed"[102] with regard to his membership of the Anglican Church.

## EVANGELICAL REACTION

Meanwhile, since the commencement of the Oxford Movement in 1833, evangelical reaction to Tractarianism had been gathering momentum. Initially, however, there was a certain sluggishness, even a certain confusion, in the response of Evangelicals to the movement. In the early days of the movement, evangelical suspicion of the Tractarians was mixed with evangelical cooperation with the Tractarians. Peter Toon, for instance, notes that within Anglican Evangelicalism in 1834 "there were those Evangelicals who were, to say the least, sympathetic to its seemingly spiritual character."[103] Thus during the first few years of the movement there was a critical delay in any serious controversy between Anglican Evangelicals and Tractarians. David Newsome, for his part, in his book *The Parting of Friends*, has shown that Gladstone was wrong in his assertion that the Evangelicals "'joined . . . in utterly condemning the Tractarian movement from the first.'"[104] Indeed Newsome asserts that "in many ways the Tractarians appeared—in the early stages of the Oxford Movement—to be the continuators of the

99. Newman, *Apologia pro Vita Sua*, 100.

100. Newman, *Apologia pro Vita Sua*, 138.

101. Cited in Reardon, *Religious Thought in Reformation*, 101.

102. Newman, *Apologia pro Vita Sua*, 99.

103. Toon, *Evangelical Theology*, 21.

104. Newsome, *Parting of Friends*, 14.

Evangelicals";[105] and Professor Owen Chadwick substantiates this idea when he writes: "There is a certain continuity of piety between the Evangelical movement and the Oxford Movement. . . . Both Newman and Pusey brought into the movement a strong element of Evangelical sensibility and language."[106] The writings of the Tractarians do indeed reveal a great insistence upon holiness, upon the loathsomeness of sin, upon the narrowness of the way, upon the vanity of this world, upon self-denial, upon unworldliness and otherworldliness, upon eternal realities "beyond the veil," upon the presence of Christ and of God. There can be no doubt but that these emphases provided a quasi-evangelical note to Tractarian teaching. However, if there was this apparent "continuity of piety" between Evangelicalism and Tractarianism, it became increasingly evident that there was not, in certain crucial areas, a continuity of doctrine. The Tractarian rule of faith, the Tractarian doctrine of justification, the "sacramental principle," and the Tractarian doctrine of "reserve"—these were the areas which proved before long that there was a great gulf fixed between the Catholic sacramentalism of the Oxford Movement on the one hand and evangelical theology on the other; and if certain Anglican Evangelicals were rather slow to recognize the dangers of Tractarianism, then this must to some extent be attributed to the Catholic undertone inherent in the formularies of Anglicanism itself.

However, if there was something of a lull before the storm, eventually the storm did break in 1837–38, and it involved a national outcry against Tractarianism. Peter Toon, in his recent work entitled *Evangelical Theology, 1833–1856: A Response to Tractarianism*, indicates that there was a tremendous output of evangelical literature in response to the Oxford Movement. "There was certainly quantity, if not quality, in the mass of material," Toon asserts.[107] Considerable quality was, however, evident in the writings of the most learned and able of the Anglican Evangelicals who responded to Tractarianism, namely, William Goode, whose scholarly writings were warmly commended by the great Scottish theologian, William Cunningham. As for the Anglican periodicals, the editor of the *Christian Lady's Magazine* described Tractarianism as an "approximation to Popery,"[108] while the *Christian Observer* spoke of "the character and evils of the system inculcated in the Oxford Tracts; which even weeping, we believe to be anti-Evangelical, anti-Protestant";[109] it was popery in disguise.

105. Newsome, *Parting of Friends*, 14.

106. Chadwick, *Mind of Oxford Movement*, 27.

107. Toon, *Evangelical Theology*, 2.

108. Cited in Toon, *Evangelical Theology*, 44.

109. Cited in Toon, *Evangelical Theology*, 32–33.

Again, an excellent critique of the Oxford Movement was produced by Merle d'Aubigné in the lecture which he delivered at the opening meeting of the Theological School of Geneva in 1842. In this lecture Aubigné argued that there had been three distinct epochs in the church prior to the Reformation—that of "Evangelical Christianity" in the first and second centuries of the church, where authority is attributed to the revealed word of God, and where it is God who reigns; that of "Ecclesiastical Catholicism," from the third to the seventh centuries, where authority is attributed to the church, and where it is man who reigns; and that of the "Roman Papacy," from the seventh to the fifteenth, where authority is attributed to the pope, and where it is Antichrist who reigns.[110] The Oxford Movement, Aubigné contended, was a "novel system of Ecclesiastical Catholicism."[111] It was "a human and sacerdotal religion"[112] which, while formally rejecting popery, "nearly approaches popery, for it already contains the germ of all the principles found there."[113] Aubigné warned that the Church of England "stood on the edge of the abyss."[114] "The Tiber flows in Oxford," he asserted; "Oxford conducts to Rome."[115]

Precisely the same note was struck by Professor James Garbett in his Bampton Lectures of 1842. "The system," he contended,

> is Romanism; not partially, but essentially; not *yet* Romanism, indeed, as historical recollections have expressed it, or as the conclusions of reason have demonstrated it to be; not Romanism in *all* its palpable and revolting incongruities to the heart and understanding. But—Romanism, as it has, in all ages, represented itself to the young and to the devout—Romanism, as it is when purified by elevated feelings, and minds originally trained in Scripture truth—Romanism, as it combines with itself all that is grand and beautiful in art, specious in reason and seductive in sentiment—Romanism, which may be safe in those scripturally-trained minds who have presented it to themselves and to the world in this beautified shape—but Romanism, still perverting the truth of the Gospel while it decorates it—Romanism, which though it looks paternally and benignly in the amiable spirits of its present advocates, involves principles ever fatal to human liberty and progression,—Romanism, with the establishment

110. Aubigné, *Geneva and Oxford*, 7.
111. Aubigné, *Geneva and Oxford*, 10.
112. Aubigné, *Geneva and Oxford*, 11.
113. Aubigné, *Geneva and Oxford*, 20.
114. Aubigné, *Geneva and Oxford*, 56.
115. Aubigné, *Geneva and Oxford*, 22.

of whose theory the Articles of the Church of England cannot coexist, and whose unseen and unavowed operations in *practice* will paralyse her spiritual power and destroy the Church of Christ, by substituting human forms for her Prophet, Priest and King.[116]

## NEWMAN'S SECESSION TO ROME

Moreover, the actual secession of John Henry Newman to the Church of Rome itself in 1845, together with a large number of his friends, may be fairly said to have settled the question of the general tendency of Tractarian or Anglo-Catholic views. "Romanism," commented William Cunningham,

> is the legitimate development of Tractarianism. . . . Tractarianism substantially agrees with Romanism in corrupting, and in the way in which it corrupts, the rule of faith, the divine method of justification, and the whole worship and government of the Church of Christ. Their agreement upon these points is great and substantial, while their differences are trifling and incidental.[117]

"It was very manifest all along," Cunningham remarked,

> that while the Tractarians expressed disapprobation of some of the particular tenets and practices of the Romanists, they had really, though probably to some extent unconsciously, embraced the whole substance, all the guiding and fundamental principles, of Popery, almost everything about it that makes it injurious to the souls of men, and ruinous to the interests of true religion.[118]

In this same article Cunningham maintained that no event of a similar nature had taken place in any Protestant Church since the Reformation, and that while individual instances of the apostasy of Protestant ministers to the Church of Rome had occurred in almost all the Reformed Churches, never before had this apostasy been exhibited on so large a scale. It was for this reason, Cunningham rightly contended, that the secession of Newman and of a large number of his friends, was "well fitted to arrest attention, and to afford useful lessons and solemn warnings to the churches of Christ."[119]

Particularly instructive are the reasons given by Newman for his joining the Church of Rome. "My one paramount reason," he wrote, "for

116. Cited in Toon, *Evangelical Theology*, 53–54.

117. Cunningham, *Church Principles*, 76.

118. Cunningham, *Church Principles*, 77.

119. Cunningham, *Church Principles*, 36.

contemplating a change is my deep, unvarying conviction that our Church is in schism, and that my salvation depends on my joining the Church of Rome.[120] . . . The simple question is, Can *I* (it is personal, not whether another, but can *I*) be saved in the English Church? Am *I* in safety, were I to die tonight? Is it a mortal sin in *me*, not joining another communion?"[121] Rome had by now cast its spell over John Henry Newman, and it was a spell that bewitched and beguiled this tragic genius, with his towering intellect, into the clutches of her bondage—a spell in which spiritual fear was mingled with Romantic attraction. Thus, in John Henry Newman we see the workings of the Catholic mind, with its great emphasis upon the visible church and upon the visible unity of the church, with its great fear of lying outside of Rome, with its conviction that salvation depends upon the church, and with its readiness to be greatly impressed and overawed by the massive historical phenomenon of Rome. "My mind fell back upon itself in relaxation and in peace," wrote Newman after joining Rome, "and I gazed at her almost passively as a great objective fact. I looked at her;—at her rites, her ceremonial, and her precepts; and I said 'This *is* a religion'; and then, when I looked back upon the poor Anglican Church, for which I had laboured so hard, and upon all that appertained to it, and thought of our various attempts to dress it up doctrinally and aesthetically, it seemed to me to be the veriest of nonentities"[122]—"a mere national institution."[123]

Moreover, the secession of John Henry Newman and of a large number of his friends served to refute the delusion that the extension of education and the spread of secular knowledge afforded of themselves an adequate safeguard and security against the extension of Romanism. William Cunningham contended that this was one of the major lessons to emerge from the Oxford Movement, namely that

> the mere diffusion of education and of general knowledge, does not, of itself, afford any adequate security against the revival and extension of Romanism. Many have been accustomed to cherish the notion that, in the midst of the light and liberty of the nineteenth century, it was quite chimerical to apprehend that Popery, with all its fooleries and absurdities, could ever again acquire any influence over the minds of men. But we have seen a system which is in substance Popery, and includes a great deal of what is usually reckoned most irrational and absurd in the

120. Newman, *Apologia pro Vita Sua*, 154.

121. Newman, *Apologia pro Vita Sua*, 155; emphasis original.

122. Newman, *Apologia pro Vita Sua*, 219; emphasis original.

123. Newman, *Apologia pro Vita Sua*, 219.

> tenets and practices of the Church of Rome, spread with marvelous rapidity among the most highly educated youth of our country.[124]

Evangelicals today must, therefore, never forget, nor ever underestimate, the natural popery of the human heart.

## ROMANTIC AESTHETICS

In this context, moreover, it must not be forgotten that a significant factor in the phenomenal growth of the Oxford Movement was the establishment in 1839 of a complementary movement in Cambridge—the Cambridge Camden Society, committed to the study of Gothic architecture and ritual arts. Romantic aesthetics ruled the day, and these Romantic aesthetics greatly favoured the Gothic, and the Gothic in turn led men back to the medievalism of the fourteenth century and to inevitable connotations of Roman Catholicism. The Camdenians felt that medieval churches possessed inner, mystical meaning; they felt that architecture possessed not only an artistic significance, but also a spiritual significance. Indeed, the Camdenians advised the modern architects of the day to make exact copies of medieval churches; they believed, writes Professor Owen Chadwick, that "Gothic was the only Christian style of architecture."[125]

Now, this new concern for beauty in architecture was again part of the Romantic spirit of the age. Professor Owen Chadwick writes, for instance, of "the sense of affection and the sensibility of beauty pervading European thought."[126] There was a desire afloat "to make the churches numinous, to transform them from bare houses of preaching into temples evocative of prayer."[127] There was this new "quest for reverence" in architecture, the feeling that churches should be made more like cathedrals, a concern more for the atmosphere of worship than the preaching of the word of God.[128] Thus, the spirit of Romanticism produced a very dangerous confusion between the artistic or aesthetic on the one hand, and the spiritual on the other hand. Back in the year 1820, for instance, the poet John Keats had written these famous words in his "Ode on a Grecian Urn":

> *"Beauty is truth, truth beauty"—that is all*

124. Cunningham, *Church Principles*, 37–38.
125. Chadwick, *Victorian Church*, 1:213.
126. Chadwick, *Mind of Oxford Movement*, 27.
127. Chadwick, *Mind of Oxford Movement*, 64.
128. Chadwick, *Victorian Church*, 1:214.

*Ye know on earth, and all ye need to know.*[129]

Keats here is asserting not only the beauty of truth, but also the truth of beauty. He is suggesting not only the beauty of holiness, but also the holiness of beauty—the naïve, Romantic, and unbiblical assumption that the beautiful is necessarily true and holy—which constituted such a powerful and dangerous idea in the hands of the Camdenians and subsequently the ritualists as they moved unerringly and inevitably in the direction of Rome.

Thus in practice the Camdenians wanted to alter the internal arrangements of most Anglican churches where hitherto the pulpit had been dominant. They introduced sanctuaries, altars, and crosses; they introduced statues, candlesticks, choirs in surplices, and stained glass windows. There was this flowering of Victorian Gothic architecture, and it coalesced very easily with the deepening Catholic sacramentalism of Oxford. Indeed, the "symbolical principle" of Cambridge developed naturally and almost inevitably out of the "sacramental principle" of Oxford. Thus Francis Close of Cheltenham, preaching on Guy Fawkes Day 1844, contended that "as Romanism is taught *Analytically* at Oxford, it is taught *Artistically* at Cambridge. . . . It is inculcated theoretically in Tracts at the one University and it is *sculptured*, *painted* and *graven* at the other."[130] It was in this way that theology and architecture acted and reacted upon one another, and mutually reinforced each other, producing an utterly unscriptural ritualism and sacerdotalism. Merle d'Aubigné's remarkable prophecy in his lecture of 1842 had been realized:

> If they put the Church above Christianity, form above life, they shall infallibly reap that which they have sown, they shall soon have for a church, an assembly of skeletons, brilliantly clothed perhaps; ranged, I grant, in admirable order, imposing to the flesh, but icy, motionless, and resembling a pale legion of the dead. If Puseyism . . . advance in the English Church, in a few years the sources of her life will be dried. The feverish excitement which the malady at first produced, will soon give pace to languor, the blood will congeal, the muscles will freeze, and that Church shall soon be no more than a dead body, upon which the eagles shall come from all quarters to feed.[131]

It was indeed not long before the quasi-evangelical note had disappeared from Anglo-Catholicism, and the smouldering fires of Tractarianism

129. Keats, "Ode on Grecian Urn," lines 49–50.

130. Toon, *Evangelical Theology*, 67; emphasis original.

131. Aubigné, *Geneva and Oxford*, 61.

developed into what J. C. Ryle was to describe as a "sensuous, histrionic, formal religion";[132] it was the living death of an extreme ritualism. Again, with the *Lux Mundi* movement of 1889, the second and third generation of Tractarians, led by Charles Gore, welded Liberalism to Catholicism, producing the double evil of a liberal sacramentalism which has become such a dominant force in world Anglicanism in the twentieth century.

## TRENDS IN CONTEMPORARY EVANGELICALISM

As we turn now to the contemporary situation in Evangelicalism today, we find that there is a very real relevance to the issues involved in the Oxford Movement of 150 years ago. The last sixteen years or so, for instance, have witnessed a quite astonishing *rapprochement* between Anglican Evangelicals and Anglo-Catholics. The tone for this new atmosphere of *détente* was set at the Keele Congress of 1967, when Anglican Evangelicals issued this statement:

> Polemics at long range have at times in the past led us into negative and impoverishing "anti"-attitudes (anti-sacramental, anti-intellectual, *etc.*) from which we now desire to shake free. We recognize that in dialogue we may hope to learn truths held by others to which we have hitherto been blind, as well as to impart to others truths held by us and overlooked by them.[133]

Since Keele in 1967 there has been this new commitment on the part of Evangelicals in the Church of England to "dialogue" and "encounter" with Anglo-Catholics, the heirs of the Oxford Movement itself. Moreover, three years later, in 1970, the first major fruit of this new relationship was published—*Growing into Union: Proposals for Forming a United Church in England*—a work that was issued jointly by two Anglo-Catholics, the Rev. Prof. Eric L. Mascall and Dr. Graham Leonard (then Bishop of Willesden, now of London), and two Evangelicals, the Rev. Colin Buchanan and Dr. James Packer. At the very outset of this work, we find quoted with approval the following statement made by Dr. A. M. Ramsey, the future Archbishop of Canterbury, in 1956:

> "Catholicism" and "Evangelicalism" are not two separate things which the Church of England must hold together by a great feat of compromise. Rightly understood, they are both facts which lie behind the Church of England and, as the New Testament

132. Ryle, *Five English Reformers*, 36.

133. Cited in C. Buchanan, *Anglo-Catholic Worship*, 8.

> shows, they are one fact. A church's witness to the one Church of the ages is a part of its witness to the Gospel of God.[134]

Now this is a quite astonishing assertion—it is quite breathtaking in its cavalier adventurism! For while it is quite true that Catholicism and Evangelicalism are "both facts which lie behind the Church of England," it is surely only a fevered Romantic imagination that can assert that "they are one fact." For this bland assertion that "they are one fact" is surely a classic example of that spirit of Romanticism which ever yearns for the synthesizing and the reconciliation of opposites. Moreover, the bland assertion, quoted with approval by two leading Anglican Evangelicals, that "the New Testament shows" that "they are one fact" is a statement which is so palpably untrue that it deserves no ordinary severity of castigation.

It is interesting, however, to notice the extent to which the shadow of John Henry Newman lies across the pages of *Growing into Union.* Very early in the first chapter, entitled "Scripture and Tradition," Newman is mentioned as the figure who, to all intents and purposes, was the first to introduce a theory of the development of Christian doctrine. This he wrote in 1845 to justify in his own mind his own imminent secession to the Church of Rome. Now the originality of Newman's famous essay lay in his assertion that truth is to be regarded as dynamic, and not static, in quality. Christian doctrine, Newman contended, was something that developed—it had this organic and dynamic quality—it was something that evolved. "Christian doctrine," he wrote, "admits of formal, legitimate, and true developments, that is, of developments contemplated by its Divine Author.[135] . . . Modern Catholicism," asserted Newman, "is nothing else but simply the legitimate growth and complement, that is the natural and necessary development, of the doctrine of the early church, and . . . its divine authority is included in the divinity of Christianity."[136] Thus when, in the context of John Henry Newman, the authors of *Growing into Union* contend that "there can be and is development in the Church's understanding of the Gospel,"[137] they are not making a harmless statement about a development in the church's *subjective* understanding of the gospel once delivered unto the saints; with a certain sleight of hand they are asserting that there has been, down through the centuries, an *objective* development of Christian doctrine itself. They speak approvingly of "the recovery of a dynamic view of Tradition as essentially

134. Cited in C. Buchanan et al., *Growing into Union*, 8.

135. Newman, *Development of Christian Doctrine*, 54.

136. Newman, *Development of Christian Doctrine*, 123.

137. C. Buchanan et al., *Growing into Union*, 31.

the process of the handing on by the Church of the faith of the Scriptures."[138] Astonishingly, both Buchanan and Packer are giving an unqualified assertion of the aforementioned position of John Henry Newman.

Evangelical Protestants are, therefore, entitled to ask Buchanan and Packer whether this endorsement of Newman's theory of the development of Christian doctrine also includes the following breathtaking assertion on Newman's part:

> The Incarnation is the antecedent of the doctrine of Mediation, and the archetype both of the sacramental principle and of the merits of Saints. From the doctrine of Mediation follow the Atonement, the Mass, the merits of Martyrs and Saints, their invocation and *cultus*. From the Sacramental principle come the Sacraments properly so called: the unity of the Church, and the Holy See as its type and centre; the authority of Councils; the sanctity of rites; the veneration of holy places, shrines, images, vessels, furniture, and vestments. Of the Sacraments, Baptism is developed into Confirmation on the one hand; into Penance, Purgatory, and Indulgences on the other; and the Eucharist into the Real Presence, adoration of the Host, Resurrection of the body, and the virtue of relics. Again, the doctrine of the Sacraments leads to the doctrine of Justification; Justification to that of Original Sin; Original Sin to the merit of Celibacy.[139]

Is *this* what Buchanan and Packer mean when they say that "there can be and is development in the Church's understanding of the Gospel"? For such is Newman's dynamic view of tradition in actual practice and such is the thorough recklessness with which he applies it. William Cunningham's comment on Newman's theory is, therefore, most relevant today:

> It seems to us, that the man who, after due investigation, has persuaded himself that the system of doctrine, government, and worship, held in the modern Church of Rome, is a legitimate development, and not a corruption, of apostolic Christianity, should be willing and ready to maintain, that the polytheism and idolatry of the ancient heathen world was a development, and not a corruption, of the patriarchal religion, and that the pharisaic system of our Saviour's days was a development, and not a corruption, of the religion which God communicated to the Jews through Moses.[140]

138. C. Buchanan et al., *Growing into Union*, 32.

139. Newman, *Development of Christian Doctrine*, 68–69.

140. Cunningham, *Church Principles*, 69.

Protestants, Cunningham rightly maintained, are the defenders of the theory of a corruption in Christian doctrine and contend that the modern Church of Rome is the ultimate product of such a corruption.

Again, the third chapter in *Growing into Union*, entitled "Church and Sacraments," reveals a quite lamentable capitulation by Buchanan and Packer to the "sacramental principle" of Anglo-Catholicism with its great emphasis upon the efficacy of the sacraments. "The language of Scripture about them," asserts *Growing into Union*,

> is the language of sheer unqualified efficacy. If the outward celebration is performed, then on the first showing the inward grace is mediated. Those who have been baptized into Christ "have put on Christ." . . . Those who receive communion receive the body and blood of Christ. . . . The simple expectation is that those who partake of the sacraments are partakers in them and by them of God's grace. . . . The overall picture is one of serene objectivity and confidence on the writers' part in the efficacy of the sacraments.[141]

Now this is surely as bold an assertion of "sacramental grace" as any Anglo-Catholic could desire, and it is both astonishing and highly regrettable that two leading Anglican Evangelicals should be signatories to such a statement which inevitably involves a radical undermining of the great evangelical and Protestant doctrines of regeneration by the sovereign Spirit of God and of justification by faith alone in the merits of Jesus Christ. It is but a further lamentable proof of the grave dangers which confront Evangelicals who are prepared to engage in ecumenical "dialogue" and "encounter."

Moreover, when we turn to *The Final Report* of the Anglican-Roman Catholic International Commission, published in 1982, we observe again the capitulation of the lone evangelical voice of the Rev. Julian Charley to the Catholic cast of thought which clearly dominates the commission. Once again the shadow of John Henry Newman lies across the pages of the report; once again we find an implicit endorsement of Newman's theory of the development of Christian doctrine in the following reference to tradition as "the growth of the seed of God's word from age to age."[142] We are assured, however, by *The Final Report* that this approach "does not necessarily contradict" the *sola scriptura* approach of never going beyond the bounds of Scripture. To this we reply that the concept of the historical development of the seed of God's word certainly does, as a mere theory, deny the sufficiency of the original revelation in the Scriptures, while in practice, as applied to

141. C. Buchanan et al., *Growing into Union*, 55.

142. Anglican-Roman Catholic International Commission, *Final Report*, 71.

the Church of Rome, it contradicts the content of that original revelation in the Scriptures. It would appear that Julian Charley and his fellow delegates in the commission have imbibed Newman's Romantic antipathy to theological logic as they strain every muscle to reconcile the irreconcilable.

With regard to *The Final Report*'s statements on papal supremacy or "universal primacy," the same note of capitulation and concession is evident. The evangelical Anglican delegate is apparently quite happy with the following statement on the See of Rome: "It seems appropriate that in any future union a universal primacy such as has been described should be held by that see";[143] and with regard to the notion of the "divine right" of the papacy, the same delegate is a signatory to the following statement: "If it is understood as affirming that the universal primacy of the bishop of Rome is part of God's design for the universal *koinonia* then it need not be a matter of disagreement."[144] And yet despite evangelical objections to this statement, Julian Charley assures us in his Grove booklet entitled *Rome, Canterbury, and the Future* that such statements are "compatible with Scripture."[145] We reply that, while such statements may be compatible with Newman's theory of development, they are certainly not compatible with Scripture.

Again, in the "Statement on Eucharistic Doctrine" of 1971, the following assertion is made by the commission: "In the eucharistic prayer the church continues to make a perpetual memorial of Christ's death, and his members . . . enter into the movement of his self-offering."[146] Now there is a vagueness, an indecisiveness about this statement; it is an ambiguous formulary, and the spirit of John Henry Newman hovers over it. Indeed, it is most significant that Julian Charley himself, in *Rome, Canterbury, and the Future*, specifically defends and specifically advocates the use of Newman's concept of "the 'elasticity' of dogma."[147] Since Vatican II, Julian Charley asserts, there has been this new vogue in "elasticity." "Possibly," he writes, "it is in the *Final Report* of ARCIC in 1982 that this 'elasticity' is most evident,"[148] and Julian Charley goes on to commend the concept of "the 'elasticity' of what once seemed wholly unchangeable. . . . It is especially necessary," he contends, "now that ecumenism has come into its own."[149] Thus according to Julian Charley, dogmas "possess an elasticity that had not hitherto been

143. Anglican-Roman Catholic International Commission, *Final Report*, 64.
144. Anglican-Roman Catholic International Commission, *Final Report*, 65.
145. Charley, *Rome, Canterbury, and Future*, 3.
146. Anglican-Roman Catholic International Commission, *Final Report*, 14.
147. Charley, *Rome, Canterbury, and Future*, 5.
148. Charley, *Rome, Canterbury, and Future*, 5.
149. Charley, *Rome, Canterbury, and Future*, 7.

appreciated; . . . they can sometimes be stretched to the point when they are barely recognizable for what they were previously thought to be"; and "they have been shown capable of being re-expressed in a way that alters their whole perspective."[150] Thus while Julian Charley himself insists that "firm theological foundations are essential to every ecumenical enterprise,"[151] he in fact believes that these foundations should be made essentially of *elastic* so that they can incorporate not only Evangelicals, but also Anglo-Catholics and the Church of Rome itself!

Again, on a somewhat different level, it is interesting to notice the reaction of the Rev. John Stott and the Bishop of Thetford, Timothy Dudley-Smith, to *The Final Report.* Writing in June 1982 as the cochairmen of the Church of England Evangelical Council, they put forward some very valid questions to the authors of *The Final Report* on the subjects of justification, the Eucharist, priesthood, authority, tradition, the Marian dogmas, and the primacy of the pope. Indeed, so valid are their questions on these vital, central issues that we find it very difficult to understand how Stott can also assert with regard to the report that "there is much in it to applaud."[152] Again, we find it very difficult to understand how two Evangelicals, with such crucial questions in their minds, can cheerfully assert the following as their opening remark: "We write in the warm afterglow of the Pope's visit."[153] But above all, we find it almost incredible, as an exercise in sheer logic, how these cochairmen can maintain that "there is nothing inconsistent about affirming the Pope as a Christian leader, while at the same time asking questions about the claims of the papacy and the dogmas of the Roman Catholic Church."[154] On the contrary, we reply, there *is* something highly inconsistent about affirming the pope as a Christian leader, while at the same time asking such fundamental questions about the claims of the papacy and the dogmas of the Roman Catholic Church. After all, Christian leadership is not just a matter of personal charisma. There is a great *sine qua non* about Christian leadership, and that is the possession of Christian truth—and that in the very areas in which Stott and Dudley-Smith are themselves now putting such relevant and crucial questions to Julian Charley and his fellow delegates.

It is, again, most significant that the 150th anniversary of the Oxford Movement has been marked by the publication, under the editorship of the

150. Charley, *Rome, Canterbury, and Future*, 4.

151. Charley, *Rome, Canterbury, and Future*, 5.

152. Stott, *Evangelical Anglicans*, 4.

153. Dudley-Smith and Stott, "Foreword."

154. Dudley-Smith and Stott, "Foreword."

Rev. Colin Buchanan, of a Grove booklet entitled *Anglo-Catholic Worship: An Evangelical Appreciation after 150 Years.* Buchanan himself describes this collection of brief articles as "our birthday present to the heirs of the Oxford Movement.[155] . . . We are deeply respectful of the catholic tradition in the Church of England,"[156] he writes. Moreover, he goes on to indicate the grounds for this *rapprochement* of Evangelicals and Catholics. "Liberalism," writes Buchanan, ". . . has often united evangelicals and anglo-catholics in defending the same ground, whilst . . . the Charismatic Movement . . . has often united them in sharing the same experience."[157] The great tendency among certain Evangelicals in recent years has been to maximize areas of common ground and to minimize crucial areas of difference. However, we must ask such Evangelicals whether a common opposition to Liberalism, coupled with a common concern for spiritual experience and holiness, is a sufficient reason for such a *rapprochement.* After all, Evangelicals of a former generation acknowledged that they were constantly fighting a battle on two fronts—against liberal theology on the one front and against sacramental theology on the other front. Moreover, we must ask whether certain Evangelicals are not guilty of confusing the supernatural with the superstitious at this point; for while it is true that the classic evangelical position does indeed involve this commitment to supernatural, biblical beliefs, it is also true that the Anglo-Catholic position involves a commitment to superstitious, unbiblical beliefs. Are these Evangelicals happy, we ask, with the "sacramental system"? Are they happy with the concept of baptismal regeneration and of the real presence of Christ? Are they happy with altars, and priests, and ritual? Are they not troubled by the concept of "God's unwritten word" and the notion of "catholic consent"? Again, are they happy with the Catholic doctrine of "reserve" and the virtual neglect of the preaching of the word? Are they really happy with the Anglo-Catholic doctrine of justification and with the denial of the principles of *sola scriptura*, *sola gratia*, and *sola fide?* And if they are *not* happy in these areas, then are these issues really so minimal and so trivial that they amount to a disagreement of only one-tenth of the whole? There is, without doubt, a strange malaise afloat among those Evangelicals whose attitude towards Anglo-Catholicism is one of deference, deep respect, concession, and capitulation. The Grove booklet *Anglo-Catholic Worship* is a prime example of such a malaise. It is essentially a historical survey of various aspects of Anglo-Catholicism and offers no real critique of a biblical or theological nature. There is an evasion

155. C. Buchanan, *Anglo-Catholic Worship*, 4.

156. C. Buchanan, *Anglo-Catholic Worship*, 8.

157. C. Buchanan, *Anglo-Catholic Worship*, 3.

of the real, fundamental doctrinal issues, and the Protestant note which characterized a former generation of Anglican Evangelicals is conspicuously absent. Indeed, it appears to be the case that certain Evangelicals today have lost all capacity for polemical theology with regard to Catholicism; indeed, it appears that the only polemic that has survived in such circles is the polemic against polemics! Let us never forget, then, that the Eternal Son of God did not shrink from polemics when he contended that the Pharisees had made the word of God of none effect through their traditions. Let us never forget that the great apostle Paul did not shrink from polemics when he contended that the Galatians had been bewitched by "another gospel, which is not another" (Gal 1:6–7). Let us never forget that the people of God are urged in the word of God to "contend earnestly for the faith once delivered unto the saints" (Jude 3).

However, the spirit which is afloat among certain Anglican Evangelicals today is one which appears all too often to pay greater deference to the fact of "Anglican comprehensiveness"[158] and the interests of visible unity than to the truth of the word of God. Julian Charley, for instance, actually warns in *Rome, Canterbury, and the Future* that "there is a danger in endeavoring to be a little more precise than the fact of comprehensiveness will allow."[159] Ecumenical activity, it seems, requires a cult of imprecision, indecisiveness, and vagueness; it requires, apparently, the concept of "elasticity" and the cult of ambiguity. It requires statements such as that on eucharistic doctrine in *The Final Report* to the effect that the members of Christ "enter into the movement of his self-offering."[160] Indeed, ecumenical activity in the realm of doctrine requires very often a spirit and an atmosphere which is one of ambiguity, subtlety, confusion, obscurity, contradiction, mystification, and fog! It requires the kind of approach which John Henry Newman described with such brilliant irony in the last century, and which can be charged upon certain Evangelicals today. "In the present day," wrote Newman,

> mistiness is the mother of wisdom. A man who can set down a half-a-dozen general propositions, which escape from destroying one another only by being diluted into truisms, who can hold the balance between opposites so skillfully as to do without fulcrum or beam, who never enunciates a truth without guarding himself from being supposed to exclude the contradictory,—who holds that Scripture is the only authority, yet that the Church is to be deferred to, that faith only justifies, yet that

158. C. Buchanan, *Anglo-Catholic Worship*, 8.

159. Charley, *Rome, Canterbury, and Future*, 28.

160. Anglican-Roman Catholic International Commission, *Final Report*, 14.

> it does not justify without works, that grace does not depend on the sacraments, yet is not given without them, that bishops are a divine ordinance, yet those who have them not are in the same religious condition as those who have,—this is your safe man and the hope of the Church; this is what the Church is said to want, not party men, but sensible, temperate, sober, well-judging persons, to guide it through the channel of no-meaning, between the Scylla and Charybdis of Aye and No.[161]

John Henry Newman has given us here a perfect description of the tactic of the modern ecumenical mind. It is in evidence in *Growing into Union*; it is in evidence in *The Final Report*—this subtle steering "through the channel of no-meaning, between the Scylla and Charybdis of Aye and No." It is a tragic thing when the great truths of the Holy Word of God are handled in this way, and when the church itself begins to speak with the voice of the oracle of Delphi!

It is evident, then, that the issues of the Oxford Movement of 150 years ago are most relevant today. Leading Evangelicals are pitching their tent toward Oxford—they are pitching their tent toward Rome; and the Tiber is now beginning to flow within Evangelicalism itself. Leading Evangelicals have put themselves into the position of Esau and are bartering and squandering their great heritage for a mere mess of pottage! They are engaged in that "vanity of vanities"—ecumenical negotiation on God's unchangeable truth. The Protestant note within Evangelicalism has been rapidly ebbing away in recent years, and one of the greatest and most urgent needs within Evangelicalism today is the recovery of that Protestant note. It must not be a cheap Protestantism—it must not be a carnal Protestantism; it must be an intelligent, cogent, spiritual Protestantism—the Protestantism of those great masters of historical theology William Cunningham and Merle d'Aubigné. It must reassert fearlessly the great principles of the Protestant Reformation—*sola scriptura*, *sola gratia*, and *sola fide*. It must protest at the damnable plus of both Anglo-Catholicism and Roman Catholicism. It must never tire of demonstrating that the epistles to the Galatians and to the Hebrews deliver a crushing death blow to the pallid "gospel" of Catholicism, exposing that "gospel" as "another gospel, which is not another." It must never cease to warn men of the spiritual bondage into which Catholicism would fain bring them; it must never cease to declare the spiritual liberty which is in Christ Jesus. It must ever proclaim the glorious perfection not only of the Person of Jesus Christ, but also of his work—that a full and perfect atonement was made once and for all at Calvary—that the work of Christ is a gloriously

161. Newman, *Apologia pro Vita Sua*, 69.

finished work—it is a work of pure gold and will not brook the dross of the additions of men. This evangelical Protestantism must declare from the Scriptures that "we *have* an altar" (Heb 13:10; emphasis added)—it is the altar of the cross of Calvary, of "Jesus Christ, and him crucified" (1 Cor 2:2). It must declare that "we *have* a great high priest, that is passed into the heavens, Jesus the Son of God" (Heb 4:14; emphasis added), and that we are "complete in Him" (Col 2:10). What need is there, then, for the sacramental principle or the sacerdotal practice of Catholicism? What need is there for the traditions of men or the weak and beggarly elements of this world? These additions of man are but an insult to the perfect work of Christ and to his perfect written word, and their effect is to make the word of God and the work of Christ of none effect. Let those, then, that are Evangelicals ensure that they do not let slip their great Protestant heritage. Let them be strong and of a good courage—let them, like Latimer and Ridley, be strong and play the man. Let them lift up their voices like trumpets in protest against the "gospel" of Catholicism which so frustrates the grace of God, and let them declare faithfully and fearlessly the everlasting and unchangeable gospel of Christ who by his "one sacrifice for sins for ever" (Heb 10:12) is able "to save them to the uttermost that come unto God by him" (Heb 7:25).

# JONATHAN EDWARDS AND THE DEISTS[1]

In *Freedom of the Will*, published in 1754, Jonathan Edwards refers to "the supposed rational and generous principles of the modern fashionable divinity"[2]—"that noble and generous freedom of thought, which happily prevails in this age of inquiry." Again, in *Original Sin*, published in 1758, Edwards comments in ironic and sardonic vein that "it must be understood, that there is risen up now at length, in this happy age of light and liberty, a set of men, of a more free and generous turn of mind, of a more inquisitive genius, and of better discernment."[3] Thus it is evident that Jonathan Edwards had firmly within his sights "a set of men" who were characterized in their thinking by the spurious generosity of the age of the Enlightenment, namely, the freethinkers or deists that were now flourishing in the age of reason.

Now it is vital that Jonathan Edwards should be understood not merely in the context of New England religion, but also in the wider context of the transatlantic intellectual community of the first half of the eighteenth century. Through his wide, eclectic reading Edwards was well aware of the rising tide of deism and the remarkable growth of scepticism in this period. In his "History of Redemption," for instance, Edwards specifically mentions England as "the principle kingdom of the Reformation," but then goes on to remark that "in this kingdom, those principles on which the power of godliness depends, are in a great measure exploded, and Arianism, Socinianism, Arminianism, and Deism, prevail, and carry almost all before them. History gives us no account of any age wherein there was so great an infidel apostasy

1. This essay was awarded first prize in the Evangelical Library Essay Competition of 1987. It was published in *Banner of Truth* (Aug.–Sept. 1988) 22–34.

2. Edwards, *Works* (Hickman), 1:86.

3. Edwards, *Works* (Hickman), 1:89.

of those who had been brought up under the light of the gospel; never was there such a disavowal of all revealed religion."[4]

The basic tenets of deism were articulated in 1624 by Lord Herbert of Cherbury (1583–1648), the man usually regarded as the father of deism. In that year he published his *De Veritate*, which identified the five following articles of deistic belief. First, there is one Supreme God. Second, this Supreme Being is to be worshipped. Third, virtue is the chief element in this worship. Fourth, repentance for sin is a duty, and upon repentance a man may cherish the hope of pardon. Fifth, there are rewards and punishments in the world to come.[5] Later deists, such as John Toland (1670–1722), Anthony Collins (1676–1729), and Matthew Tindal (1655–1733), built upon this foundation. There was this denial of supernatural revelation. Christianity, it was declared, was "not mysterious"; it was "as old as the creation" and was simply "a republication of the law of nature." Man himself was exalted, and above all, God was removed to a great distance from the world.

## REASON AND THE LIGHT OF NATURE

Both in his sermons and his theological treatises Jonathan Edwards reveals a remarkable preoccupation with the threat of deism. In *Original Sin* he refers to "the folly and great evil of deism."[6] Again, in his sermon on "Man's Natural Blindness in the Things of Religion," he contends that the rise of deism soon after the Reformation was itself an example of "the sottish blindness and folly of the heart of men"[7]—a classic illustration of man's proneness "to fall into such gross delusions, soon after they have been favoured with clear light."[8] Edwards stresses not only the fallenness of man, but also the fallenness of man's reason. Deism was simply one manifestation of man's extreme natural blindness. Thus, Edwards emphasized very strongly the inadequacy and insufficiency of human reason and the light of nature. Indeed, Edwards' works provide a very detailed and thorough critique of the optimistic concept of reason as entertained by the mind of the Enlightenment. "Mere reason,"[9] "unassisted reason,"[10] he contended, could never bring fallen men to the knowledge of God.

4. Edwards, *Works* (Hickman), 1:233.
5. Herbert, *De Veritate.*
6. Edwards, *Works* (Hickman), 1:197.
7. Edwards, *Works* (Hickman), 2:249
8. Edwards, *Works* (Hickman), 2:249.
9. Edwards, *Works* (Hickman), 2:462.
10. Edwards, *Works* (Hickman), 2:461.

With regard to specific doctrines of the Christian faith Edwards argued that the doctrine of the Trinity, the method of the sinner's justification, and even the doctrine of a future general judgment are not discoverable by the light of nature, but depend upon a revelation from God. Again, with regard to the immortality of the soul Edwards argues interestingly that "there is no one probable opinion in the world which mankind, left entirely to themselves, would have been more unlikely to have started. Who, if he was not assured of it by good authority, would ever take it into his head to imagine, that man, who dies, and rots, and vanishes for ever, like all other animals, still exists? It is well, if this, when proposed, can be believed; but to strike out the thought itself, is somewhat, I am afraid, too high and difficult for the capacity of men."[11] Indeed, it is interesting to note the extent to which Edwards minimizes the light of nature. "It is one thing," he writes in his *Miscellanies*, "to work out a demonstration of a point, when once it is proposed; and another, to strike upon a point itself. I cannot tell whether any man would have considered the works of creation as effects, if he had never been told they had a cause."[12] Certainly, Edwards concedes, man's reason and learning prove to be "an excellent handmaid to divinity,"[13] but it is essential that man's reason should first be enlightened. Only then can those truths which are above reason be seen to be agreeable to reason. "Reason may greatly confirm truths revealed in the Scriptures."[14] Reason confirms revelation, it undergirds revelation, it elucidates revelation. But a revelation from God himself is absolutely indispensable.

In his *Miscellanies* Edwards puts considerable emphasis on the connection between revelation and certainty. "Were it not for divine revelation," he writes, "I am persuaded, that there is no one doctrine of that which we call natural religion, which, notwithstanding all philosophy and learning, would not be for ever involved in darkness, doubts, endless disputes, and dreadful confusion."[15] Natural religion, he maintains, leads only to "abundance of uncertainty,"[16] "infinite confusion,"[17] "ten thousand different schemes."[18] Now Edwards' critique of deism is twofold here. First, he argues that the heathen darkness of the gentile nations is in itself a great and lasting proof

11. Edwards, *Works* (Hickman), 2:477.
12. Edwards, *Works* (Hickman), 2: 476.
13. Edwards, *Works* (Hickman), 1:601
14. Edwards, *Works* (Hickman), 2:100.
15. Edwards, *Works* (Hickman), 2:462.
16. Edwards, *Works* (Hickman), 2:462.
17. Edwards, *Works* (Hickman), 2:462.
18. Edwards, *Works* (Hickman), 2:462.

of the utter inadequacy and insufficiency of man's natural reason. Indeed, Edwards draws an interesting parallel between the light of the heathen and the light of the deists: "Those nations, who all that time lay in such gross darkness, and in such a deplorable helpless condition, had the same natural reason that the deists have."[19] Again, "it is strange, that the natural light should be so clear, and yet the natural darkness so great, that in all unassisted countries the most monstrous forms of religion, derogatory to God, and prejudicial to man, should be contrived by some, and swallowed by the rest, with a most voracious credulity. I could wish most heartily, that all nations were Christians: yet, since it is otherwise, we derive this advantage from it, that we have a standing and contemporary demonstration of that which nature, left to herself, can do."[20] Then, second, Edwards contends that the deist's light of nature in fact flows from God's revelation! "It was the Christian religion," he maintains, "that opened the eyes of the polite nations of Europe, and even of the deists of this age."[21] "All the right speculative knowledge of the true God, which the deists themselves have, has been derived from divine revelation."[22] In effect, Edwards charges the deists here with taking divine revelation for granted. The deists, he claims, borrow from Christianity. Natural religion, while rejecting revelation, in fact rides upon the back of revelation. Natural religion, so vaunted by the deist, in fact builds its flimsy edifice on the very foundations laid by the Christian religion itself. Indeed, Edwards extends this argument back in time to the heathen nations in the Old Testament era. "Judea," he asserts, "was a sort of light among the nations, though they did not know it."[23] Rome, Greece, Egypt, Syria, and Chaldea were to some extent beneficiaries of that light which God imparted to the nation of Israel. Those nations that lay in close proximity to Israel thus enjoyed a kind of reflected light from divine revelation itself; they learned from the principles and practices of the Jews, so that that which is hailed as the light of nature has in fact been handed down, via tradition, from revelation. Edwards reminds the deists of the significance of "Eastern traditions."[24] Thus he asserts, in effect, that pagan moral philosophy and also deistic moral philosophy were unconscious imitators of God's revelation to

19. Edwards, *Works* (Hickman), 2:253.
20. Edwards, *Works* (Hickman), 2:479.
21. Edwards, *Works* (Hickman), 2:477.
22. Edwards, *Works* (Hickman), 2:253.
23. Edwards, *Works* (Hickman), 2:463.
24. Edwards, *Works* (Hickman), 2:477.

Moses and of God's revelation through Christ respectively. In each case, the light of nature in fact consisted of "relics of revelation."[25]

## MAN AND ORIGINAL SIN

For Jonathan Edwards, one of the most significant features of the rationalistic mind was its doctrine of man and sin. By the mid-eighteenth century the optimistic Enlightenment view of man, with its belief in man's ability and goodness, had engulfed much of Europe and England, and was now, Edwards felt, encroaching dangerously upon America. Edwards' own view of man—essentially Calvinistic—is well summarized by this statement of his in "Thoughts on the Revival": "What a poor, blind, weak, and miserable creature is man, at his best estate!"[26] However, as Clyde Holbrook points out, by the 1750s "the notion of man as a fundamentally rational, benevolently inclined individual was emerging as the unquestionable postulate for the expansionist mood of Western culture. But the doctrine of original sin marred this flattering image. It stood for everything the spirit of the Enlightenment detested."[27] Thus the New England stage was well set for a clash between the Enlightenment view of man and the Reformation view of man—a clash that is epitomized in the 1750s by the controversy between Dr. John Taylor and Jonathan Edwards.

Dr. John Taylor (1694–1761) of Norwich was initially an orthodox Presbyterian, but in the 1730s he appears to have moved in the direction of Arianism and Unitarianism. In 1738 Dr. Taylor openly identified himself with the rising tide of Arminianism and Pelagianism by his attack on the doctrine of original sin. His influential *Scripture Doctrine of Original Sin* enjoyed a wide circulation in England, Scotland, and America, and did much to undermine the foundations of Calvinism in New England and to reinforce the rationalism and the moralism of the Enlightenment. As far as John Wesley was concerned, Taylor's work was "old deism in new dress."[28] Edwards' aim in *Original Sin* was to establish "the innate sinful depravity of the heart."[29] He therefore took up his initial position on ground conceded by Dr. Taylor himself, namely, that men "universally run themselves into that which is, in effect, their own utter eternal perdition."[30] From this fact,

25. Edwards, *Works* (Hickman), 2: 463.

26. Edwards, *Works* (Hickman), 1:420.

27. Clyde Holbrook, in Edwards, *Original Sin*, 1.

28. Clyde Holbrook, in Edwards, *Original Sin*, 69.

29. Edwards, *Works* (Hickman), 1:146

30. Edwards, *Works* (Hickman), 1:148.

established by both Scripture and experience, and also acknowledged by Dr. Taylor, Edwards goes on to conclude that there is in man a natural tendency or propensity to sin. "The natural dictate of reason," he writes, "shows, that where there is an effect, there is a cause, and a cause sufficient for the effect; because, if it were not sufficient, it would not be effected; and that therefore, where there is a stated prevalence of the effect, there is a stated prevalence in the cause. A steady effect argues a steady cause." Since there is in mankind "a propensity that is invincible, or a tendency which really amounts to a fixed, constant, unfailing necessity," this tendency or propensity must lie, not in any external circumstances, but in something inherent in man himself; it is seated, Edwards maintains, in "that nature which is common to all mankind."[31] It is thus that Edwards reasons, step by step, and with irresistible logic, from premises conceded by Dr. Taylor to a conclusion most unwelcome to Dr. Taylor!

It is particularly interesting to note the way in which Edwards disposes of Dr. Taylor's argument that man's own free will, rather than any depravity of nature, is sufficient to explain the great and general wickedness of the world. Here Edwards turns his opponent's arguments back upon his opponent.

> But I would ask, how comes it to pass that mankind so universally agrees in this evil exercise of their free will? If their wills are in the first place as free to good as to evil, what is it to be ascribed to, that the world of mankind, consisting of so many millions, in so many successive generations, without consultation, all agree to exercise their freedom in favour of evil? If there be no natural tendency or preponderation in the case, then there is as good a chance for the will being determined to good as to evil. If the cause be indifferent, why is not the effect in some measure indifferent? If the balance be no heavier at one end than the other, why does it perpetually preponderate one way? How comes it to pass that the free will of mankind has been determined to evil, in like manner before the flood and after the flood; under the law and under the gospel; among both Jews and Gentiles, under the Old Testament, and since then, among Christians, Jews, Mahometans; among papists and protestants; in those nations where civility, politeness, arts and learning most prevail, and among the Negroes and Hottentots in Africa, the Tartars in Asia, and Indians in America, towards both the poles and on every side of the globe; in greatest cities and obscurest villages; in palaces and huts, wigwams, and cells underground? Is it enough to reply, it

31. Edwards, *Works* (Hickman), 1:150.

> happens so, that men everywhere, and in all times, choose thus to determine their own wills, and so to make themselves sinful, as soon as ever they are capable of it, and to sin constantly as long as they live, and universally to choose never to come up halfway to their duty?[32]

It is thus, with relentless logic, that Edwards exposes the weaknesses, the inconsistencies, and intrinsic absurdities of Dr. Taylor's own avowed principles, and indeed appears to have entirely baffled and confounded his opponent with superior force of argument. It is not in the least surprising that the great Scottish theologian of the nineteenth century, William Cunningham, asserted of Edwards' *Original Sin* that it "never has been, and never can be, successfully assailed."[33]

## HELL AND THE HUMANITARIANS

For Jonathan Edwards, another dangerous feature of deism was its scepticism of the orthodox doctrine of hell. The doctrine of the eternal torment of the damned, so clearly taught in the Bible and in the great Calvinistic confessions, was under attack. John Tillotson (1630–94), for instance, who was appointed Archbishop of Canterbury in 1691, had sought to tone down the Calvinist doctrine of strict reprobation by emphasizing God's mercy at the expense of his justice. In 1690, Tillotson had preached before the Queen a most significant sermon on "The Eternity of Hell Torments." This was a subtle, suggestive, insinuating sermon in which Tillotson, while purporting to defend the doctrine of the everlasting misery of the damned, in fact deliberately subverted this very doctrine. He cast doubt upon the everlasting nature of God's punishment of sinners. Everlasting punishment, he suggested, was not so much a certainty as a possibility. He suggested that the Bible's teaching on eternal punishment was given to "deter men"; it was a deterrent rather than retributive.[34] Moreover, by using the example of Nineveh, Tillotson suggested that while God is obliged to fulfil his promises, he is not obliged in fact to fulfil his threatenings. "For there is this remarkable difference between promises and threatenings," wrote the future Archbishop of Canterbury, "that he who promiseth passeth over a right to another, and thereby stands obliged to him in justice and faithfulness to make good his promise, and if he do not, the party to whom the promise is

32. Edwards, *Original Sin*, 169.
33. Cunningham, *Reformers*, 373.
34. Tillotson, *Works*, 3:84.

made is not only disappointed, but injuriously dealt withal: but in threatenings it is quite otherwise. He that threatens keeps the right of punishing in his own hand, and is not obliged to execute what he hath threatened any further than the reasons and ends of government do require: and he may without injury to the party threatened remit and abate as much as he pleaseth of the punishment that he hath threatened: and because in doing so he is not worse but better than his word, nobody can find fault, or complain of any wrong or injustice thereby done to him."[35] In this same sermon, moreover, Tillotson flirts and toys with the heterodox notions of the Greek father Origen who held that punishment in the world to come is reformatory and rehabilitative, and who suggested that such punishment may last for only a thousand years.

It is important to note that in 1714 Tillotson's writings arrived in New England; and it is not surprising that as a famous preacher and as a former Archbishop of Canterbury, his writings should exercise a considerable influence among New England divines. The historian Perry Miller has characterized Tillotson's approach as "moderate,"[36] "reasonable,"[37] "latitudinarian."[38] Anthony Collins, the freethinker and deist, regarded Tillotson as the head of all freethinkers. For Jonathan Edwards, however, Tillotson was the fountainhead of much that was objectionable in eighteenth-century liberal Christianity, and in April 1739, almost fifty years after the preaching of Tillotson's own sermon, Edwards himself preached a sermon on "The Eternity of Hell Torments" that was based on Tillotson's own text from Matt 25:46—"And these shall go away into everlasting punishment." Indeed, the Northampton divine specifically mentions the Canterbury divine in this sermon—"Archbishop Tillotson, who has made so great a figure among the new-fashioned divines."[39] Both here, and also in his *Miscellanies*, Edwards launches a brilliant counterattack upon "the infidel humour"[40] of the age. Reasoning both from the Scriptures and also from the philosophical premises of opponents such as Tillotson and the third earl of Shaftesbury, Edwards attacks the psychological optimism and the sentimental humanitarianism of the benevolist school. He strongly rejects the ethics of pity and compassion with its emphasis on "a God of universal benevolence."[41] He

35. Tillotson, *Works*, 3:84–85.

36. Miller, *New England Mind*, 465.

37. Miller, *New England Mind*, 249.

38. Miller, *New England Mind*, 241.

39. Edwards, *Works* (Hickman), 2:86–87.

40. Cited in Fiering, *Jonathan Edwards's Moral Thought*, 200.

41. Edwards, *Works* (Hickman), 2:521.

dismisses the notion of the punishment of hell as a "kind and benevolent chastisement.[42] . . . This life," Edwards insists, "is the only state of trial. . . . There is no other day of trial after this life."[43] There is, Edwards maintains, an inalienable connection between the nature of sin and the nature of hell. "Our obligation to love, honour, and obey God being infinitely great, sin is the violation of infinite obligation, and so is an infinite evil. Once more, sin being an infinite evil, deserves an infinite punishment, an infinite punishment is no more than it deserves: therefore, such punishment is just."[44] Edwards thus rejects the Origenist notion that the torments of hell are simply "purifying pains"; they are not "medicinal," Edwards contends—they are not reformatory or rehabilitative.[45] Edwards totally rejects the idea that there are "offers of mercy" in hell and that there is any possibility of repentance in hell.[46] He also proceeds to destroy Tillotson's suggestion that although God threatens eternal punishment, he may not in fact fulfil his threatenings. "The doctrine of those who teach, that it is not certain that God will fulfil those absolute threatenings, is blasphemous another way; and that is, as God, according to their supposition, was obliged to make use of a fallacy to govern the world. . . . But what an unworthy opinion does this convey of God and his government, of his infinite majesty, and wisdom, and all-sufficiency!—Beside, they suppose that though God has made use of such a fallacy, yet it is not such an one but that they have detected him in it."[47] Now Archbishop Tillotson was not, of course, himself a deist, but he was a precursor of the deists, and Edwards did not underestimate the threat posed by Tillotson's "moderate" and "reasonable" Christianity. He regarded the "generosity" of Tillotson's views as a spurious and dangerous generosity; and in combating the views of the Archbishop, Edwards sought to provide a reasoned and scriptural counterblast to the benevolist and humanitarian pull of the age.

## THE IMMEDIACY OF THE LIVING GOD

"'Tis a strange disposition that men have," Edwards insists, "to thrust God out of the world, or to put him as far out of sight as they can, and to have in no respect immediately and sensibly to do with Him. Therefore, so many

42. Edwards, *Works* (Hickman), 2:516.
43. Edwards, *Works* (Hickman), 2:517.
44. Edwards, *Works* (Hickman), 2:83.
45. Edwards, *Works* (Hickman), 2:515.
46. Edwards, *Works* (Hickman), 2:518.
47. Edwards, *Works* (Hickman), 2:86.

schemes have been drawn to exclude, or extenuate, or remove at a great distance, any influence of the Divine Being in the hearts of men, such as the scheme of the Pelagians, the Socinians, etc."[48] Edwards does not specifically mention the deists here, but there can be no doubt that he had the scheme of the deists very much in mind. For the great tendency of the deists was precisely that of putting God at a distance. The deists believed, of course, in the existence of God, but their God was a God that was distant, passive, inert, and remote. God was the Supreme Being—the great Architect or Mechanic who had created the universe in the beginning but who then left the universe to run its own course as a self-operating machine. God was not involved in the world—he did not intervene or interfere in the affairs of men. The deists denied supernatural revelation; they denied miracles, the incarnation, God's moral government, his providence, the communication of his Spirit. The God of the deists was a Deity in absentia, a depersonalized God, the unmoved Mover of the universe.

Now it is vital to remember that Jonathan Edwards lived in the age of Newtonian physics. Sir Isaac Newton died in 1727, when Edwards was twenty-three, but Newton had already opened up a universe which was governed by natural law. The Newtonians, however, tended to move in a distinctly deistic direction. The post-Newtonian universe was conceived by Newton's followers as a mechanical, mathematical universe. God's creation was conceived as an intricate, impersonal, inert machine. Science was now dominated by the notions of mechanical causation and the uniformity of natural law. This new emphasis ruled out the immediate activity of God in the world, and God was thus pushed to the remote edge of the universe. Dr. Douglas J. Elwood comments that "the chief problem of the eighteenth century became one of relocating God in a post-Newtonian universe."[49] The deists were seeking to put God at a great distance from the world, while Edwards, with his remarkable emphasis upon divine immediacy, was consciously opposing this deistic notion of a First Cause operating at a remote distance from its effects. For Edwards, deism was the very acme of those related schemes, "Arianism, Socinianism, Arminianism, and Deism," which all sought, in varying degrees, to distance man from God.[50] The deists denied the immediacy of God, but for Edwards the immediacy of God was a great and glorious reality. Indeed, Dr. Elwood has argued very cogently that Edwards' concept of divine immediacy is the controlling idea or principle of correlation that runs throughout his works. "His whole theology," writes

48. Edwards, *Treatise on Grace*, 53.

49. Elwood, *Philosophical Theology*, 51.

50. Edwards, *Works* (Hickman), 1:233.

Dr. Elwood, "stands out against all forms of deism. . . . It rises in opposition to any view that tends to separate God from the world he has made."[51] This emphasis of Edwards is evident, for instance, in his remarkable doctrine of creation. Edwards believed in continuous creation—he believed in "the continued immediate efficiency of God."[52] In *Original Sin* he makes the following assertion, which stands in such stark contrast to the emphasis of the deists:

> As the child and the acorn which come into existence according to the course of nature, in consequence of the prior existence and state of the parent and the oak, are truly immediately created by God, so must the existence of each created person and thing, at each moment, be from the immediate continued creation of God. It will certainly follow from these things, that God's preserving of created things in being, is perfectly equivalent to a continued creation, or to his creating those things out of nothing at each moment of their existence. If the continued existence of created things be wholly dependent on God's preservation, then those things would drop into nothing upon the ceasing of the present moment, without a new exertion of the divine power to cause them to exist in the following moment.[53]

Edwards' insistence upon the immediacy of God emerges also in his understanding of God's moral government over the world of mankind. In contradistinction to the deists, who separated the concept of God as Creator from the concept of God as Moral Governor of the world, Edwards explained that God is not "an indifferent spectator" of the conduct of his highest creatures, nor will he "act as a perfectly indifferent spectator."[54] Edwards insists that "the Creator of the world is doubtless also the Governor of it."[55] For Edwards any divorce between God as Creator and God as Moral Governor of the world is unthinkable. Indeed, so intense is Edwards' determinism and his concept of the sovereignty of God, that all question of Arminian contingency, conditionalism, or self-determination in human affairs is excluded. God is "the supreme Orderer of all things";[56] God is "the all-wise Determiner of all events."[57] Edwards' insistence on "an universal

51. Elwood, *Philosophical Theology*, 9.
52. Edwards, *Works* (Hickman), 2:512.
53. Edwards, *Works* (Hickman), 2:512.
54. Edwards, *Works* (Hickman), 2:51.
55. Edwards, *Works* (Hickman), 1:79.
56. Edwards, *Works* (Hickman), 1:79.
57. Edwards, *Works* (Hickman), 1:87.

determining Providence" coheres very well with his insistence upon the involvement and immediacy of God in the world.[58]

Again, this same correlating principle emerges in Edwards' doctrine of regeneration. In his *Treatise on Grace* Edwards again takes the offensive against the deistic tendencies of those that deny the immediate influence of the Spirit of God. "This doctrine of a gracious nature being by the immediate influence of the Spirit of God, is not only taught in the Scriptures, but is irrefragable to reason. Indeed there seems to be a strong disposition in men . . . to disbelieve and oppose the doctrine of immediate influence of the Spirit of God in the hearts of men, or to diminish and to make it as small and remote a matter as possible, and put it as far out of sight as may be."[59] Moreover, in one of the early sermons entitled "A Divine and Supernatural Light, Immediately Imparted to the Soul by the Spirit of God, Shown to Be Both a Scriptural and Rational Doctrine," Edwards maintained that this light is imparted in regeneration without the use of any intermediate natural causes. In this sense it is quite different from other knowledge. "This is a kind of intuitive and immediate evidence," Edwards contends. "It is a kind of emanation of God's beauty."[60] "It is as immediately from God, as light from the sun."[61]

Dr. Elwood's central thesis that the works of Jonathan Edwards are characterized by the correlating principle of divine immediacy can in fact be extended into Edwards' theology of revival. For Edwards, revival involved "remarkable communications of the Spirit of God, . . . remarkable effusions at special seasons of mercy."[62] In times of revival or awakening, the Spirit of God himself is poured out—the Spirit of God himself is communicated. Thus, the outstanding characteristic of revival is the presence of God. "God appears unusually present," writes Edwards. "God . . . is then extraordinarily present."[63] Edwards had personally witnessed the phenomenon of revival in Northampton in 1734–35, and in the Great Awakening in New England in 1740–42. Moreover, it is clear that Edwards regarded one's attitude towards these awakenings as a touchstone of one's theology: "Can any good medium be found," he writes in his "Thoughts on the Revival," "where a man can rest with any stability, between owning this work, and being a deist? If indeed this be the work of God, does it not entirely overthrow their scheme of

58. Edwards, *Treatise on Grace*, 52.

59. Edwards, *Works* (Hickman), 2:14.

60. Edwards, *Works* (Hickman), 2:16.

61. Edwards, *Works* (Hickman), 2:15.

62. Edwards, *Works* (Hickman), 1:539.

63. Edwards, *Works* (Hickman), 1:393.

religion; and does it not infinitely concern them, as they would be partakers of eternal salvation, to relinquish their scheme? Now is a good time for Arminians to change their principles."[64] Edwards had in mind here men such as Charles Chauncy and those who were known as the "Old Lights"—rationalistic Arminians opposed to the concept of divine immediacy and whose Arminianism was virtually incipient deism. "With remarkable prescience," writes C. C. Goen, "Edwards foresaw that the Great Awakening was to become a decisive watershed in American religious thought. As history would eventually reveal, many of the rationalistic opposers were really pre-Unitarians who would develop an ever more self-conscious antithesis to evangelicalism until the result could fairly be called Deism."[65]

Inseparably linked to Edwards' theology of revival is his concept of "divine discoveries" to the soul of the believer. "God sometimes is pleased to remove the veil, to draw the curtain, and to give the saints sweet visions. Sometimes there is, as it were, a window opened in heaven, and Christ shows himself through the lattice; they have sometimes a beam of sweet light breaking forth from above into the soul; and God and the Redeemer sometimes come to them, and make friendly visits to them, and manifest themselves to them."[66] Jonathan Edwards himself had known such experiences; Sarah Edwards, his wife, had known such experiences also; so too had Abigail Hutchinson in the awakening in Northampton in 1734–35. Such "discoveries" were in Edwards' mind "a kind of beatific vision of God."[67]

Such, then, is Edwards' concept of the immediacy of the divine presence. There is in his writings this remarkable emphasis upon the immanence of God, the reality of God, even the visibility of God. "God is a communicating Being,"[68] Edwards insists. "With his vision," comments Dr. Joseph Haroutunian, "he demolished deism."[69] And while certain aspects of Edwards' thought—notably, perhaps, his doctrine of continuous creation—can be explained in terms of his recoil from deism, yet essentially his vision of the immediacy of God in his providence, his moral government, in redemption, regeneration, and revival, and indeed in the possibility of the beatific vision in this world, is to be traced to the Scriptures. "Whither shall I flee from Thy presence?" (Ps 139:7). "Behold, the heaven and the heaven of heavens

64. Edwards, *Works* (Hickman), 1:422–23.

65. C. C. Goen, in Edwards, *Great Awakening*, 78.

66. Edwards, *Works* (Hickman), 2:889–90.

67. Edwards, *Works* (Hickman), 1:360.

68. Townsend, *Philosophy of Jonathan Edwards*, 130.

69. Cited in Elwood, *Philosophical Theology*, ix.

cannot contain Thee" (1 Kgs 8:27). For God is "not far from every one of us: for in Him we live, and move, and have our being" (Acts 17:27–28).

# JONATHAN EDWARDS AND THE THEOLOGY OF REVIVAL[1]

"It may here be observed," writes Jonathan Edwards, "that from the fall of man, to our day, the work of redemption in its effect has mainly been carried on by remarkable communications of the Spirit of God. Though there be a more constant influence of God's Spirit always in some degree attending his ordinances; yet the way in which the greatest things have been done towards carrying on this work, always have been by remarkable effusions, at special seasons of mercy."[2] Now this statement, written in his treatise *A History of the Work of Redemption*, contains, I believe, the key to an understanding of Jonathan Edwards' theology of revival. It contains the key for this reason, that as this great theologian surveyed the vast panorama of biblical and ecclesiastical history, he noticed two major patterns. On the one hand there was, as he puts it, a more constant influence of God's Spirit always attending upon the church; that remains constant. But in addition to this more constant influence of God's Spirit there were special times and special seasons when God's Spirit was poured out, when God came, as it were, when God descended in mighty power. Therefore, Edwards speaks also of "remarkable communications of the Spirit of God" and of "remarkable effusions at special seasons of mercy." In other words, as he surveyed the history of the Bible and the history of the Christian church, he could see the heights as well as the more normal periods; he could see the heights as well as the times of declension. He sees this pattern of ebb and flow in the Spirit's dealings with the church.

But who was Jonathan Edwards and why should we consider him here today? Jonathan Edwards was born in New England in the year 1703.

1. This lecture was given at the Spring Family Bible Conference at Westminster Presbyterian Church, Jacksonville, FL, Mar. 8, 1997.

2. Edwards, *Works* (Hickman), 1:539.

He died, prematurely, of a smallpox vaccination in 1758. However, during that brief life Edwards experienced, on two remarkable occasions, the great phenomenon of revival. Not only did he experience revival twice, but he, above all other men, analyzed revival and bequeathed to us a theology of revival, that we might see the mighty acts of God and understand the way in which God works during these wonderful, special seasons of mercy. The vast majority of the ministry of Jonathan Edwards was spent in the town of Northampton in Massachusetts. Edwards was called there to be the assistant to his grandfather, Solomon Stoddard—a man who had had a very lengthy and influential ministry in that same pulpit in Northampton. Now, Jonathan Edwards is widely regarded as the greatest philosopher that America has ever produced. He is certainly the greatest theologian that America has ever produced, and he is also one of America's greatest preachers. It is a sad reflection upon the days in which we live that all too often his name is vilified, that he is dismissed merely as the preacher of that particular sermon, "Sinners in the Hands of an Angry God," and when men who have not studied him are very ready to dismiss him. He was a distinctly great man of God, a distinctly great servant of God, and well deserves the title of "*the* theologian of revival."

Now I mentioned that Jonathan Edwards' predecessor was Solomon Stoddard; and Edwards himself, describing Solomon Stoddard's ministry, says this concerning him: "He had five harvests."[3] What does he mean by that striking phrase? He means this, that as you look at the ministry of Solomon Stoddard—a ministry that stretched over almost sixty years—there were five years that stand out. They were seasons of remarkable blessing. "Five harvests," he calls them—five years of remarkable ingathering. I emphasize that for this reason, that there is in the theology of Jonathan Edwards this concept of *periodicity*. In other words, there are these times, these seasons when God comes in a special, remarkable, extraordinary manner, when his Spirit is given, when his Spirit is communicated and poured out, when there is this remarkable phenomenon of widespread conviction of sin, when sinners are brought savingly to the Lord Jesus Christ. This is the phenomenon that Edwards is describing—"five harvests." We notice, then, this concept of periodicity, this ebb and flow, in the history of the Christian church.

Now then, Solomon Stoddard died in 1729, shortly after Jonathan Edwards had come to be his assistant in the pulpit at Northampton; and Edwards comments that the time following Solomon Stoddard's death was in fact "a time of extraordinary dullness in religion."[4] It was a time of declen-

3. Edwards, *Works* (Hickman), 1:347.

4. Edwards, *Works* (Hickman), 1:347.

sion; it was not a time of harvest; it was not a time of ingathering. Rather it was a season of "extraordinary dullness." However, before long a remarkable revival—one of the great historical revivals of all time, the revival that occurred in 1734–35—was to break out in the town of Northampton. What were the circumstances that led up to that particular revival? Well, in and of themselves they may seem insignificant. Edwards says this, that there were two significant deaths in the town which solemnized the people. One was a young man, the other was a young woman; and these deaths had an awakening and solemnizing effect upon the people in the town, and acted as a kind of harbinger of the revival that was shortly to follow. In addition to that, he mentions this: the threat of Arminianism. Arminianism is, of course, that system of theology which does not do justice to the sovereignty of God or to the absolute nature of God's mighty work in redemption. This Arminianism involved an emphasis upon human effort and moral striving, and it was beginning to infiltrate the situation in New England. Even though the Pilgrim fathers had arrived only some one hundred years earlier, already there was the threat of Arminianism; and this was taken seriously by the people of God in that particular area. And this threat—the spectre of corrupt, heterodox principles—again caused concern and had a quickening and awakening effect. Now, it was because of this threat of Arminianism that Jonathan Edwards began to lecture on the great doctrine of justification by faith alone—that doctrine which Martin Luther once described as "the article of the standing or the falling of the church." Edwards comments that it seemed to be "a word spoken in season."[5] It seems to have been vindicated of God, because it was in the wake of this series on justification by faith alone that God's Spirit began to set in. Edwards speaks of a climate of "religious concern."[6] The time of extraordinary dullness had given way now to an awakened and quickened spirit and atmosphere. "And *then* it was," says Edwards, "in the latter part of *December*, *that the Spirit of God* began extraordinarily to set in, and *wonderfully* to work amongst us; and there were, very suddenly, one after another, five or six persons, who were to all appearance savingly converted, and some of them wrought upon in a very remarkable manner."[7] Edwards is describing December 1734. This revival was to last some six months, and Edwards is describing the beginning of the revival. Notice how he puts it that the Spirit of God began in the latter part of December to "set in." He was poured out from on high; and you will notice immediately the effect: there were convictions, there were

5. Edwards, *Works* (Hickman), 1:347.

6. Edwards, *Works* (Hickman), 1:347.

7. Edwards, *Works* (Hickman), 1:348; emphasis original.

conversions. Some five or six persons, he says, one after the other, were very wonderfully converted.

Now Edwards then describes the conversion of a young woman. This particular young woman he describes as "one of the greatest company keepers in the town." It appears that she may well have had a very bad reputation. But this young woman was wonderfully converted and brought home savingly to the Lord Jesus Christ; and the effect of this particular conversion was quite dramatic. It was "like a flash of lightning" upon the people. The news of it spread; it had a powerful effect; and this is what Edwards says about this conversion: it was "a glorious work of God's infinite power and sovereign grace."[8] And he goes on to speak of the revival in this way:

> Presently upon this, a great and earnest concern about the great things of religion, and the eternal world became *universal* in all parts of the town, and among persons of all degrees, and all ages. The noise amongst the *dry* bones waxed louder and louder; all other talk but about spiritual and eternal things, was soon thrown by; all the conversation, in all companies, and upon all occasions, was upon these things only, unless so much as was necessary for people carrying on their ordinary secular business. Other discourse than of the things of religion, would scarcely be tolerated in any company. The minds of people were wonderfully taken off from the *world*, it was treated amongst us as a thing of very little consequence. They seemed to follow their worldly business, more as a part of their duty than from any disposition they had to it; the *temptation* now seemed to lie on that hand, to *neglect* worldly affairs too much, and to spend too much time in the immediate exercise of religion. . . . But although the people did not ordinarily neglect their worldly business; yet *religion* was with all sorts the great concern, and the *world* was a thing only by the bye. The only thing in their view was to get the kingdom of heaven, and every one appeared pressing into it.[9]

Notice that—his emphasis upon this spiritual concern—this concern to press into the kingdom of God. You see, this is what happens in a revival. It is a quickening, it is a divine touch, it is an awakening, it is a shower of blessing from on high. God's Spirit comes, God's Spirit is poured out. Sinners are convicted; they are converted; they turn to Christ. The people of God are enhanced in holiness and in sanctification; they too press forward in the things of God. There is this general quickening of the pulse of religion

8. Edwards, *Works* (Hickman), 1:348.

9. Edwards, *Works* (Hickman), 1:348; emphasis original.

among the people of God; and sinners are affected, and they press into God's kingdom.

Now what kind of preaching was it that produced this awakening? What kind of preaching was it that God used? It is very important, I think, to see the connection between the kind of preaching that was heard from Edwards' pulpit and the quickening and the awakening that occurred under that preaching. I want therefore to give you an example—a sample, if you like, of his preaching at that particular time; and therefore I am going to quote from one particular sermon that was greatly used of God: "The Justice of God in the Damnation of Sinners." The text was this, "That every mouth may be stopped." He was preaching from Romans chapter 3. Notice the searching, pointed nature of Jonathan Edwards' preaching:

> You have not only neglected your salvation, but you have willfully taken direct courses to *undo* yourself. You have gone on in those ways and practices that have directly tended to your damnation, and have been perverse and obstinate in it. You cannot plead ignorance; you had all the light set before you that you could desire; God told you that you was undoing yourself; but yet you would do it: he told you that the path you was going in led to destruction, and counseled you to avoid it; but you would not hearken: how justly therefore may God leave you to be undone! You have obstinately persisted to travel in the way that leads to hell for a long time, contrary to God's continual counsels and commands, till it may be at length you are got almost to your journey's end, and are come near to hell's gate, and so begin to be sensible of your danger and misery; and now account it unjust and hard, if God won't deliver you! You have destroyed yourself, and destroyed yourself willfully, contrary to God's repeated counsels, yea, and destroyed yourself in fighting against God: now therefore why do you blame any but yourself, if you are destroyed? If you will undo yourself in opposing God, and while God opposes you by his calls and counsels, and, it may be too, by the convictions of his Spirit, what can you object against it, if God now leaves you to be undone? You would have your own way, and did not like that God should oppose you in it, and your way was to ruin your own soul: how just therefore is it, if now at length, God ceases to oppose you, and falls in with you, and lets your soul be ruined, and as you would destroy yourself, so should put to his hand to destroy you, too! The ways you went on in had a natural tendency to your misery: if you would drink poison, in opposition to God, and in contempt of him and his advice, who can you blame but yourself if you are

> poisoned, and so perish? If you would run into the fire against all restraints both of God's mercy and authority, you must e'en blame yourself if you are burnt.[10]

Notice, then, the very searching nature of this preaching that the people of Northampton were hearing. Let me just give you one more extract from this sermon:

> God may justly show greater respect to others than to you, for you have shown greater respect to others than to God. You have rather chosen to offend God than men. God only shows a greater respect to others, who are by nature your equals, than to you; but you have shown a greater respect to those that are infinitely inferior to God than to him. You have shown a greater regard to *wicked* men than to God; you have honoured them more, loved them better, and adhered to them rather than to him. Yea, you have honoured the devil, in many respects, more than God: you have chosen his will and his interest, rather than God's will and his glory: you have chosen a little worldly pelf, rather than God: you have set more by a vile lust than by him: you have chosen these things, and rejected God. You have set your heart on these things, and cast God behind your back: and where is the injustice if God is pleased to show greater respect to others than to you, or if he chooses others and rejects you. You have shown great respect to vile and worthless things, and no respect to God's glory; and why may not God set his love on others, and have no respect to your happiness? You have shown great respect to others, and not to God, whom you are laid under infinite obligations to respect above all; and why may not God show respect unto others, and not to you, who never have laid him under the least obligation?[11]

That was the kind of preaching that the people in Northampton were hearing at the time of the revival; and Edwards goes on to describe this revival, this remarkable outpouring of God's Spirit, in this way:

> This work of God . . . soon made a glorious alteration in the town: so that in the spring and summer following, *anno* 1735, the town seemed to be full of the presence of God: it never was so full of *love*, nor of *joy*, and yet so full of distress, as it was then. There were remarkable tokens of God's presence in almost every house. It was a time of joy in *families* on account of salvation

10. Edwards, *Sermons and Discourses, 1734–1738*, 371–72.

11. Edwards, *Works* (Hickman), 1:679.

> being brought unto them; *parents* rejoicing over their children as new born, and *husbands* over their wives, and *wives* over their husbands. *The goings of God* were then *seen in his sanctuary*, God's *day* was *a delight*, and his *tabernacles* were *amiable*. Our public assemblies were then beautiful: the congregation was *alive* in God's service, every one earnestly intent on the public worship, every *hearer* eager to drink in the words of the *minister* as they came from his mouth; the assembly in general were, from time to time, *in tears* while the word was preached; *some* weeping with sorrow and distress, *others* with joy and love, *others* with pity and concern for the souls of their neighbours.[12]

This, then, was the revival that occurred—this famous revival which Jonathan Edwards has recorded for us in great detail in his *Faithful Narrative of the Surprising Work of God*. Let me, in passing, commend that work to you. It is one of the great seminal works on the subject of revival and it had a remarkable influence upon Great Britain. Edwards had this work published; it was sent to Great Britain and published there and, as a result, the news of this revival kindled a desire for further revival in Great Britain. Notice too the way in which Edwards describes this revival. He speaks of "this shower of divine blessing,"[13] "this remarkable pouring out of the Spirit of God."[14]

Now, how extensive was the work of conversion? I have emphasized that conviction of sin and conversion is one of the great hallmarks of revival. How extensive was this? Well, remember that the town of Northampton at that particular time consisted, Edwards tells us, of some two hundred families. He tells us that there were probably "more than 300 souls"[15] converted out of these two hundred families. Indeed, he gives details as to the age and the age range involved. There were two above the age of seventy who were converted at this time; about ten above the age of sixty; more than twenty above the age of fifty; more than fifty above the age of forty; about two hundred between the ages of fifteen and forty; nearly thirty between the ages of ten and fourteen; two aged about nine and ten; and remarkably there was one who was aged four—a little girl who was aged four. Now, Edwards goes into some detail. He mentions "two *particular instances*"[16] and he describes them in great detail. I want, first, to tell you about this little girl who was aged four. Her name was Phebe Bartlet. She had a number of brothers and sisters; and

12. Edwards, *Works* (Hickman), 1:348; emphasis original.
13. Edwards, *Works* (Hickman), 1:349.
14. Edwards, *Works* (Hickman), 1:349.
15. Edwards, *Works* (Hickman), 1:350.
16. Edwards, *Works* (Hickman), 1:359; emphasis original.

she was, apparently, greatly affected by the conversion of her brother at this time. Her parents had not particularly addressed their remarks on spiritual things to her, because they considered her too young. But then they began to notice that Phebe would retire regularly to her closet five or six times a day. Her mother would hear her praying out loud; and this is what her mother heard: "PRAY, BLESSED LORD, *give me salvation!* I PRAY, BEG, *pardon all my sins!*"[17] This, my good friends, a little girl aged four! There were some weeks that elapsed before she was actually converted, it seems. At first she was seeking, and then wonderfully she found the Savior. This is what happened—she came out of her bedroom on one occasion and, after a period of considerable distress, suddenly said this: "*Mother, the kingdom of heaven is come to me!*" A little later she came out of her closet again and said, "*I can find God now!*"[18] On one occasion she said this, "I have been talking to *Nabby* and *Eunice. . . . I told them they must pray, and prepare to die*; that they had *but a little while to live in this world, and they must always be ready.*"[19] Now, I want you to listen to Jonathan Edwards' assessment of this young girl. He speaks of "a very remarkable abiding change in the child. . . . She seems to delight much in hearing religious conversation. . . . She seems to have very much of the fear of God before her eyes, and an extraordinary dread of sinning against him. . . . She has often manifested a great concern for the good of others' souls: and has been wont many times affectionately to counsel the other children. . . . She has discovered an uncommon degree of a spirit of charity. . . . She has manifested great love to her minister. . . . She still continues very constant in secret prayer."[20] My dear friends, this is not just a surprising conversion; this is an absolutely astonishing and staggering conversion, and the experience of this young child at this particular time is really quite amazing. It is very interesting to note that in 1789 Phebe Bartlet was still alive and still witnessed a good confession and profession. She had the character of a true and sound convert.

The second person that Edwards describes in his narrative is Abigail Hutchinson. This young woman was in fact sickly and infirm, and before long was going to die. But she was very wonderfully converted. She was awakened by the news of the conversion of the other young woman—the company keeper whom I mentioned earlier. She began to seek; she began to search the Scriptures; and before very long there was a deep and profound conviction of sin in the heart and soul of Abigail Hutchinson. "Her *great*

17. Edwards, *Works* (Hickman), 1:361.

18. Edwards, *Works* (Hickman), 1:362.

19. Edwards, *Works* (Hickman), 1:363; emphasis original.

20. Edwards, *Works* (Hickman), 1:362–63.

*terror*, she said, was *that she had sinned against God*; her distress grew more and more for three days, until she saw *nothing but blackness and darkness before her, and her very flesh trembled for fear of God's wrath*; she *wondered and was astonished at herself, that she had been so concerned for her body, and had applied so often to physicians to heal that, and had neglected her soul*."[21] This woman was undergoing what our forefathers have described as "the pangs of the new birth." We seldom hear that phrase today. I commend it to your attention—"the pangs of the new birth." For just as there are pangs when a child comes into the world, so there are often pangs when a sinner is born again and presses into the kingdom of God. But before long this deep, profound conviction of sin had turned into joy and rejoicing; and this is what Edwards says: "She had many extraordinary discoveries of the glory of God and Christ. . . . Her mind was so swallowed up with a sense of the glory of God's *truth* and other perfections, that she said, *it seemed as though her life was going*, and that she *saw it was easy with God to take away her life by discoveries of himself*." And Edwards makes this comment: "It seemed to me she dwelt for days together in a kind of *beatific vision* of God."[22]

This woman, as I have mentioned, was very sick and infirm. She had a condition of the throat which ultimately meant that she could not eat or drink, and Edwards tells us that basically she died of famine. But, my dear friends, she died well! Just as the Methodists described by John Wesley were said to "die well," so too Abigail Hutchinson died well; and these were the words frequently upon her lips at the end: "*God is my friend!*" She knew that she was reconciled to God by the Person and work of the Lord Jesus Christ; and Edwards says concerning her that she was a "very eminent instance of Christian experience."[23]

Now Edwards mentions some very interesting social consequences of this remarkable revival. He comments on the health of the people of Northampton: "It was," he says, "the most remarkable time of health that ever I knew since I have been in the town."[24] The reason for that is this: the relationship between the soul and the body—the way in which the soul can affect the body in a number of different respects. But he also makes another social comment with regard to the tavern. He says, "The place of resort was now altered, it was no longer the tavern, but the minister's house that was thronged far more than the tavern had ever been wont to be."[25] The people

21. Edwards, *Works* (Hickman), 1:359; emphasis original.

22. Edwards, *Works* (Hickman), 1:360.

23. Edwards, *Works* (Hickman), 1:361; emphasis original.

24. Edwards, *Works* (Hickman), 1:363.

25. Edwards, *Works* (Hickman), 1:351.

were pressing into the kingdom of God, and they were now pressing into the minister's house rather than into the tavern.

Now Edwards describes not only the setting in of the Spirit of God, but also the withdrawing of the Spirit of God. He says this: "In the latter part of May"—that is 1735—"it began to be very sensible that the Spirit of God was gradually withdrawing from us, and after this time *Satan* seemed to be more let loose, and raged in a dreadful manner. The first instance wherein it appeared, was a person putting an end to his own life by cutting his throat." A man committed suicide, and this was one of the marks of Satan's raging against them and of the withdrawing of the influence of God's Spirit at that particular time. How long did this revival last? Well, it lasted some six months, from December 1734 through to May 1735; and Edwards' overall assessment of the revival is in these words: "In the main, there has been a *great and marvelous work of conversion and sanctification* among the people here. . . . And we are evidently a people blessed of the Lord! For here, *in this corner of the world*, God dwells, and manifests his glory."[26]

I want to mention now an experience which Jonathan Edwards himself had in the year 1737, some two years after the revival itself. He says this:

> Once, as I rid out into the woods for my health, *anno* 1737; and having lit from my horse in a retired place, as my manner commonly has been, to walk for divine contemplation and prayer; I had a view, that for me was extraordinary, of the glory of the Son of God, as mediator between God and man; and his wonderful, great, full, pure and sweet grace and love, and meek and gentle condescension. This grace that appeared to me so calm and sweet, appeared great above the heavens. The person of Christ appeared ineffably excellent, with an excellency great enough to swallow up all thought and conception. Which continued, as near as I can judge, about an hour; which kept me, the bigger part of the time, in a flood of tears, and weeping aloud. I felt withal, an ardency of soul to be, what I know not otherwise how to express, than to be emptied and annihilated; to lie in the dust, and to be full of Christ alone; to love him with a holy and pure love; to trust in him; to live upon him; to serve and follow him, and to be perfectly sanctified and made pure, with a divine and heavenly purity. I have several other times, had views very much of the same nature, and that have had the same effects.[27]

26. Edwards, *Works* (Hickman), 1:363; emphasis original.

27. Edwards, *Letters and Personal Writings*, 801.

I want to emphasize that this was not some vision with the bodily eyes; Edwards had no brief for such things. Rather this was a vision to the eyes of the soul, a vision to the eyes of the mind, if you like, of the glory of the blessed and eternal Son of God, as he meditated upon him, of his infinite transcendence and glorious efficacy, as the Mediator between God and men, and as Edwards meditated upon this, so he was utterly broken down with weeping, and yet with joy. My dear friends, what you see here in Jonathan Edwards is, I suggest, a touch of the revival in him personally, so that what happens in revival is really the multiplication synchronously of this same experience in the lives of many, many people. Edwards puts this in the category of "discoveries of Christ"—Christ revealing himself in this remarkable way to the mind and the soul of the believer; and he describes such experiences as "prelibations of heaven's glory given upon earth."[28]

I want to look now at the Great Awakening, which broke out in 1740 and which lasted roughly until 1742. By now the great English preacher George Whitefield had come and had joined Edwards and the Tennents and others, and an even more remarkable revival had broken out in New England. It was during the Great Awakening that Edwards had preached that sermon which is so famous and even notorious, "Sinners in the Hands of an Angry God." Let me read to you an extract from this sermon, because it shows the connection between the preaching and the revival that occurred. This what Edwards says about the condition of those that are now in hell:

> If we could speak with them, and inquire of them, one by one, whether they expected, when alive, and when they used to hear about hell, ever to be the subjects of that misery, we, doubtless, should hear one and another reply, "No, I never intended to come here: I had laid out matters otherwise in my mind; I thought I should contrive well for myself: I thought my scheme good. I intended to take effectual care; but it came upon me unexpected: I did not look for it at that time, and in that manner; it came as a thief: Death outwitted me: God's wrath was too quick for me. O my cursed foolishness! I was flattering myself, and pleasing myself with vain dreams of what I would do hereafter; and when I was saying, Peace and safety, then sudden destruction came upon me."[29]

Now this sermon had a most remarkable effect upon the people, and there is a description, which has been passed down to us, of the effect of this particular sermon which he delivered at Enfield in Connecticut in the year

28. Edwards, *Works* (Hickman), 1:380.

29. Edwards, *Works* (Hickman), 2:9.

1741. Benjamin Trumbull informs us that "before the sermon was ended, the assembly appeared deeply impressed and bowed down with an awful conviction of their sin and danger. There was such a breathing of distress and weeping, that the preacher was obliged to speak to the people and desire silence, that he might be heard. This was the beginning of the same great and prevailing concern in that place, with which the colony in general was visited."[30]

My dear friends, I want to ask you this question: When did you last see someone truly, powerfully under conviction of sin? When did you last see weeping under the preaching of the word of God? When did you last see sinners pressing with a holy violence into God's kingdom? When did you last hear the word of God going forth with such power that men were bowed down before it, and could not evade it, but had to press into the kingdom of God? This is what happens in times of revival. This is why we should read about these things; this is why we should long for these things; this is why we should pray for these things. Jonathan Edwards puts it in this way, that revival involves "the outpouring of God's Spirit"—"remarkable effusions at special seasons of mercy." "God appears unusually present" at such times, he writes. "God . . . is then extraordinarily present."[31] It is the remarkable, unusual, extraordinary presence of God that characterizes a revival; and there are, I suggest, two hallmarks of this in particular: first, a deep, profound sense of sin that constrains men and drives them to go to Jesus Christ for salvation; and second, this "joy unspeakable and full of glory" (1 Pet 1:8) as they press into God's kingdom and as they find the Savior.

You know, Jonathan Edwards' wife had some most remarkable experiences. She had been a Christian for many years, but you see this "joy unspeakable and full of glory" in Sarah Edwards. Edwards describes her, interestingly, as "the person." He says,

> The person has more than once continued for five or six hours together, without interruption, in a clear and lively view or sense of the infinite beauty and amiableness of Christ's person, and the heavenly sweetness of his transcendent love; so that (to use the person's own expressions) the soul remained in a kind of heavenly elysium, and did as it were swim in the rays of Christ's love, like a little mote swimming in the beams of the sun that come in at a window. The heart was swallowed up in a kind of glow of Christ's love, coming down as a constant stream of sweet light, at the same time the soul all flowing out in love to him; so

30. Cited in Tracy, *Great Awakening*, 216.

31. Edwards, *Works* (Hickman), 1:393.

> that there seemed to be a constant flowing and reflowing from heart to heart.[32]

With regard to his wife, Edwards says that she experienced "a kind of paradise," that she experienced "a kind of omnipotent joy," as if her soul was so powerful that it would leap up and almost leave the body.[33] These things, my dear friends, are really quite remarkable, are they not? They are strange to our ears because we have not experienced them. This is why it behooves us to read about revival, to long for it, and to pray for it.

Listen to the way in which Edwards defends these experiences against the charge of "enthusiasm":

> Now if such things are enthusiasm, and the fruits of a distempered brain, let my brain be evermore possessed of that happy distemper. If this be distraction, I pray God that the world of mankind may be all seized with this benign, meek, beneficent, beatifical, glorious distraction. . . . And what notions have they of religion, that reject what has been described, as not true religion. What shall we find to answer those expressions in Scripture, 'The peace of God that passeth all understanding; rejoicing with joy unspeakable and full of glory, in believing in and loving an unseen Saviour.—All joy and peace in believing; God's shining into our hearts, to give the light of the knowledge of the glory of God, in the face of Jesus Christ; With open face, beholding as in a glass the glory of the Lord, and being changed into the same image, from glory to glory, even as by the Spirit of the Lord;—Having the love of God shed abroad in our hearts, by the Holy Ghost given to us;—A being called out of darkness into marvelous light; and having the day-star arise in our hearts'—I say, if those things which have been mentioned, do not answer these expressions, what else can we find out that does answer them?[34]

Now, Jonathan Edwards, during the Great Awakening, was in fact fighting a battle on two fronts; and this is where you see the balance and the judiciousness of this great man of God and of this great theologian. On the one hand there were those who, like Charles Chauncy, the pastor of the First Church in Boston, were opposers of the revival and who engaged in a rationalistic dismissing of the phenomena of the revival. Edwards had to oppose them and resist them. Equally, he had to oppose certain friends of the revival—in particular, James Davenport, who went to extremes, who

32. Edwards, *Works* (Hickman), 1:376.

33. Edwards, *Works* (Hickman), 1:376.

34. Edwards, *Works* (Hickman), 1:378.

was guilty of excesses, who basically succumbed to fanaticism at times. What you find in Jonathan Edwards is a resistance to both these extremes—a resistance to the rationalistic opposers and a resistance to the fanatical friends of the revival—those that were liable to bring the revival itself into disrepute.

In his treatise *The Distinguishing Marks of a Work of the Spirit of God*, Edwards lays down very valuable criteria by which we can judge and assess and evaluate a revival. First of all he gives *nine negative signs*. These signs are negative in this sense, that if they are present, they are no sign that the work in general is not a revival:

1. That the work is carried on in an unusual and extraordinary way.
2. That it produces strong effects upon the bodies of its subjects.
3. That it occasions "a great deal of noise about religion".
4. That it produces lively impressions upon people's imaginations.
5. That it is promoted very much by the influence of example (i.e., by imitation).
6. That it results in imprudent and irregular conduct.
7. That errors of judgment and "delusions of Satan" intermingle with it.
8. That some of its professed converts later fall into gross errors or scandal.
9. That its preachers insist very much on the terrors of God's wrath.[35]

Nine negative signs—these things do not prove that the work in general is not of the Spirit of God.

But in addition to giving some nine negative signs, he also gives *five positive signs*; and how important they are. It is a work of God, Edwards says, if:

1. It raises men's esteem of Jesus as Son of God and Savior of the world.
2. It leads them to turn from their corruptions and lusts to the righteousness of God.
3. It increases their regard for the Holy Scriptures.
4. It establishes their minds in the objective truths of revealed religion.
5. It evokes genuine love for God and man.[36]

35. Edwards, *Works* (Hickman), 2:261–65.

36. Edwards, *Works* (Hickman), 2:266–68.

These are the hallmarks, positively, says Edwards, which establish whether a particular work is indeed a work of revival.

Now Edwards acknowledges that mistakes were made in the Great Awakening; he acknowledges that there were blemishes and imprudences. He says that this is not surprising; it is only to be expected. But the very existence of blemishes and mistakes and imprudences does not invalidate the revival in and of itself; and so he gives us this very important defence of the revival:

> Whatever imprudences there have been, and whatever sinful irregularities; whatever vehemence of the passions, and heats of the imagination, transports, and ecstasies: whatever error in judgment, and indiscreet zeal; and whatever outcries, faintings, and agitations of body; yet, it is manifest and notorious, that there has been of late a very uncommon influence upon the minds of a very great part of the inhabitants of *New England*, attended with the best effects. There has been a great increase of seriousness, and sober consideration of eternal things; a disposition to hearken to what is said of such things, with attention and affection; a disposition to treat matters of religion with solemnity, and as of great importance; to make these things the subject of conversation; to hear the Word of God preached, and to take all opportunities in order to it; to attend on the public worship of God, and all external duties of religion, in a more solemn and decent manner; so that there is a remarkable and general alteration in the face of *New England* in these respects. Multitudes in all parts of the land, of vain, thoughtless, regardless persons, are quite changed, and become serious and considerate. There is a vast increase of concern for the salvation of the precious soul, and of that inquiry, "*What shall I do to be saved?*"[37]

But Edwards, with his remarkable balance and judiciousness, gives this warning to the friends of the revival: "If we look back into the history of the church of God in past ages, we may observe that it has been a common device of the devil, to overset a revival of religion; when he finds he can keep men quiet and secure no longer, then he drives them to excesses and extravagances. He holds them back as long as he can; but when he can do it no longer, then he will push them on, and, if possible, run them upon their heads. . . . Yea, the principal means by which the devil was successful, by degrees, to overset the grand religious revival of the world, in the primitive ages of Christianity . . . was to improve the indiscreet zeal of Christians, to drive them into those three extremes of *enthusiasm*, *superstition*, and *severity*

37. Edwards, *Works* (Hickman), 1:374; emphasis original.

*towards opposers*; which should be enough for an everlasting warning to the Christian church."[38] You can see, then, how that Edwards is steering a very balanced and judicious course here. He is defending the revival against its rationalistic opposers; but equally he realizes the dangers that come from the other wing, from men like James Davenport and the fanatical element, who were in danger of bringing the revival into disrepute.

Now one of the most striking things about Edwards' theology of revival is this, that he emphasizes that revival is indeed a *mixed* work, that there are blemishes and irregularities that mingle with this remarkable work of grace; and the analogy that he provides for that is this, that just as in the most godly of men there are remaining elements of sin and corruption which, in a sense, spoil the profession, so too in revival there are these elements of remaining sin and corruption, mistakes and errors, imprudences and irregularities which mingle with the work of God. Revival, then, is inevitably a mixed work. What we must be careful, however, to do is this: we must not *condemn* "all in the lump"; as Edwards puts it, merely because of the existence of these irregularities and blemishes and faults. We must not condemn "all in the lump"; but equally we must not *approve* "all in the lump."[39] We must learn to distinguish—to distinguish between things that differ. It is a mixed work; and yet it is a glorious and sovereign work of the sovereign Lord himself.

My dear friends, I want to emphasize that in the Great Awakening there were, in New England, it is estimated, some fifty thousand sinners who were converted. That is one fifth of the then-population of New England. If you were to apply those statistics to America today—that is to say, if a revival were to break out in America today on the same scale—it would mean this, that some fifty million sinners would press into the kingdom of God. I ask you, then: Do you not see the importance of revival? Do you not see anything of the wonder of it? Do you not see how desperately we need it? This is undoubtedly a "day of small things" (Zech 4:10). We do not "despise the day of small things"; there is indeed this "more constant influence of God's Spirit." But equally we should go to him and ask him for more; and we should pray for an outpouring and an effusion of God's gracious Holy Spirit. My dear friends, I ask you: Do you ever pray for revival? Do you pray for it privately? Do you pray for it in your churches? There can be no doubt about it, that one of the great hallmarks of revival is the prayer and the prayers of God's people that so often precede it and accompany it. Jonathan Edwards was raised up by God, I believe, not only to experience revival, but

38. Edwards, *Works* (Hickman), 1:397–98; emphasis original.

39. Edwards, *Works* (Hickman), 1:371.

also to record it and to analyze it and to give us this wonderful theology of revival. He was raised up to defend it, to protect it, to pass it on; and he was also greatly concerned to promote it. He was concerned that it should be promoted by the friends of religion, above all by the means of prayer; and this is what he says about the need for prayer in promoting this great cause of revival. "So is God's will, through His wonderful grace, that the prayers of His saints should be one great and principal means of carrying on the designs of Christ's kingdom in the world. When God has something very great to accomplish for his church, it is his will that there should precede it the extraordinary prayers of his people. . . . And it is revealed that, when God is about to accomplish great things for his church, he will begin by remarkably pouring out the spirit of grace and supplication"; and he goes on to say this: "There is no way that Christians in a private capacity can do so much to promote the work of God, and advance the kingdom of Christ, as by prayer. By this even women, children, and servants may have a public influence. . . . A poor man in his cottage may have a blessed influence all over the world. God is, if I may so say, at the command of the prayer of faith; and in this respect is, as it were, under the power of his people; *as princes, they have power with God, and prevail.*"[40]

My dear friends, do you pray for revival? Do you see what a wonderful thing it would be for our land, for Great Britain, and for Europe, and for all the needy nations of the world, if God were, in our day, to surprise us and astonish us by pouring out of his Spirit in response to our prayers? Do you not see what wonderful blessing would result? And does it not behoove us, therefore, to go to God time and time again with a continual coming and with great importunity and ask and seek and knock until he opens the door and gives us that for which we long—the coming of his kingdom in great and mighty power? My dear friends, I encourage you to read about these things; I encourage you to have an interest in them; and I encourage you also to go back to your homes and back to your churches and to pray for this—this sovereign divine intervention of the living God at special seasons of mercy! Amen.

40. Edwards, *Works* (Hickman), 1:426; emphasis original.

# THE HOLY SPIRIT AND REVIVAL[41]

On September 23, 1857, there occurred in New York City an event of seemingly relative insignificance. A prayer meeting had been arranged by the city missioner of New York City by the name of Jeremiah Lanphier, a man of some forty years of age and a devoted servant of the Lord Jesus Christ. The Lord had laid upon the heart of this man that something additional was needed. He had been preaching God's word; he had been seeking God's face in prayer; but he longed to be able to reach the masses of the unconverted men and women, young people and children of New York City, and the Lord laid it upon his heart to arrange for a noonday prayer meeting for businessmen.

Thus, on the twenty-third of September, 1857, at noon, this prayer meeting was convened. When the hour of noon struck, nobody had, in fact, arrived; but by twelve thirty some six men in all had arrived and sought God's face in prayer. The number of six increased to twenty, one week later. One week later still the number had increased to approximately thirty-five, and a week later, which, interestingly, in the providence of God coincided with a financial crash, one hundred people were gathering together in Fulton Street, New York City, to seek the face of God in prayer. Before long, these weekly meetings had become daily. Before long they were meeting not only in Fulton Street, but in other parts of New York City; and within some six months we find this remarkable phenomenon that ten thousand people were meeting daily in New York City as well as in other parts of the United States in prayer, seeking the great blessing of revival.

Revival is, I believe, a phenomenon. It is not the norm; it is unusual; it is remarkable; it is extraordinary. God goes out of his way, as it were, and rends the heavens and comes down in great blessing upon his church. J. Edwin Orr, one of the experts on the whole issue of revival, has spoken of

41. This lecture was given during the annual spring conference of Greenville Presbyterian Theological Seminary, Taylors, SC, Mar. 10, 2011.

this revival as "an incredible movement of the people to pray."[1] This revival was carried on through prayer; it was initiated through prayer. Hundreds and thousands of people were converted in prayer meetings; and the net result, according to judicious historians on the subject, was that approximately one million people pressed into the kingdom of God at that time. The fires of revival spread across the Atlantic. They reached Ulster; they reached Wales; they reached parts of Scotland. England was touched and also parts of the continent. It had been estimated that perhaps as many as a further one million people were converted and entered into the kingdom of God on the other side of the Atlantic, resulting in approximately two million conversions in all in this remarkable outpouring of God's Spirit.

It is important to note that revival always begins in the church. God revives his church; he quickens his church; he enlivens his church. He pours out his Spirit; and seemingly lethargic, perhaps even seemingly moribund church members, suddenly become alive with a new power. Here in this remarkable revival it was manifested supremely through this astonishing movement of the people in prayer.

Now, where do we find in the Scriptures the phenomenon of revival? Well, we could, I believe, go to many different parts and portions. I want just briefly to touch on one. You see here, I believe, the significance of a little phrase in Acts 3:19. The apostle Peter, preaching just after the healing of the man lame from his mother's womb, says this: "Repent ye therefore, and be converted, that your sins may be blotted out, when the times of refreshing shall come from the presence of the Lord" (Acts 3:19). Now notice that little phrase: "the times of refreshing"—these seasons of refreshing. I believe we have here in this brief phrase a concept that deals with the whole notion and reality of God's reviving of his work. They are times of refreshing which come from the presence of the Lord.

The context of this statement, the context of this exhortation to repent and the reference to the times or seasons of refreshing is, of course, quite simply, that of the healing of the man lame from his mother's womb. Peter and John, you remember, were about to enter into the temple at the hour of prayer. It is the ninth hour—it is three o'clock in the afternoon. But sitting there by the Beautiful Gate of the temple is a man who is a cripple, a man who is a beggar. He is begging his living, as he must; and his eyes fasten upon Peter and John. He hopes for alms from them. But Peter says to him, "Silver and gold have I none; but such as I have give I thee: In the name of Jesus Christ of Nazareth rise up and walk" (Acts 3:6). Thus, through the power of

1. Orr, *Light of the Nations*, 105.

the risen Christ, the apostle Peter is able to raise up this poor crippled man and restore him to perfect soundness.

The people are filled with wonder and amazement at this miracle which has been performed in the name of the Lord Jesus Christ. But Peter focuses not so much upon the miracle as upon the Lord Jesus Christ. He preaches Christ. He emphasizes the God of Abraham, the God of Isaac, the mighty God of Jacob. He is the one who has glorified his Son Jesus. "Ye denied him; ye crucified him; but God has raised him up. God has glorified him; and he is the one responsible," says Peter, deflecting any attention away from himself. "He is the one responsible for raising up this poor crippled man in this astonishing way."

Thus, as he preaches to the people and tells them to repent, he refers to these times of refreshing which come from the presence of the Lord. I want to emphasize, in passing, that the word "when" in Acts 3:19 is not the ideal translation. It should be "that," or "so that," or "in order that." In other words, the apostle Peter says, "Repent ye, therefore, and be converted, that your sins may be blotted out, so that the times of refreshing shall come from the presence of the Lord." I want to speak this morning upon these times, these seasons of refreshing, which God in his goodness and in his sovereignty, chooses to bestow upon his church and, therefore, upon the world; and I want you to notice that implicit in what the apostle Peter says is a description of the entire inter-adventual period, that is to say, a description of the entire period between the two advents of Christ. This inter-adventual period will be marked, says the apostle Peter, by these times or seasons of refreshing from the presence of the Lord.

Now what exactly does the apostle Peter mean when he refers to "refreshing"? The word in the original is an interesting word. Literally it means "cooling." Remember that this is a hot, oriental climate and, therefore, the time of cooling is, in fact, that of refreshing. The idea here is that of times of relief, times of recovery. Think of a hot, arid, desert wilderness climate where the sun beats down relentlessly day after day. How welcome would be the cooling breezes that come, perhaps, from the north and which bring relief and recovery to those that are oppressed by the heat in those conditions. My mind goes back to the first week in July 1999. Some of you may remember that during that time temperatures in the United States soared into the hundreds. People were dying. There was a tremendous pressure upon the purchase of air conditioners. People were dousing themselves with water. They were buying cold drinks. There was a concern even to stay alive precisely because of the oppressive nature of the heat. How refreshing a time of northerly breezes would have been, bringing a cooling of the temperature at such a time.

"Now," says the apostle Peter in effect, "there are such times in the spiritual realm. There are times when God comes, times when God pours out his Spirit and grants this relief, this recovery, this refreshment to his church—these times of cooling which come from the presence of the Lord, as the church passes through the wilderness of this world; and as the sun beats down upon her in persecution, in tribulation, in trouble, and in the day of small things, there are times of spiritual enjoyment and refreshment."

Now, what exactly do we mean by "revival"? The word is misused today and is often misunderstood. I think that it is important that we should understand what the apostle Peter says on the day of Pentecost, because there is an inextricable connection between true revival, the day of Pentecost, and the Spirit that was given on that occasion. "But this is that which was spoken by the prophet Joel; and it shall come to pass in the last days, saith God, I will pour out of my Spirit upon all flesh. . . . I will pour out in those days of my Spirit" (Acts 2:16–18). Joel puts the emphasis upon the pouring out of the Spirit of God. The apostle Peter repeats it—he is citing Joel. This outpouring of the Spirit is, I believe, not limited to the day of Pentecost. There are other later outpourings of the Spirit of God in revival at certain times and seasons. Dr. Martyn Lloyd-Jones described revival in this way: "Revival is an outpouring of the Spirit. It is something that comes upon us, that happens to us. We are not the agents, we are just aware that something has happened."[2] It is a visitation of God's Spirit, an outpouring of God's Spirit. It is essential, I believe, that we connect revival to the immediate activity of the Third Person of the Godhead.

The term "revival" is often misused and even abused today. You might be driving along the road in some town unknown to you and on the church notice board you see advertised, "Revival!" "Revival: November 4, 5, and 6 at 7:30 p.m.!" Now that is, I believe, a misuse of the term. It is synonymous here with an evangelistic campaign, a series of evangelistic meetings. There is nothing wrong with such things. They can be used in the providence of God and in his kingdom. But they are not the same as revival. You can never preannounce revival. It is something that happens, something that God sends. So this is a misuse of the term that has led many, I think, into a dismissing of revival, into a disillusionment, perhaps, with it, into a failure to understand what revival is. But I would emphasize that this misuse of the term is scarcely two hundred years old. It dates from the early decades of the nineteenth century and, in particular, from the New Measures controversy involving Charles Grandison Finney.

2. Lloyd-Jones, *Puritans*, 368.

It is important to note that prior to the 1830s, revival was understood quite differently. Prior to the 1830s the church was imbued with an Edwardsean concept of revival. The church has lost sight of this; the church needs to recover this Edwardsean tradition, which emphasized what Edwards describes as "remarkable communications of the Spirit of God," "remarkable effusions, at special seasons of mercy." This is what he says in his "History of Redemption":

> It may here be observed, that from the fall of man, to our day, the work of redemption in its effect has mainly been carried on by remarkable communications of the Spirit of God. Though there be a more constant influence of God's Spirit always in some degree attending his ordinances; yet the way in which the greatest things have been done towards carrying on this work, always have been by remarkable effusions, at special seasons of mercy.[3]

Note in particular the concept of periodicity here in Edwards' view of revival. He is widely regarded as "the theologian of revival." He experienced revival twice, in 1734–35 in Northampton and the Connecticut River Valley and also in the Great Awakening in the 1740s, when he was joined by George Whitefield and by the Tennent brothers and others. He wrote extensively on revival. No one has analyzed revival more than he. Notice the concept of periodicity, this idea of that which is occasional, that which is sporadic. It doesn't occur all the time. It is not the norm. It is something that God sends and gives at certain times and seasons. He speaks of "a more constant influence of the Spirit of God." But in addition to this more constant influence of the Spirit of God, there are these special times, these remarkable seasons of special mercy and grace. This is clearly something uncommon, something unusual, something quite out of the ordinary.

Dr. Lloyd-Jones says this: "A revival is something that comes, lasts for a while, and then passes."[4] We have noticed the concept of periodicity. But consider that also implicit in Edwards' view of revival is the concept of degree—the degree or the measure in which the Spirit of God is given; there is "a more constant influence of God's Spirit always in some degree attending his ordinances," but in addition to this, there are these "remarkable effusions." So his terminology here clearly denotes this idea of periodicity and also the concept of measure or degree.

Edwards illustrates this in his "History of Redemption" as he traces the mighty works of God through the Old Testament and on into the New. In

3. Edwards, *Works* (Hickman), 1:539.

4. Lloyd-Jones, Revival, 105.

the first place he refers to the days of Enos, the grandson of Adam. "Then began men to call upon the name of the LORD" (Gen 4:26). There is something new here, something unusual, something different in degree. Edwards says this: "And this in the days of Enos, was the first remarkable pouring out of the Spirit of God that ever was. There had been a saving work of God on the hearts of some before; but now God was pleased to bring in a harvest of souls to Christ."[5] That is it—this idea of something unusual, something wonderfully new and extraordinary in degree.

We see, then, this seasonal element; indeed, the element of unpredictability. No man knows the times or the seasons which God has put in his own power. Therefore, we can never ever announce a revival. It is something that simply happens. You look back historically upon it. You cannot announce it in advance. These words in Acts 3 were spoken in the midst of such times. On the day of Pentecost there were some three thousand conversions; shortly afterwards some five thousand conversions. These conversions were inextricably connected with the giving, the pouring out of the Spirit of God. Edwards says this: "God also has his days of mercy, accepted times, chosen seasons, wherein it is his pleasure to show mercy, and nothing shall hinder it; times appointed for the magnifying of the Redeemer and his merits, and for the triumphs of his grace."[6] This is the peculiar work of the Spirit of God.

Let me remind you of the fundamental work of the Spirit of God: it is to testify to Christ; it is to glorify Christ. How does he do that? By convincing men of sin, and of God's righteousness, and of the judgment to come. That is how he does it. He convicts men and women such as you and me of their sin, of God's righteousness, of the judgment to come. He testifies to the Lord Jesus Christ; he glorifies Christ. He leads men to Christ unerringly and irresistibly and, thus, they enter into the kingdom of God. That is the great task of the Holy Spirit, to lift up, to magnify the Lord Jesus Christ in the conversion and the sanctification of men.

Let me demonstrate this historically. The apostle Peter speaks of these times, these seasons of refreshing, these remarkable periods of cooling, if you like, when God greatly blesses his church. Think of the Reformation of the sixteenth century. We tend not to think of the Reformation primarily in terms of revival, but I believe it was, among other things, just that—a mighty, mighty movement of God's Spirit across the face of Europe, beginning essentially in 1517, though there were, of course, precursors to that in the providence of God. Martin Luther nails his Ninety-Five Theses to the church door in Wittenberg in 1517, and before long the progress proves to be

5. Edwards, *Works* (Hickman), 1:539.

6. Edwards, *Works* (Hickman), 2:294.

absolutely astonishing. Before long the gospel is being disseminated across the nations of Europe. Yes, a mighty work of reformation; but a mighty work of revival also. The gospel goes forth in power. Men are convicted; they are converted. They are humbled under the mighty hand of God; and they press into God's kingdom. God's kingdom comes with power at such times. This great revolt, this mighty revolution of the sixteenth century, which we call the Protestant Reformation, was, I believe, among other things, a reviving of God's work.

Take, then, the Great Awakening of the 1740s. There was, of course, a kind of precursor to the Great Awakening. You could, in fact, include it in the Great Awakening—I am referring to the revival in Northampton under Edwards' ministry in 1734–35. It began in December 1734 and continued until about May 1 of 1735, a period of some six months, when God poured out his Spirit in great and wonderful blessing upon that town. It wasn't only Northampton; other parts, towns, villages in the Connecticut River Valley were also affected. Of the two hundred families there in Northampton, some three hundred souls, in Edwards' judgment, pressed into the kingdom of heaven at that time. This is how he describes it: "In the main, there has been a great and marvelous work of conversion and sanctification among the people here. . . . And we are evidently a people blessed of the Lord! For here, in this corner of the world, God dwells, and manifests his glory."[7]

In 1740, just a few years later, Edwards was joined, of course, by the young George Whitefield, whose seraphic preaching of the word of God on either side of the Atlantic was such that men rushed to hear him. Read Nathan Cole's astonishing account of the mere announcement that Whitefield will preach and you will soon see how astonishing this phenomenon was.

Edwards himself says this concerning the Great Awakening. He is describing revival. "God appears unusually present. . . . [God] is then extraordinarily present."[8] There is an emphasis upon the presence of God in revival. Listen again to our text: "seasons of refreshing from the presence of the Lord"—seasons of cooling and refreshment, which are marked by the presence of God, so that men are now conscious of the presence of God in a remarkable and unusual way. Indeed, historians estimate that approximately fifty thousand people were converted in New England during the Great Awakening—as many as one in five, approximately—and entered into God's kingdom. This is how Edwards describes this work: he speaks

7. Edwards, *Works* (Hickman), 1:364.

8. Edwards, *Works* (Hickman), 1:393.

of "so glorious and wonderful a display of his power and grace in the late outpourings of His Spirit."[9]

It is undeniable that there were those that resisted the Great Awakening. There were those who were opposed to it, such as Charles Chauncy, and even some believers. The Old Side, for instance, tended to resist the Great Awakening on the whole; but this was Edwards' defence of the Great Awakening: "The great weakness of the greater part of mankind, in any affair that is new and uncommon, appears in not distinguishing, but either approving or condemning all in the lump."[10] Now this, of course, is a common error in the thinking of men, a tendency innate in our minds by nature, either to approve all in the lump or to condemn all in the lump. There is something we don't like—we dismiss it in its entirety; we like it—we approve of everything. "No," says Edwards, "this is wrong. We need to be more discriminating. We need to distinguish between the wheat and the chaff. We must neither approve nor condemn all in the lump, but distinguish between things that differ." There can be no doubt that this great man of God, this theologian of revival, this man with this remarkable, astonishing, discriminating mind, uses a scalpel to distinguish between that which is good and of God and that which is not.

Listen to what Edwards says as he defends the essence of the Great Awakening:

> Whatever imprudences there have been, and whatever sinful irregularities; whatever vehemence of the passions, and heats of the imagination, transports, and ecstasies: whatever error in judgment, and indiscreet zeal; and whatever outcries, faintings, and agitations of body; yet, it is manifest and notorious, that there has been of late a very uncommon influence upon the minds of a very great part of the inhabitants of *New England*, attended with the best effects. There has been a great increase of seriousness, and sober consideration of eternal things; a disposition to hearken to what is said of such things, with attention and affection; a disposition to treat matters of religion with solemnity, and as of great importance; to make these things the subject of conversation; to hear the Word of God preached, and to take all opportunities in order to it; to attend on the public worship of God, and all external duties of religion, in a more solemn and decent manner; so that there is a remarkable and general alteration in the face of *New England* in these respects. Multitudes in all parts of the land, of vain, thoughtless, regardless persons, are

9. Edwards, *Works* (Hickman), 1:427.

10. Edwards, *Works* (Hickman), 1:371.

> quite changed, and become serious and considerate. There is a vast increase of concern for the salvation of the precious soul, and of that inquiry, "*What shall I do to be saved?*"[11]

You see, Edwards concedes that there were blemishes. He doesn't approve all in the lump, nor does he dismiss or reject all in the lump. He discriminates carefully; but he is very careful also to insist that, in the main, this was a great and wonderful and astonishing work of God's Spirit. Indeed, he describes it as "a strange revolution" that led to "a visible reformation" among the people of God.[12]

Did you know that at the same time as the Great Awakening here in this country there was a remarkable revival in England? God had raised up the young George Whitefield—at the age of twenty-one he was preaching to thousands in the open air! Before long John Wesley joined him and other great evangelists—there was a remarkable evangelical revival in England. It is important to note that the Puritan era had long disappeared over the horizon. In 1662 some two thousand godly ministers had been ejected from their livings, and the period between 1662 and (let us say) the 1730s or 40s was one of terrible decadence and increasing corruption in England. Read Arnold Dallimore's fine account of this in his biography of George Whitefield. But there can be no doubt about it, that in the 1730s and 40s, something astonishing begins to happen. Listen to the Oxford historian John Richard Green in his fine *Short History of the English People*:

> A religious revival burst forth . . . which changed after a time the whole tone of English society. The church was restored to life and activity. Religion carried to the hearts of the people a fresh spirit of moral zeal, while it purified our literature and our manners. A new philanthropy reformed our prisons, infused clemency and wisdom into our penal laws, abolished the slave trade, and gave the first impulse to popular education.[13]

It is not only the Oxford historian John Richard Green who makes this point—the French historian Elie Halévy (1870–1937) says this: "Evangelical religion was the moral cement of English society."[14] He contrasts what happened in France in 1789, and all that preceded it, with what happened in England in these decades. He makes the point that, but for this evangelical

11. Edwards, *Works* (Hickman), 1:374; emphasis original.

12. Edwards, *Works* (Hickman), 1:379.

13. Green, *Short History*, 718.

14. Halévy, *History of English People*, 166.

revival, England might well have suffered a revolution analogous to the bloodbath of the French Revolution in 1789.

I come now to what is known as the Second Great Awakening in the early nineteenth century. We are dealing now with the years 1800 to 1825—some historians say 1800 to 1831, a period of some twenty-five to thirty years where there were these periodic revivals of religion. Iain Murray, in his fine work *Revival and Revivalism* (notice he distinguishes between the two), points out that this Second Great Awakening differs from the first Great Awakening in that it was greater in length, more extensive geographically, and also more extensive denominationally. Thousands upon thousands of people entered into the kingdom of God and into the churches of Christ. We see again what Iain Murray calls "this mysterious periodicity,"[15] which is itself a reflection of the sovereignty of God. He is the one who gives this. He is the one who sends it at certain times and seasons, and they lie within his power.

Interestingly, there were some precursors to this period of awakening between 1800 and 1825, or 1831. A very interesting and significant precursor occurred in Virginia and North Carolina known as the Great Revival of 1787–89. Iain Murray makes this very interesting observation concerning this Great Revival in Virginia: "The Great Awakening had largely missed Virginia in the 1740s and left her one of the most materialistic of all the colonies, but in the Virginia of the 1780s an impetus for biblical religion affected large numbers of people and prepared the way for a major spiritual change in the South. For the first time, religion became identified in the public mind with evangelical Christianity."[16]

We need to remember that, in the early nineteenth century, America was on the move; there was this movement westward. You had the developing frontier in Kentucky, especially, and also Tennessee. These two states were "the mother of the West." Men, women, children were on the move. They were migrating westward, hundreds and thousands; and in this particular context, of course, you had hundreds and thousands of people assembled in the area. You have the beginning, in the 1800s, of what is known as "camp meetings."

According to Iain Murray, these camp meetings originated in the context of Presbyterian communion seasons. We can easily imagine the scene: masses of people are there; they are there in their tents; they are there with their wagons; the word of God is preached and proclaimed; there is prayer; there is preaching; you have these prayer societies. There can be no doubt

15. I. Murray, *Revival and Revivalism*, 201.

16. I. Murray, *Revival and Revivalism*, 87.

about it that there was revival. Now equally—and I emphasize this—there were excesses, especially during this Second Great Awakening—excesses and disorders. There were fallings; there was hysteria. This brings us to a very important point made by Dr. Packer: "Revival . . . is a *mixed* work," he insists.[17] Revivals vary; they vary in purity; they vary in power; they vary in methodology in many respects. It is a mixed work. But we should neither approve all in the lump nor condemn all in the lump. There is no doubt about it that thousands upon thousands of people were converted during the Second Great Awakening. We also acknowledge some of the weaknesses and some of the excesses by which this was marked.

Listen, again, to John B. Boles. You southerners will like this!

> The Great Revival altered the course of Kentucky and southern history. . . . Evangelical Protestantism was placed on such a foundation that never again was Protestant dominance threatened in the South. . . . Much that is associated with the southern character may be linked to conservative religion, and the Great Revival, beginning in Kentucky, and spreading into the remainder of the South, was largely responsible.[18]

In the 1830s, however, you have the rise of a man by the name of Charles Grandison Finney. Finney is often referred to as "the father of modern evangelism." In 1834–35 Finney gave his lectures on revivals of religion and he became engaged in the New Measures controversy. The other leader in the controversy was the great Asahel Nettleton, described by some as "a second Whitefield." It has been estimated that the preaching of this great man of God, Asahel Nettleton, was such that some thirty thousand people were saved under his ministry. Asahel Nettleton belonged to the old school. Finney belonged to these New Measures. These two men were engaged in this significant controversy over the New Measures.

What were the New Measures? Well, the anxious seat, the altar call, decisionist evangelism. Asahel Nettleton rightly resisted these and showed how dangerous they were. The problem was that Charles Grandison Finney's theology was not merely Arminian; it was basically Pelagian. He says that God commands (this is his logic)—God commands men to repent; therefore, they must be able to repent. That is a classic Arminian and even Pelagian argument. There is, in Finney, a complete disregard of the utter inability of the sinner to save himself, the utter inability of the sinner to respond to the gospel apart from the saving work of God's Spirit. Indeed,

17. Packer, *1960–1962*, 41; emphasis original.

18. Cited in I. Murray, *Revival and Revivalism*, 173.

Finney's theology is not just Arminian, or semi-Pelagian; it is essentially Pelagian. These Pelagian errors were spreading significantly in the 1830s.

Listen to Finney: "Regeneration consists in the sinner changing his ultimate choice, intention, preference."[19] Could you have a more Arminian, a more Pelagian expression of conversion than that? You see, under Finney conversion becomes reduced to a decision of the will. You have this introduction of decisionist evangelism, with all that that involves; and this Pelagian element clearly affected his theology of revival. Listen to the way in which Finney describes revival. "A revival is not a miracle."[20] That is, it is not an extraordinary work of God's Spirit. "A revival is the result of the right use of the appropriate means."[21] In other words, you can get up a revival. You simply have to use the means; and if you use the means in a correct manner, then you will have a revival as a result. You can easily see that the whole idea of the sovereignty of God in revival is being eroded here by Finney, and the concept of revival as a sovereign work of God's Spirit is being replaced by the concept of an evangelistic campaign or a series of evangelistic meetings.

Iain Murray makes this observation in his book *Revival and Revivalism*: "There can be no question that by 1900 the impression was almost universal that Charles Grandison Finney had introduced revivals in nineteenth-century America."[22] But he had not. What Finney had introduced was revivalism, these new measures which undermine true revival, indeed, undermine evangelism: the anxious seat, the altar call, the decisionism, his pathetically weak theology of regeneration. He introduced revivalism.

Revivalism is not quite two hundred years old; these New Measures are not quite two hundred years old. Iain Murray, in distinguishing revivalism from revival, says this: "Revivalism contains no real element of mystery. . . . Revivalism is marked by the predictable."[23] Revival, you see, is always marked by the unpredictable. It is a sovereign work of God, something God gives, something God sends at special times and seasons. Do you not see the difference between the theology of Jonathan Edwards on the one hand and the theology of Charles Grandison Finney on the other? W. G. McGloughlin compares these two men and their respective influences in this way: "One saw God as the center of the universe, the other saw man. One believed that revivals were 'prayed down,' and the other that they were 'worked up.'" In other words, Edwards saw God as the center of the universe; Finney saw

19. Finney, *Systematic Theology*, 411.

20. Finney, *Revivals of Religion*, 20.

21. Finney, *Revivals of Religion*, 21.

22. I. Murray, *Revival and Revivalism*, 297.

23. I. Murray, *Revival and Revivalism*, 380.

man. Edwards believed that revivals were prayed down. If they were sent at all, it was in response to prayer. He didn't have some kind of *ex opere operato* view. But he did believe—and I quote him—that God "puts himself at the command of prayer." So, one believed that revivals were prayed down—that is Edwards' view; the other that they were worked up—that is Finney's view.

I come back briefly to the 1857–58 revival in this country which is often referred to as the 1858–59 revival in Great Britain. It was the same revival in its transatlantic phases. Notice again the role of prayer in that great revival. John L. Girardeau was ministering in Charleston, South Carolina, largely to black people. He had a wonderful ministry of the gospel among black people; and at this time, namely, the revival of 1857–58, he had introduced, as many others had in different places, special prayer meetings. He was asked the question, "What about special preaching services?" He delayed; he resisted initially. But then there came a point in the revival where he said, "The Holy Spirit has come; we will begin preaching tomorrow evening."[24] For eight weeks, night after night, Girardeau preached the gospel because he recognized that the Spirit of God had come and that he must make use of this remarkable opportunity—this special season of refreshing from the presence of the Lord.

Dr. Martyn Lloyd-Jones says this. "So the two main characteristics of revival are, first, this extraordinary enlivening of the members of the Church, and second, the conversion of masses of people who hitherto have been outside in indifference and sin."[25] Thus, once again, we see that revival always begins in the church. Revival doesn't begin in the world; it begins in the church. You can't quicken something that doesn't have life. No, the church is quickened; the church is enlivened. As a result, this spreads to those that are outside the church. J. Edwin Orr makes this observation: "The awakening of 1857–58 was the most thorough and most wholesome movement ever known in the Christian Church."[26] This is a remarkable accolade. There was this transatlantic quality to that particular revival.

Take the land of Wales, which has often been described as "the land of revivals." Did you know that between 1762 and 1862 there were at least fifteen major, outstanding revivals in the land of Wales, connected, of course, with the great preachers which God, in his providence, raised up in that particular country? Read the book *Some of the Great Preachers of Wales*. It is a remarkable work and it shows how God's Spirit rested upon the labors of these men. "The land of revivals"! Well, this revival reached

24. Cited in I. Murray, *Revival and Revivalism*, 420.

25. Lloyd-Jones, *Revival*, 2.

26. Cited in I. Murray, *Revival and Revivalism*, 332.

Wales in 1858, and it has been estimated by Eifion Evans that as many as perhaps one hundred thousand people entered into the kingdom of God at that time. Evans says that the Welsh revival was "born in prayer."[27] It was stimulated, you see, by the prayers of God's people, by the news of revival. This stimulated prayer in other places. You see it here in the United States. Did you know that in this country it wasn't merely limited to New York City. No; before long the revival of 1857–58 spread from the north to the south, from the Atlantic to the Pacific, and affected all the major towns and parts of this mighty nation.

We come now to the revival in Wales in 1904–5. This, too, was a remarkable revival, although it was marked by some weaknesses and some blemishes. But I want to emphasize that David Lloyd George (his name is, perhaps, familiar to you—he was the prime minister of Great Britain at the time of the First World War), who was not a believer, he was not a godly man, said that this particular movement of God's Spirit was, in his view, "like a mighty earthquake." He said that it was "like a tornado sweeping the country." It has been said that one of the great features of this revival was the universal, inescapable sense of the presence of God.

I want to tell you of something quite extraordinary that occurred in the revival in Wales in 1904–5—I want to tell you about the pit ponies down the mines. These pit ponies knew that something remarkable was occurring. How, you say? In this way—these poor, dumb, brute beasts were so used to being kicked and beaten and cursed by the rough, ungodly miners that, when these men were converted in large numbers, the poor, brute beasts didn't know whether they were coming or going! They didn't know how to respond! They testify, you see, to the power of this revival, to the power of the work of the Spirit of God in the hearts and lives of men that hitherto were unconverted and dead in their sins.

It is undeniable that there were some significant mistakes made in the 1904–5 revival. Evan Roberts, the leader, became far too mystical, far too subjective. There was a neglect of preaching as the revival developed. I remind you, once again, that revival is a mixed work. But we must neither condemn all in the lump nor approve all in the lump, but finely discriminate between that which is good and that which is bad, between the wheat and the chaff, as Edwards himself does.

Let me remind you of the origin of these times of refreshing. They come "from the presence of the Lord." Yes, and they bring with them the presence of God. Revival is something that God gives, something that God sends. That means that you can never organize a revival. This idea that you

27. Evans, *Revival Comes to Wales*, 40.

can announce that a revival is going to occur on November 4, 5, and 6 is totally fatuous! It is a complete misuse and abuse of the term. No, this is something that God gives. You cannot organize a revival. Why, you might just as well speak of organizing a thunderstorm! You might just as well speak of organizing an earthquake! You might just as well speak of organizing a volcanic eruption! You might just as well speak of organizing a tornado! You might just as well speak of organizing a hurricane! Let's speak of organizing a tsunami! These "acts of God"—that is how the old insurance companies used to view them—are analogous to these times, these "seasons of refreshing from the presence of the Lord." They are the mighty acts of God! They are totally unpredictable. No man knows the time or the place or even the instrumentalities that will be used.

So revival is, in the final analysis, a matter of the sovereignty of God. I sometimes think this: there is a sense in which nothing demonstrates the sovereignty of God more than revival itself. He chooses the men; he chooses the times; he chooses the place; he chooses the instruments. They are outside of our hands. All we can do is beseech him. It is the sovereignty of the Spirit! Remember how the Lord Jesus Christ puts it: "The wind bloweth where it listeth" (John 3:8). That is to say, the wind blows where it wills. Have you ever reflected upon the sovereignty of the wind—the power of the wind, the direction of the wind, the temperature of the wind? You and I have utterly no control over these at all. You and I cannot control its power, its temperature, its direction. It lies outside of our control. These things are in the hands of God. "The wind bloweth where it listeth." It is the same with God's Spirit. He moves where he will. So there is a sovereignty of the Spirit in revival in terms of time and place and instrumentalities.

Revival is, therefore, peculiarly a work of the Spirit of God. Yet, characteristically, the Spirit doesn't focus upon himself. As Dr. Packer puts it, "The Holy Spirit's distinctive new covenant role, then, is to fulfill what we may call a floodlight ministry in relation to the Lord Jesus Christ."[28] His aim is always to testify to the Lord Jesus Christ, always to glorify the Lord Jesus Christ; and to that end he convicts and convinces men of sin and of righteousness and of judgment to come. It is peculiarly a work of the Spirit of God.

We see here the significance of the day of Pentecost—the significance of the prophet Joel and his great prophecy: "And it shall come to pass afterwards, that I will pour out my Spirit upon all flesh. . . . In those days I will pour out my Spirit" (Joel 2:28–29). I believe that this concept of the outpouring of the Spirit, which is so integral to the great Edwardsean

28. Cited in Justin Taylor, "Holy Spirit's Hidden Floodlight," para. 1.

tradition that affected this country and Scotland and other parts of the world, is very, very important to our understanding as to what happens in revival. Dispensationalists dismiss the concept. George Smeaton noted that in his very fine work on the Spirit of God—he takes the dispensationalists to task over this very issue:

> And no more mischievous and misleading theory could be propounded, nor any one more dishonoring to the Holy Spirit, than the principle adopted by the Plymouth Brethren, that because the Spirit was poured out at Pentecost, the Church has no need, and no warrant to pray any more for the effusion of the Spirit of God. On the contrary, the more the Church asks the Spirit and waits His communication, the more she receives.[29]

It is an interesting fact that some Reformed men are, at this point, strange bedfellows with our dispensationalist brethren in that they don't want any prayer for God's Spirit. They dismiss the notion, as the dispensationalists do, that we have any right, any warrant, any need to pray for the influences of God's Spirit. But listen to the Lord Jesus Christ: "If ye then, being evil, know how to give good gifts unto your children: how much more shall your heavenly Father give the Holy Spirit to them that ask him?" (Luke 11:13). We have, I believe, every right and every warrant from Christ's own teaching to pray for, to ask for the Spirit of God. "If ye then, being evil . . . "—and we are! Nevertheless, we know how to give good gifts unto our children—"how much more shall your heavenly Father give the Holy Spirit to them that ask him?" Moreover, the great aim—and we say this with an eye upon our Pentecostal and charismatic friends—should be not to focus upon the things upon which they tend to focus, but upon the fact that the Spirit of God testifies to Christ, glorifies Christ, convinces men of sin, of God's righteousness, and of the judgment to come.

So then we have these times of refreshing—the history of the church shows it; the word of God shows it—times when God moves in an unusual, uncommon, extraordinary way; and as we live today in a day of small things (although we do not despise that), it behooves us to remember these days of great things, these days when God has made bare his mighty arm, when he stretched forth his mighty hand, when he has rent the heavens and come down and brought this remarkable blessing upon his church—always to testify to Christ, to glorify Christ, and to bring hundreds and thousands of sinners, who were dead in their trespasses and their sins, into the kingdom of God.

29. Smeaton, *Doctrine of Holy Spirit*, 288–89.

Do you believe that there are such times? Do you believe that there have been such times? Do you believe that in God's sovereignty there could be such times again? Do you ever read about revival? Do you ever pray for revival? You that preach God's word, do you ever preach about revival? There is, sadly, in Reformed circles a resistance sometimes to the concept of revival. These things ought not so to be. We recognize that revival is a mixed work. We don't approve of everything; we don't condemn everything. There are blemishes. But we recognize also that there are these times and seasons of remarkable power, of the presence of God manifest among men.

And so, we should have this desire to pray that God's kingdom might come. Now, there is, of course, as the Lord Jesus himself shows, a very real place for praying in our prayer meetings for this one that is sick, for that one that is in need, for a job for this person—for temporal, material needs. But is it not the case that, all too often, our prayer meetings have become saturated with requests of that nature, and we have forgotten to pray for that which our Lord puts first, namely, the coming of God's kingdom—that God's kingdom might come with power, that it might come with power in mighty revival? That, surely, should be our great priority, while we do not for one moment dismiss these other secondary matters. They also are important, and we have a right to pray for them. But this is even more important—that God's kingdom should be extended and come with great power. Therefore, I urge you to bid God awake, to bid God arise, to bid God to pluck his hand out of his bosom, to visit us, to quicken us, to rend the heavens, to come down, to pour out his Spirit, to testify to the Lord Jesus Christ, to glorify him by convicting men and women in their hundreds and their thousands of sin, and of righteousness, and of judgment to come. Amen.

# REDEMPTIVE-HISTORICAL PREACHING: A CRITIQUE[1]

"PREACHING that lacks application," remarks Geoffrey Thomas, "is the bane of the modern reformed pulpit."[2] In some Reformed pulpits this lack of application is inadvertent and a matter of neglect; in other Reformed pulpits, as in the case of the more extreme wing of the redemptive-historical school, this lack of application is deliberate and a matter of principle. But whether it is a matter of neglect, or whether it is a matter of principle, such lack of application always constitutes a serious deficiency and a serious failure on the part of the preacher. Traditionally Reformed theology, following the analogy of the Scriptures, has defined preaching as *explicatio et applicatio verbi Dei*, that is to say, the explication and the application of the word of God. Thus, *explicatio verbi Dei* (the explication of the word of God) is not enough. It is essential that *explicatio verbi Dei* be complemented and supplemented by *applicatio verbi Dei* (the application of the word of God). Robert Lewis Dabney is, we believe, quite correct when he insists that the great aim and end of preaching of the word of God is "to produce a definite practical volition in the hearer"; it is "to make men do."[3]

Historically, this tendency on the part of the redemptive-historical school to suppress, or even to eliminate, the note of exhortation in preaching emerged, with particular prominence, during the course of a homiletical controversy in the *Gereformeerde Kerken* of the Netherlands in the 1930s and 1940s. This controversy is generally referred to as "the exemplary/redemptive-historical" controversy. The central issue in this debate was whether or not it was valid for the preacher to utilize the characters or

1. This lecture was delivered during the annual spring conference of Greenville Presbyterian Theological Seminary, Taylors, SC, Mar. 8, 2002.

2. Thomas, "Powerful Preaching," 380.

3. Dabney, *Evangelical Eloquence*, 33–34.

the events of the Bible as examples or models for believers today. As the name suggests, the exemplary or exemplaristic school of preachers took the position that such a use of the characters or the events of the Bible was valid, that the Scriptures themselves demonstrated both the right and the duty of exemplification. The redemptive-historical school took the position that such a use of the characters or the events of the Bible was not valid and that such preaching would inevitably tend to be atomistic, subjectivist, anthropocentric, and moralistic.

One of the major charges leveled by the redemptive-historical school against the exemplaristic school was the charge of atomism. "'Atomistic,'" explains Sidney Greidanus, "refers to the isolation of certain 'atoms' within the text from the inner coherence, the central thrust of the text."[4] The temptation is, as Greidanus puts it, that "a few elements ('atoms' again) are lifted out of the text and context."[5] In other words, the redemptive-historical school regarded the atomistic approach as leading inevitably to arbitrary and subjective selection on the part of the preacher. It must be conceded that there is a style of preaching, sadly often heard from evangelical pulpits today, which in its concern to be relevant, practical, and applicatory, adopts a selective and even manipulative approach to the text and ultimately distorts and trivializes the message of the text. It is a vital principle of both hermeneutics and homiletics that the text should be considered in its context. Nevertheless, the central question ultimately is this: Do the Scriptures themselves ever select certain "elements" or "atoms" from historical passages in the Old Testament as examples for New Testament believers? The answer to this question is unquestionably in the affirmative.

Another charge leveled by the redemptive-historical school against the exemplaristic school in this historical controversy was that of moralism—a charge that persists to this day. This charge of moralism is, of course, inextricably connected with the charge of anthropocentricity or man-centeredness. Again we can see there is an element of justice in this charge. The preacher who directs the attention of his hearers to Bible saints, without directing his hearers to the Lord Jesus Christ, is guilty of moralistic preaching. If a sermon, or if a man's ministry, is acceptable to a Jewish rabbi or to a Unitarian, then it clearly is unevangelical and has lost the savor of Christ and of the gospel. One of the problems, however, in the contemporary debate is that some in the redemptive-historical school tend to bandy the charge of moralism about without actually defining the term itself. Professor John Frame contends that the charge of moralism is often unjust and sometimes

4. Greidanus, *Sola Scriptura*, 63.

5. Greidanus, *Sola Scriptura*, 78.

even slanderous. "'Moralism' was a term associated particularly with social-gospel liberals of the Ritschlian school of the nineteenth and twentieth centuries. They had no gospel at all. To use that term of principled evangelicals of our own time, I believe, is an injustice."[6] In other words, moralism is essentially Pelagianism, whether deliberate or unintentional. It ignores the crucial indicatives of the gospel, which are rooted and grounded in "Jesus Christ and him crucified." If, however, Jesus Christ is made the great foundation and presupposition of appropriate exhortation that follows, then the charge is, as Professor Frame contends, manifestly unjust.

It is evident, then, that one of the central issues in this controversy was, and still is, the issue of application. There can be no doubt that the homiletical ideal of the balance between explication and application, or between the objective and the subjective aspects of the truth of God, is one which is clearly in accord with the analogy of Scripture, as evidenced by the apostolic preaching in the Acts of the Apostles and supremely, perhaps, by the epistles of the apostle Paul himself. It should be noted that the apostle always moves from indicatives to imperatives; he always moves from doctrine to practice. Greidanus summarizes the position of the exemplaristic school in this way: "The objections raised by the exemplary side to exclusive historical-redemptive preaching center on the lack of application."[7] Indeed, Greidanus refers to "the frequent charges that the exclusive use of the redemptive-historical method leads to objective sermons, mere explication, lectures on redemptive history, sermons without tangible relevance."[8] Redemptive-historical preaching was, it was alleged by its critics in the original controversy, a genre of preaching that was all too often characterized by objectivism, intellectualism, and scholasticism.

It is interesting to note some of the more recent criticisms which redemptive-historical preaching in general has attracted. Professor Frame again: "Some redemptive-historical preachers seem to have an antipathy to the very idea of application. . . . I get the impression that some who stress redemptive history really want to avoid 'practical' application. They want the whole sermon to focus on Christ, not on what works the believer should do. They want it to focus on gospel, not on law. So they want the sermon to evoke praise of Christ, not to demand concrete change in people's behavior. In their mind, Christocentricity excludes any sustained focus upon specific practical matters."[9]

6. Frame, "Ethics, Preaching," para. 22.

7. Greidanus, *Sola Scriptura*, 152.

8. Greidanus, *Sola Scriptura*, 43.

9. Frame, "Ethics, Preaching," paras. 10, 12.

Dr. Hendrik Krabbendam has expressed similar criticism of redemptive-historical preaching:

> Preaching in the redemptive-historical tradition is often comparable to a ride in a Boeing 747 high above the landscape with its hot deserts, its snowpeaked mountains, its wide rivers, its dense forests, its open prairies, its craggy hills and its deep lakes. The view is panoramic, majestic, impressive, breathtaking and always comfortable. But there is one problem. The Christian is not "above" things. He is in the middle of things. He is trekking through the landscape. As such he experiences heat, or cold, or pain, or failure. Sometimes the journey seems interminable, or monotonous, or cheerless, or impossible. At times the traveler loses his sense of direction, or his strength to continue, or his hope of success, or his will to endure. At other times, he lacks wisdom, or expertise, or resources, or support. At all times he is engaged in battle. That is why "aesthetic contemplation" is simply not sufficient fare for the Christian on his way through life. All by itself, it is a starvation diet.[10]

Where, then, has redemptive-historical preaching gone astray? It has gone astray, we believe, through its failure to note and to implement in its preaching the indicative-imperative pattern or structure of New Testament Christianity. Listen to Dr. J. Gresham Machen: "Christianity begins with a triumphant indicative."[11] Machen makes this observation in his great work *Christianity and Liberalism.* He is contrasting two rival systems, namely, liberalism and Christianity, and he highlights the essential difference between these two systems in terms of the fundamental grammatical mood in which each system operates. "Christianity," he says, "is religion founded not on aspirations, but on facts. Here is found the most fundamental difference between liberalism and Christianity—liberalism is altogether in the imperative mood, while Christianity begins with a triumphant indicative."[12] In other words, liberalism begins by telling the sinner what he must do, whereas Christianity begins by telling the sinner what God has done in Christ Jesus.

Let me demonstrate the latter: "For there is born to you this day in the city of David, a Savior, which is Christ the Lord" (Luke 2:11). This is a great announcement, a great annunciation, a declaration of a *fait accompli*, the declaration of an event, namely, the incarnation of Christ. Listen again:

10. Krabbendam, "Hermeneutics and Preaching," 235–36.

11. Machen, *Christianity and Liberalism*, 47.

12. Machen, *Christianity and Liberalism*, 47.

"Christ died for our sins according to the Scriptures, and . . . He was buried, and . . . He rose again the third day according to the Scriptures" (1 Cor 15:3–4). "The liberal preacher offers us exhortation," comments Machen. "The Christian evangelist . . . offers . . . not exhortation but a gospel." That gospel begins, as Machen puts it, with this "triumphant indicative."[13]

It is, however, vital to understand that although Christianity begins with a triumphant indicative, it does not end with a triumphant indicative. It always moves on to the imperative. In other words, Christianity is not altogether in the indicative mood. Dr. Sinclair B. Ferguson puts it this way: "Indicatives lead to imperatives."[14] He is commenting both upon the pattern or the structure that we find in the Scriptures and also on the pattern or structure that should govern our homiletics: "Indicatives lead to imperatives." Thus, although there is a fundamental primacy and priority about the indicative mood in preaching, there is actually an incompleteness and an insufficiency about the indicative mood considered in isolation. The indicative mood must be complemented and supplemented by the imperative mood. Proclamation must be complemented and supplemented by appeal. *Explicatio verbi Dei* must be complemented and supplemented by *applicatio verbi Dei.* True preaching always involves, in the Reformed tradition, *explicatio et applicatio verbi Dei.*

Interestingly, what we find in the New Testament is not so much a single indicative followed by a single imperative, as in fact a double indicative into which a double imperative is interwoven or intertwined. Thus, the theology of the New Testament reveals the following sequence.

1. Indicative: "Christ died for our sins" (1 Cor 15:3).
2. Imperative: "Repent, and believe in the gospel" (Mark 1:15).
3. Indicative: "We . . . died to sin" (Rom 6:2).
4. Imperative: "Reckon yourselves to be dead indeed to sin" (Rom 6:11).

Professor John Murray's observation, in the context of definitive sanctification, concerning "the interweaving of the indicative and the imperative"[15] is an observation applicable to the theology of the gospel as a whole. Indicatives and imperatives "lie in each other"; they are interwoven and intertwined.[16]

13. Machen, *Christianity and Liberalism*, 121.

14. Ferguson, "Exegesis," 193.

15. J. Murray, *Collected Writings*, 2:280–81.

16. Ridderbos, *Paul*, 255.

With regard to this indicative-imperative pattern or structure of the Christian life, it is important to note the following two principles recently articulated by Dr. Richard B. Gaffin Jr. of Westminster Seminary in Philadelphia: First, the principle of *irreversibility.* There is an irreversibility in the relationship between the indicative and the imperative; you cannot transpose them. Dr. Gaffin says this: "The indicative has the priority; the indicative is foundational. It grounds the imperative—not the imperative somehow grounding the indicative. . . . Paul never writes in the imperative without first of all, either explicitly or implicitly, writing in the indicative."[17]

Second, the *inseparability* within the relationship between the indicative and the imperative moods. "Christianity begins with a triumphant indicative," not with an urgent imperative. Nevertheless, it does move on to the imperative. Christianity does not end with a triumphant indicative; it moves on to the urgent imperatives. In other words, the indicative and the imperative are inseparable in the theology and in the preaching of the New Testament. Dr. Gaffin puts it this way: "Paul never writes in the indicative without having the imperative in view, either explicitly or implicitly. . . . Imperative and indicative are given together; and the imperative is a consequence or attestation apart from which the indicative does not exist."[18]

John Stott is thus quite correct when he insists, on the basis of the analogy of the Scriptures, that in preaching there must be a balanced emphasis upon God's action and man's response, or, in other words, a balanced emphasis upon proclamation and appeal: "From this coupling together of proclamation and appeal, we may learn two complementary lessons. First, we must never issue an appeal without first making the proclamation. . . . The second lesson we must learn from this Biblical coupling together of proclamation and appeal is the complementary one; we must never make the proclamation without then issuing an appeal."[19] It should be noted that Stott has simply expressed, in his own words, Dr. Gaffin's principles of the irreversibility and the inseparability of the indicative and the imperative moods.

With regard to the issue of the use of example, which lay at the very center of the original controversy in the Netherlands, there can be no doubt that the exemplaristic school of thought was able to appeal to precedent and tradition in justification of its own position. Sidney Greidanus, in his *Sola Scriptura*, concedes "the deep-seated nature of the exemplary approach

17. Gaffin, *Reformed Hermeneutics*, cass. 3.

18. Gaffin, *Reformed Hermeneutics*, cass. 3.

19. Stott, *Preacher's Portrait*, 48, 50.

in Reformed theology."[20] Dr. C. Trimp, in his *Preaching and the History of Salvation*, emphasizes that both Luther and Calvin made use of exempla in their preaching. "Luther . . . himself had made generous use of exemplum.[21] . . . Calvin did indeed preach 'exemplaristically.'"[22] Moreover, it is evident that the Puritans made frequent and extensive use of examples from the Scriptures in order to illustrate and to apply their doctrine. It is important to note that, although the redemptive-historical side in the original controversy wished to exclude the exemplary element in preaching, the exemplaristic side, for its part, did not wish to exclude the redemptive-historical element. "Not one of us is opposed to the redemptive-historical method as such," insisted J. Douma. "What we object to is the exclusive redemptive-historical method."[23]

Of greater cogency still, of course, was the appeal by the exemplaristic school to the Scriptures themselves. Take, for instance, the crucial passage in 1 Corinthians 10:5–11. Here the apostle Paul uses the word "examples" twice in referring to the experiences of the Israelites in the wilderness: "Now these things became our examples, to the intent that we should not lust after evil things as they also lusted. . . . Now all these things happened to them as examples, and they were written for our admonition, on whom the ends of the ages have come" (1 Cor. 10:6, 11).

The examples adduced here in the Scriptures by the apostle Paul are indeed negative examples; they are warnings. Moreover, we should note exactly what the apostle has done here. He has drawn a straight line from the experience of the Israelites in the wilderness to the experience of the Corinthians—a straight line from the past to the present. He has, in fact, turned indicatives into imperatives. Indeed, he has issued a series of imperatives to the Corinthian believers which are based on the evident parallelism which obtains between "the church in the wilderness" and the church of the New Testament. The apostle's desire is clearly that the Corinthian believers should learn the lessons of sacred history from the Scriptures. The observation of the great English Puritan theologian John Owen is most relevant at this point: "Old Testament examples are New Testament instructions."[24]

In turning from the passage in 1 Corinthians 10 to the passage in Hebrews 11, we turn from a consideration of those with whom "God was not well pleased" (1 Cor 10:5) to a consideration of those who "obtained a

20. Greidanus, *Sola Scriptura*, 120.

21. Trimp, *Preaching and the History*, 102.

22. Trimp, *Preaching and the History*, 109.

23. Trimp, *Preaching and the History*, 45.

24. Owen, *Hebrews*, 49.

good testimony" (Heb 11:2, 39). We pass from examples to be avoided to examples to be emulated. The writer to the Hebrews specifies Abel, Enoch, Noah, Abraham, Sarah, Isaac, Jacob, Joseph, Moses, Rahab, Gideon, Barak, Samson, Jephthah, David, Samuel, "the prophets," and alludes to many others who are unnamed. It is evident that the Epistle to the Hebrews is powerfully Christocentric; it is also powerfully exemplaristic. The writer to the Hebrews clearly saw no dichotomy between holding up Christ on the one hand as the sole object of, and the supreme example for, faith and holding up the Old Testament saints on the other hand as supplementary examples of faith. In effect, his message is this: "Consider them! But supremely consider him!"

When we come to the Epistle of James, we see that James, for his part, adduces the example of Elijah in order to illustrate and exemplify the duty of earnest prayer: "The effective fervent prayer of a righteous man avails much. Elijah was a man with a nature like ours, and he prayed earnestly that it would not rain; and it did not rain on the land for three years and six months. And he prayed again, and the heaven gave rain, and the earth produced its fruit" (Jas 5:16b–18). James' reference here to Elijah is crucial; it is clearly exemplary in nature. Huyser's observation concerning this passage in the original controversy in the Netherlands is surely unanswerable. "If Scripture itself derives an example from 1 Kings 18:42 ff., this is irrefutable proof that there is in fact an example in this history, otherwise it could not have been drawn from it. . . . The preacher not only has the right to do this, but it is his biblical duty. He neglects this duty if he fails to bring out the 'exemplary' element. . . . Whoever refuses to interpret and apply this history in the light cast upon it by the Spirit through James 5, violates Scripture and purposely suppresses the truth."[25]

Dr. Gaffin, in his recent lectures on Reformed Hermeneutics, goes even further than Huyser here. He points out that James, in his adduction of 1 Kings 18, has seized upon "an incidental aspect"—"a quite subordinate point," namely, Elijah's earnest praying, and has turned this into "a primary point" in his own epistle. Dr. Gaffin observes that the fact of Elijah's praying receives so little emphasis in 1 Kings 18 that one might well not even notice it in a cursory reading of the text itself. Dr. Gaffin draws this tentative conclusion: "A minor point of the text may on occasion legitimately be a major emphasis of the sermon."[26] Indeed, James' reference to Elijah raises a very interesting question, which we put to the redemptive-historical school: Does the redemptive-historical school regard James' reference to Elijah as

25. Cited in Greidanus, *Sola Scriptura*, 118.

26. Gaffin, *Reformed Hermeneutics*, cass. 2.

atomistic and moralistic, or not? If it does, it is clearly claiming to be wiser than the inspired authors of the word of God. If it does not, it is conceding the very point at issue in the original controversy. One of the major problems with the charge made by some within the redemptive-historical school to the effect that an exemplary use of an Old Testament or of a New Testament passage will inevitably be atomistic, subjectivist, anthropocentric, and moralistic is that this charge actually recoils upon James himself—it recoils upon the Holy Scriptures of God.

There can be little doubt that, if the issue of application is the Achilles' heel of some redemptive-historical preaching, the root of this deficiency is to be found in the failure of the redemptive-historical school to grasp fully the biblical concept of example. The fact that Christ is supremely a Savior does not mean that he is not also an Example. It is important to remember that Christ is not only Prophet, Priest, and King to the believer; He is also clearly the believer's Example. In John chapter 13 the Lord Jesus Christ says to the disciples, "For I have given you an example, that you should do as I have done to you." Moreover, Peter in his First Epistle says that the sufferings of Christ not only have atoning value; they also have exemplary value. "For to this you were called, because Christ also suffered for us, leaving us an example, that you should follow His steps . . . who, when He was reviled, reviled not again. When He suffered, He did not threaten, but committed Himself to Him who judges righteously; who Himself bore our sins in His own body on the tree" (1 Pet 2:21–24). Trimp contends: "The unique character of Christ's work does not eliminate the exemplaristic character of His life and death, but rather governs it."[27] The fact that believers are to look supremely to Christ as their Savior and Example does not mean that they are not also to learn from the example of "so great a cloud of witnesses." The fact that liberal theology with its naïve Pelagianism has perniciously overemphasized the concept of example does not mean that there is no role nor place for the concept of example in Reformed preaching. We believe that there has been an overreaction on the part of the redemptive-historical school to the concept of example, that Schilder himself—described by Greidanus as "the originator of the redemptive-historical approach"[28]—was guilty at times of a certain extremism in some of his statements in this respect, and that the paranoia with regard to moralism evident in some proponents of the redemptive-historical approach is a further manifestation of this extremism. We believe that Trimp is correct when he charges the redemptive-historical school with operating "under the influence of exaggerated sensitivity regarding the

27. Trimp, *Preaching and the History*, 106.

28. Greidanus, *Sola Scriptura*, 24.

word 'example.'"[29] We believe that Trimp is also correct when he alleges, with regard to the redemptive-historical school, that "there was a certain narrowness of perspective in dealing with the important passage of Hebrews 11."[30] Indeed, we believe that the redemptive-historical school has yet to provide a satisfactory refutation of the position that the writer to the Hebrews in chapter 11, the apostle Paul in 1 Corinthians 10, James in chapter 5, and the Lord Jesus Christ in Luke 17 ("Remember Lot's wife") all endorse the validity and the spiritual value of scriptural examples. Christocentricity is indeed vital in our preaching; but Christocentricity must not be permitted to degenerate into Christomonism. The Christocentric does not and must not exclude the exemplary; the indicatives of history do not and must not exclude the imperatives of ethics.

This tendency to suppress or to eliminate the imperative mood is evident more recently both in the homiletical philosophy and the published expositions of *Kerux: A Journal of Biblical-Theological Preaching*, first published in 1986 under the editorship of James T. Dennison Jr. *Kerux* magazine is profoundly committed to the hermeneutical methodology of Geerhardus Vos, and thus to the disciplines of biblical theology and redemptive-historical preaching. *Kerux* reveals a striking emphasis upon the centrality of Christ and upon the believer's union with Christ; it reveals a striking emphasis upon what we might call the double indicative of Christianity. *Kerux* also reveals a striking lack of emphasis upon the need for repentance and sanctification; in other words, it manifests a striking lack of emphasis upon the double imperative of Christianity. The expositions and reviews in *Kerux* reveal a remarkable diffidence with regard to the issue of application in general and the use of the imperative mood in particular. In an article entitled "Some Thoughts on Preaching" Charles G. Dennison asserts:

> Good preaching is God-centered, not man-centered. . . . Good preaching is Christ-centered, not morality or behavior-centered. . . . Good preaching does not make the text meaningful for us in our contemporary situation; rather good preaching makes us and our contemporary situation meaningful in the text. In other words, good preaching doesn't pull the word into our world as if the word were deficient in itself and in need of our applicatory skills. Instead good preaching testifies and declares to us that we have been pulled into the word which has its own marvelous sufficiency.[31]

29. Trimp, *Preaching and the History*, 111.
30. Trimp, *Preaching and the History*, 115.
31. C. Dennison, "Some Thoughts on Preaching," 6.

The antithesis posited here between God-centeredness and man-centeredness, between Christ-centeredness and morality or behavior is, we believe, a false antithesis. It is a false antithesis that sets up a false dichotomy. It is abundantly evident from "the Pauline theology" itself that theocentricity and Christocentricity do not exclude the addressing of issues of morality or behavior.

It is significant that many of the contributors to *Kerux* make the steady insinuation that all concern for relevant application and practical Christianity in preaching essentially originates in liberal, rationalistic presuppositions. Professor Frame has demonstrated the fallacy of this position:

> James Dennison objects to the term "application," because he believes it had bad connotations in theologies like Schleiermacher's and Bultmann's. But criticizing language on such grounds is an instance of the genetic fallacy. And Dennison's proposed alternatives, "participation in the text," "identification with the text," have also been used in non-Christian philosophies, particularly those of Plato and the mystics. And the alternative "living in the text" is really too vague to denote a purposeful ethical preaching thrust.[32]

Indeed, the quasi-applicatory phrases which are commonly found in the expositions in *Kerux*—phrases such as "pulled into the word which has its own marvelous sufficiency,"[33] "find your story within the structure of John's story of Jesus,"[34] "find your life in the text of the word of God"[35]—are surely little more than vague, meaningless generalities. Professor Frame again: "It is simply wrongheaded to deny the importance of concrete, practical, ethical application."[36]

There can be no doubt that Geerhardus Vos is the hero of the more extreme wing of the redemptive-historical school. James T. Dennison Jr., for instance, demonstrates his predilection for both the hermeneutical and the homiletical method of the Princeton theologian in his article "What Is Biblical Theology? Reflections on the Inaugural Address of Geerhardus Vos." Vos gave this address on the occasion of his installation as professor of biblical theology at Princeton on May 8, 1894. Dennison comments as follows:

32. Frame, "Ethics, Preaching," para. 11.

33. C. Dennison, "Some Thoughts on Preaching," 6.

34. J. Dennison, "John 2," 12.

35. J. Dennison, "Paul on Damascus Road," 27.

36. Frame, "Ethics, Preaching," para. 12.

> The insights gathered from Vos's inaugural mean that our preaching can never be the same again. For Vos has alerted us to the Copernican revolution in hermeneutics—eschatology is prior to soteriology; and all soteriology is eschatologically oriented. Through the Scriptures, God has invited us into the very arena which he himself inhabits. With Paul, we are caught up to the "heavenly places." Never again can we isolate or abstract a part of God's Word from its biblical-theological and organic context in the history of redemption. The people of God are hungry and thirsty for Christ Jesus. The poor lambs of Christ yearn for the streams of living water that flow by the throne of God. The vessels of grace long to be lifted to the right hand of the glory on high. Biblical-theological preaching will bring our people to the arms of Jesus. It will direct their gaze toward the crystal sea mirroring the lapis lazuli throne. It will draw them to find their life hidden with Christ in God.
>
> Preaching which does any less is bankrupt. For anything less is not an exaltation of God in his glory, or the Son of God in his mercy, or the Spirit of God in his heavenly motions—anything less is the promotion of the earthly agenda of the preacher.[37]

We would make the following observations on James Dennison's statement. First, the hermeneutical methodology of biblical theology is not the only hermeneutical theology available to the theologian or the preacher. It is essential that the claims of systematic theology should not be neglected in this respect. Indeed, it is very interesting to note that in his inaugural address Vos himself specifically warns against any relegation of systematic theology at the hands of biblical theologians, or any elevation of biblical theology at the expense of systematic theology:

> Biblical Theology is of the greatest importance and value for the study of Systematic Theology. It were useless to deny that it has been often cultivated in a spirit more or less hostile to the work in which Systematic Theology is engaged. The very name Biblical Theology is frequently vaunted so as to imply a protest against the alleged un-Biblical character of Dogmatics. I desire to state most emphatically here, that there is nothing in the nature and aims of Biblical Theology to justify such an implication. For anything pretending to supplant Dogmatics there is no place in the circle of Christian Theology. . . . Dogmatics is the

37. J. Dennison, "What Is Biblical Theology," 40–41.

> crown which grows out of all the work that Biblical Theology can accomplish.[38]

Thus, to focus exclusively upon one particular hermeneutical methodology, namely, that of biblical theology, is to invite imbalance. A great deal of redemptive-historical preaching demonstrates, we believe, such an imbalance. It demonstrates a particular hermeneutic driving a particular homiletic. Indeed, it often demonstrates an unbalanced hermeneutic driving an unbalanced homiletic. Dr. W. Robert Godfrey, president of Westminster Seminary in California, is surely correct when he accuses the extreme wing of the redemptive-historical school of being "hyper-Vosian."

Second, the extreme wing of the redemptive-historical school demonstrates a preoccupation with the eschatological which almost amounts to an obsession. James T. Dennison Jr., as noted above for instance, asserts that, according to Vos, "eschatology is prior to soteriology."[39] Dennison asserts that "the Vosian genius" lies in this emphasis upon "the priority of the eschatological."[40] It is important to note, however, that this preoccupation with eschatology on the part of the extreme wing of the redemptive-historical school is, in fact, a preoccupation with only one particular aspect of eschatology, namely, with what Geerhardus Vos calls the "semi-eschatological"[41] or the "semi-celestial."[42] We concur with Vos that this "semi-eschatological" perspective is "characteristic of the Epistles of the First Imprisonment, Ephesians, Colossians, Philippians."[43] That this is part of the counsel of God, we do not deny; that this is not the whole counsel of God, we most emphatically insist. Indeed, it is not even the whole of eschatology. We note with interest that Vos's own treatment of eschatology is not restricted to this aspect of eschatology; it is much more full orbed and includes, for instance, a strong emphasis upon the second coming of Christ. We find little or no emphasis in redemptive-historical preaching, however, upon the second coming of Christ. The emphasis falls repeatedly, indeed repetitiously, upon this semi-eschatological note. Thus, it is difficult to avoid the conclusion that those redemptive-historical preachers who constantly harp on this semi-eschatological note are, in fact, no more balanced in their ministry than those dispensationalist preachers who constantly harp on the second coming of Christ. Both sets of preachers are characterized by

38. Vos, "Idea of Biblical Theology," para. 41.

39. J. Dennison, "Geerhardus Vos," paras. 2, 12.

40. J. Dennison, "Geerhardus Vos," para. 3.

41. Vos, *Pauline Eschatology*, 38.

42. Vos, *Pauline Eschatology*, 54.

43. Vos, *Pauline Eschatology*, 38.

a serious imbalance which flows from their extrapolation of one particular doctrine from the whole corpus of Christian truth.

Third, this overemphasis upon the eschatological on the part of the extreme wing of the redemptive-historical school goes hand in hand with an underemphasis upon the ethical. It should be noted that James T. Dennison's assertion that "eschatology is prior to soteriology" is his own phrasing, not the words of Vos. Moreover, the phrase "prior to" is the critical phrase here precisely because it contains a potential ambiguity. It is one thing to assert that eschatology is prior to soteriology in sequence (i.e., logically prior); it is quite another thing to assert that eschatology is prior to soteriology in importance. The danger of this particular slogan is that, potentially at least, it smuggles in, by means of an intrinsic ambiguity in the phrase "prior to," a conclusion that is actually foreign to the statements adduced from Vos to support it.[44]

Moreover, this underemphasis upon the ethical flies in the face of a colossal emphasis placed upon ethics in the New Testament itself. Professor John Frame makes the following observation:

> I believe that it is possible to go too far in our emphasis on the history of redemption. Although the two-age structure of Pauline ethics is important, it does not by any means exhaust the biblical teaching relevant to our ethical decisions. There are pages and pages of Scripture devoted to the details of God's law, to proverbs about the practical life of the believer, to the heart motivations of love and faith that should impel our passion for holiness.[45]

This underemphasis upon the ethical also flies in the face of Vos's own characterization of Pauline theology as that of an "already/not yet" structure. The "already" aspect of Pauline theology reflects the eschatological aspect of Christian truth; it coheres with the indicative mood in Christianity. The "not yet" aspect of Pauline theology reflects the ethical aspect of Christian truth; it coheres with the imperative mood in Christianity. We contend strongly that, in their emphasis on the "already" aspect of the Christian life, the more extreme redemptive-historical preachers demonstrate a significant neglect of the ""not yet" aspect of the Christian life—the ethical imperatives with which the New Testament unquestionably teems. Professor Frame contends: "When a preacher avoids concrete ethical application in his sermons, he is

44. See J. Dennison, "Geerhardus Vos." Note also that Dennison asserts that "as eschatology is prior to soteriology, so eschatology is prior to ethics."

45. Frame, "Ethics, Preaching," para. 3.

not preaching the whole counsel of God, and he is not adequately edifying his people."[46]

Fourth, the extreme wing of the redemptive-historical school demonstrates an idealization—indeed, almost an idolization—of Geerhardus Vos as a preacher which must be challenged. We recognize most readily the erudition and profundity of Vos as a theologian and the richness and profundity of Vos's sermons. We do not, however, regard Geerhardus Vos as an ideal model for preachers for two *reasons.* In the first place, his homiletical style is essentially too heavy, too theological, too demanding, and it savors too much of the essayist. In the second place, Vos's sermons manifest a minimal level of application. It would be incorrect to assert that Vos engages solely in *explicatio verbi Dei* to the total exclusion of *applicatio verbi Dei.* Indeed, it is an interesting fact that Vos engages somewhat more in application than many of his modern adherents! Nevertheless, it is a striking fact that the imperatival note is significantly suppressed in Vos's preaching. It is for these two reasons that we regard Dr. J. Gresham Machen as unquestionably correct when, as a student at Princeton Seminary, he made this general observation concerning Vos's preaching: "He is usually rather too severely theological for Sunday morning."[47]

In his valuable critique of redemptive-historical preaching, Dr. C. Trimp charges the redemptive-historical school with a certain imbalance and even reductionism in its homiletical methodology. "It involves the reduction of salvation history to the single, advancing work of God in and toward Christ."[48] Indeed, Trimp charges the redemptive-historical school with "overlooking man."[49] In other words, in his emphasis on the eschatological drive of history, the redemptive-historical preacher is too prone to forget that, as Trimp puts it, "in salvation history God is dealing with people."[50] It is evident that the Scriptures themselves, in their focus on the coming Messiah, do not suppress the human element; they do not suppress the personal element, indeed, what we might even call the popular element. Thus to assert, as M. B. van't Veer did in the original controversy in 1944, that "Elijah's soul is no more or less significant for us than his mantle,"[51] is

46. Frame, "Ethics, Preaching," para. 15.

47. Stonehouse, *J. Gresham Machen*, 72. The fact that this statement is made in the context of an expression of great admiration on Machen's part for one particular sermon by Vos does not detract from the significance of the statement itself. The exception simply tends to prove the rule.

48. Trimp, *Preaching and the History*, 121.

49. Trimp, *Preaching and the History*, 53.

50. Trimp, *Preaching and the History*, 122.

51. Trimp, *Preaching and the History*, 122.

really quite preposterous. The bilateral nature of the covenant means that collateral with the emphasis upon Christ is an emphasis upon men and women in relationship with Christ.

This balance between the divine aspect and the human aspect of the bilateral covenant requires, as Dr. Gaffin has pointed out, a balanced emphasis upon both *historia salutis* and *ordo salutis*. The *historia salutis* (the history of salvation) focuses upon the accomplishment of redemption; it focuses upon the unique epochal events involved in Christ's humiliation and exaltation. These events are described, indeed, they are announced in the Scriptures, by means of the "triumphant indicative." Conversely, the *ordo salutis* (the order of salvation) focuses upon the application of redemption; it focuses upon the ongoing appropriation of Christ's work in the life and the experience of Christ's people. Many of the various acts and processes involved in the application of redemption are expressed by means of an urgent imperative. It is at this point that a certain imbalance is discernible in some redemptive-historical preaching, where there is a tendency to emphasize the *historia salutis* at the expense of the *ordo salutis*. In other words, there is a tendency in redemptive-historical preaching to emphasize redemption accomplished by Christ at the expense of redemption applied to Christ's people. In short, there is a tendency in the redemptive-historical school to emphasize the indicative at the expense of the imperative. It is the paradox of the indicative mood that it constitutes at one and the same time both the great strength and the great weakness of much redemptive-historical preaching.

Dr. Gaffin has recently expressed his concern over some redemptive-historical preaching in this way: "Very often it seems to involve a conception of preaching that is unduly . . . exclusive, narrow, restrictive, even straight-jacketing in a way, so that it loses sight of—inhibits legitimate room for—diversity and flexibility in preaching."[52] Gaffin goes on:

> The one-sidedness or imbalance of some redemptive-historical preaching perhaps lies along this line—that it has an eye only for the unique typological moments of Old Testament history. It only has an eye for that which is bound up with the theocratic institutions that are in play through Israel's history in its ongoing forward movement to the fulfillment of Christ. . . . Some redemptive-historical approaches in preaching are so focused on the unique typological in the Old Testament that it [*sic*] downplays and at least practically ignores what is common with

52. Gaffin, *Reformed Hermeneutics*, cass. 1.

> the New Testament—with New Testament believers. As James says, "Like us!"[53]

Dr. Gaffin develops his reference to Elijah here by emphasizing that Elijah should be viewed not merely as the theocratic prophet, but also as a believer. Similarly, David should be viewed not merely as the theocratic king, but also as a believer. In other words, Old Testament characters such as Elijah and David should be considered not merely in their theocratic and typological role as prophet and king respectively, who point forward to Christ, but also as believers in Christ—as Old Testament Christians—who, as such, share a great deal in common with New Testament believers today. Dr. Gaffin emphasizes that these Old Testament characters should be viewed in two dimensions:

> The concern here is that we don't polarize legitimate concerns. . . . Preaching from the Old Testament must do justice to covenant history in both dimensions. It has to honor the redemptive-historical—honor that which is unrepeatable and epochal in the movement forward toward Christ—and that, I would even say, is primary. (Remember, the main point is Christ, not the Christian—or God, not his people.) But also, while that is true, preaching from the Old Testament must honor the covenant history in its *ordo salutis* constancy and commonality with the New Testament church in terms of the principle of faith—*sola fide*—a faith alone that gives rise to a life of faith working by love.[54]

We have already noted both the irreversibility and the inseparability of the indicative and the imperative moods in the theology and preaching of the New Testament. It is in particular the implications of the inseparability between the indicative and the imperative that are relevant to redemptive-historical preaching. In a recent article in *Kerux* entitled "Redemptive-Historical Preaching," Lee Irons has contrasted "redemptive-historical preaching" and "modern preaching" in the following way: "'Redemptive-historical preaching' is characterized by the 'indicative-grounded imperative,' whereas 'modern preaching' is characterized by the 'bare imperative.'"[55] This is, we contend, a caricature of modern preaching. We do not deny that some "modern preaching" is characterized by the "bare imperative." But to imply that all non-redemptive-historical preaching belongs to this sweeping

53. Gaffin, *Reformed Hermeneutics*, cass. 2.

54. Gaffin, *Reformed Hermeneutics*, cass. 2.

55. Irons, "Redemptive-Historical Preaching," 44.

category of modern preaching and that it is, therefore, by definition characterized by this bare imperative, is a gross misrepresentation. We personally have no brief for exclusive redemptive-historical preaching; but neither do we have any brief for preaching that is characterized by the "bare imperative." Our brief is for expository preaching, and we believe passionately that such preaching should be both governed by and should reflect this indicative-imperative pattern for the Christian life. Indeed, it is precisely because we believe passionately in this indicative-imperative pattern or structure of New Testament Christianity (and by implication, in the *de jure* necessity of indicative-imperative preaching) that we lament the very significant extent to which redemptive-historical preaching is characterized by a *de facto* bare indicative!

Dr. Gaffin asserts: "Some so-called redemptive-historical preaching has fallen to the pattern of accenting the indicative in a way in which the imperative has not had adequate justice done to it." Speaking of the moral consequences of justification by faith alone, Dr. Gaffin emphasizes that "those consequences do not follow as a form of automatism. . . . The exhortations of the New Testament are the clear indication that new obedience does not result automatically in the life of the justified."[56] Dr. Gaffin is unquestionably right. It is not enough to focus on the great, central, epochal events in the history of redemption. It is not enough to speak almost exclusively in the indicative mood. It is not enough to reduce the imperatives of the New Testament to the vague generality, which is so often heard, namely, "Look to Christ!," and to leave the application of the preached word to the Spirit of God. There is, says Dr. Gaffin, a concreteness and a specificity about the imperatives and the exhortations of the New Testament, and this concreteness and specificity should be reflected in our preaching. The analogy of Scripture should be reflected not merely in our hermeneutics, but also in our homiletics.

The classic Reformed position concerning preaching is that of *explicatio et applicatio verbi Dei*. This balance between the explication and the application of the word of God is, we believe, irrefutably established by the analogy of Scripture and powerfully confirmed by the history of Reformed preaching. It is for that reason that we regard that wing of the redemptive-historical school which, on principle, eschews application of the word of God as having introduced into the Reformed Churches a homiletical innovation. Indeed, it has, in the name of homiletical reformation, introduced into the Reformed Churches a species of homiletical revisionism. Moreover, the significance of Dr. Gaffin's recent penetrating

56. Gaffin, *Reformed Hermeneutics*, cass. 3.

and cogent critique of some redemptive-historical preaching lies in this, that Dr. Gaffin is himself unashamedly a passionate exponent of biblical theology. Thus Dr. Gaffin is clearly making a very important conceptual distinction between the particular hermeneutic of biblical theology on the one hand and the particular homiletic of redemptive-historical preaching on the other. Dr. Gaffin's recent acute critique demonstrates that an espousal of the hermeneutical methodology of biblical theology does not inevitably entail an endorsement of all the shibboleths of the homiletical methodology of redemptive-historical preaching.

True preaching, then, always involves a balance between the indicative and the imperative moods. True preaching, we maintain, always involves both proclamation and appeal. True preaching always involves *explicatio et applicatio verbi Dei*—the explication and the application of the word of God. The indicative mood is the native sphere of the explication of the word of God; the imperative mood is the native sphere of the application of the work of God. It is evident that true preaching is not mere explication; nor is it mere exhortation. Explication and exhortation must coexist in proper tension and balance. Dr. Gaffin again: "A proper grasp, a proper maintenance of the relationship between the indicative and the imperative get us right to the heart of the Christian life, whereas where that relationship is not properly maintained, deviations—distortions of a more or less serious character—are going to enter the picture."[57] If the indicative is permitted to predominate to the exclusion of the imperative, the result will tend in the direction of quietism or antinomianism. If the imperative is permitted to predominate to the exclusion of the indicative, the result will tend in the direction of moralism or legalism. It is a regrettable fact that much Reformed preaching, indeed, much redemptive-historical preaching, operates in a virtual mono-mood—that of the indicative—to the virtual exclusion of the imperative. It must be noted that, in this context, the corollary of tension is balance. In other words, the theological tension that subsists between the indicative and the imperative moods implies a homiletical balance between these two moods. The preacher, therefore, if he is to sustain a ministry that is balanced, must see to it that he preaches sermons that are balanced. The doctrinal must be balanced by the practical; the historical must be balanced by the ethical; *historia salutis* must be balanced by *ordo salutis*; the work of Christ must be balanced by the work of the Spirit. It is absolutely essential that the great indicatives of Christ's accomplishment of redemption be balanced by the great imperatives of the Spirit's application of redemption. It is vital to the health of preaching, and it is vital to the health of the church

57. Gaffin, *Reformed Hermeneutics*, cass. 3.

that this delicate relationship between the indicative and the imperative be implemented and maintained. It is part of the great calling of the preacher that in this vital matter he learn to "negotiate the razor's edge."[58]

58. Gaffin, *Reformed Hermeneutics*, cass. 3.

# THE EXTEMPORANEOUS MODE OF PREACHING[1]

THE Stuart king, Charles II, was, certainly in his lifetime, no saint; nor, it can be presumed, was he any great lover of the word of God or of the gospel of our Lord and Savior, Jesus Christ. But in 1674, in a proclamation to the University of Cambridge, he demonstrated a remarkable insight into the true nature of preaching. He forbad "on pain of his majesty's displeasure the practice of reading sermons," which practice he called "a supine and slothful way of preaching"[2] and which he commanded to be laid aside when men preached before the university and before himself. This interesting fact demonstrates, I believe, that there is, on the part of the popular mind, an almost instinctive preference for the extemporaneous mode of preaching; it is something that is taught even by the light of nature.

I want, therefore, to lecture this evening on this very important subject—*the extemporaneous mode of preaching.* We are dealing here obviously with the *manner* in which the word of God ought to be proclaimed. It seems to me that there are two crucial elements in the preaching of the word of God: there is, on the one hand, the *matter*, and there is, on the other hand, the *manner*. On the one hand, there is the content, the material—what the preacher actually says, what would be reported if the sermon were taken down, printed, and published in a book; but then, that which cannot in fact be captured on the written page—the actual manner of the preaching itself. We could describe these two important aspects of the sermon in this way: the light and the heat. Both are essential in the preaching of the word of God. Preaching, it seems to me, is no more *light without heat* than it is *heat*

1. This lecture was given as the inaugural lecture on my appointment as professor of homiletics at Greenville Presbyterian Theological Seminary, Taylors, SC, Dec. 4, 2009.

2. Broadus, *Preparation and Delivery*, 435–36.

*without light.* Light and heat must be emitted together in the true preaching of the word of God.

Now, with regard to the *matter*, which I will deal with briefly, it is interesting to note that Robert Lewis Dabney describes "instructiveness" as one of the "cardinal requisites of the sermon."[1] He is absolutely right. A man must have something to say, and what he says must be of quality. "The instructive sermon," says Dabney, "is that which abounds in food for the understanding. It is full of thought, and richly informs the mind of the hearer." It is "rich in matter."[2] It is, therefore, undeniable that light is essential; instructiveness is essential. But there is something additional that is also crucial in the preaching of the word of God, namely, the *manner* in which the word of God is proclaimed. The delivery is crucial. Listen to Dabney again in his fine work on preaching: "Eloquence is not the mere communication of a set of dry notions; it is a sympathy, a spiritual infection, a communion of life and action between two souls, a projection of the orator's thought, conviction, emotion and will into the mind and heart of the audience. Nothing, therefore, is a true oration which is not a life, a spiritual action, transacted in the utterance."[3]

What, then, is the best method or mode of delivery? How is that method or mode of delivery related to the arduous task of preparation on the part of the preacher? There is, I believe, broad, general consensus that there are three options—three methods or modes available to the preacher. First, there is the possibility of *writing and reading*; second, there is the possibility of *writing and memorizing*; and third, there is the option of *extemporizing*. We are going to consider this issue in detail here this evening, and I intend to give a ringing endorsement of the third option, namely, that of the extemporaneous mode of utterance.

First, then, there is the option of *writing and reading*. I choose to call this "the *verbatim* reading method." What happens here is this: the preacher writes the sermon out in full, he takes a full manuscript into the pulpit, and he then proceeds to read that manuscript from beginning to end to those that are gathered in front of him. Now, there can be no doubt that there have been, in the history of the Christian church, some very famous preachers that have adopted this mode of preaching. We can call them, as they have been called, "reading preachers"—preachers who read their sermons. Two notable names immediately spring to mind—Jonathan Edwards and Thomas Chalmers. But let me just say a word with regard to Jonathan Edwards: he

1. Dabney, *Evangelical Eloquence*, 105.
2. Dabney, *Evangelical Eloquence*, 117.
3. Dabney, *Evangelical Eloquence*, 333.

is often accused of being lamely dependent upon a manuscript; he is often accused of preaching from a manuscript in a monotone. This reputation, however, is something of a caricature. Certain stereotypical caricatures have come down through history. There are, in fact, two very significant turning points in his ministry: in 1729, a minor turning point, and in 1741, which captures the heart of the Great Awakening, a very significant major turning point. It is very evident that Edwards did not always read his sermons; it is very evident that he moved increasingly towards an extemporaneous mode of utterance. I happen to think that he was not particularly adept at that more difficult and demanding type of delivery. Nevertheless, there are these significant turning points, and it is, therefore, a misrepresentation of his ministry to say that he was lamely dependent upon a manuscript. He developed and he evolved; and his sermons, as you move through the 1740s and into the 1750s, are much more likely to be found in outline than in the full manuscript.[4]

I also want to concede that there are many good men today, many godly men, many fine pastors and adequate preachers who use this method. It is my judgment, however, that this method of writing and reading is not the best method. It is not the ideal method; and, regrettably, it has become really rather common in evangelical circles and even in Reformed circles.

It is interesting to trace something of the history of the development of this trend towards the reading of sermons. In 1888, William G. Blaikie (1820–99), one of the professors at New College, Edinburgh, delivered the Cunningham Lectures on "The Preachers of Scotland." He emphasized the fact that it was not until the era of Moderatism in the Church of Scotland in the eighteenth century that this tendency to read sermons developed and held sway. Under the influence of Moderatism there was this "recoil from evangelical doctrine"—this "decline of the evangelical spirit." Blaikie says this: "The fact is, that up till now the reading of sermons in the pulpit was hardly known in Scotland. . . . It is beyond doubt . . . that it was under the moderate *régime* that the practice of reading sermons became general in Scotland."[5] Under the moderate régime you have what Blaikie calls "mild discourses"[6]—discourses devoid of life and of fervor; and the moderates, who adopted widely this method of reading their sermons, "preached without life or power."[7] It is an interesting fact that, historically, there is a

4. On the issue of Edwards's delivery, see Carrick, *Preaching of Jonathan Edwards*, ch. 26.

5. Blaikie, *Preachers of Scotland*, 228–29.

6. Blaikie, *Preachers of Scotland*, 222.

7. Blaikie, *Preachers of Scotland*, 219.

connection between the rise of Moderatism on the one hand and the setting in of this tendency and trend on the other.

But how effective is this particular method? The problem is that it tends to promote the "essay style"; it tends to promote what has been termed the "essay sermon." There is always the tendency in this particular method to reduce the sermon to an essay or to a lecture. Indeed, I would say that there are too many sermons in our evangelical and Reformed circles that savor of one of those two *genres*. I concede that the matter may be good; I concede that the sermon may be well structured; I concede it may be delivered with a degree earnestness and passion and fervor. Nevertheless, I also insist upon it that there is, in that particular method, something missing, something wanting, something almost indefinable, which must nevertheless be defined. What is it? It is *the living, dynamic element*—that is what is missing in sermons that are read. I will put it this way: there is, in general terms and in a relative sense, a dryness, a deadness, a lameness, a tameness, and a flatness about sermons that are written out and read verbatim from the pulpit.

I have no hesitation in saying that reading is never conducive to eloquence in the pulpit; and if a man really aspires to be truly eloquent in a spiritual sense, then he must adopt some form of the extemporaneous mode of delivery. Moreover, in my research recently I have not found one single major preacher, I have not found one single major homiletician who advocates, endorses, or even defends the practice of reading sermons. Listen to Dabney again, writing in 1870:

> Reading a manuscript to the people can never, with any justice, be termed preaching. Even if the matter and style are rhetorical, the action cannot be. . . . In the delivery of the sermon there can be no exception in favour of the mere reader. How can he whose eyes are fixed upon the paper before him, who performs the mechanical task of reciting the very words inscribed upon it, have the inflections, the emphasis, the look, the gesture, the flexibility, the fire, or oratorical action? Mere reading, then, should be sternly banished from the pulpit.[8]

Notice that—Dabney says this: "Even if the matter and the style are rhetorical, the action cannot be."[9]

Listen also to John A. Broadus, writing in 1870 in his fine work on *The Preparation and Delivery of Sermons*: "Greater coldness of manner is almost inevitable. . . . The gestures are nearly always unnatural.[10] . . . This is

8. Dabney, *Evangelical Eloquence*, 328.

9. Dabney, *Evangelical Eloquence*, 328.

10. Broadus, *Preparation and Delivery*, 444.

not living speech."[11] Listen to Charles Haddon Spurgeon, writing in 1875: "Very strongly do I warn all of you against reading your sermons."[12] Listen Dr. Martyn Lloyd-Jones lecturing at Westminster Theological Seminary in 1969:

> Surely preaching involves . . . a direct contact between the people and the preacher, and an interplay of personalities and minds and hearts. There is the element of "give and take." It is good therefore that the preacher be looking at the people; and you cannot be looking at the people and reading a manuscript at the same time. Such reading is bad for you and bad for the people. You lose their attention and your grip on them, and they lose grip on you and what you are saying. Surely, by definition, preaching is speech addressed to people in a direct and personal manner. It is not something theoretical or an academic lecture; it implies a living contact. Anything that makes you lose that is bad in and of itself.[13]

In the course of his treatment Dr. Lloyd-Jones compares what he calls "the mechanical element" inherent in the reading of the sermon and "the living element" inherent in the extemporaneous mode of utterance. Al Martin endorses the same position: "The man of God should never read a full manuscript from the pulpit."[14]

Indeed, it is my judgment that any preacher who adopts throughout his ministry this particular method of reading his sermons verbatim will be inevitably *settling for mediocrity* in terms of his delivery. I am not saying that he cannot be edifying; I am not saying that he cannot, in one sense, preach good sermons. But I am saying that, in terms of the delivery, he is settling inevitably for a certain mediocrity. This falls far short of the ideal set for us by the great preachers of the past. The first method, then, is that of *writing and reading*.

The second method is that of *writing and memorizing*. I shall call this "the *verbatim memoriter* method." What happens here is this: the preacher writes the sermon out and then commits it, astonishingly, to memory and delivers it verbatim from memory. Dabney says this: "The second method is that of writing a discourse and committing it to memory *verbatim*, to be

11. Broadus, *Preparation and Delivery*, 445.

12. Spurgeon, *Lectures to My Students*, 141.

13. Lloyd-Jones, *Preaching and Preachers*, 227.

14. Borgman, *My Heart*, 243.

recited in the pulpit."[15] We are dealing here with recitation; we are dealing here with a repetition from memory. Now, I think it must be conceded that this, of the three methods, is the least common. Apparently, it has been found more in Europe, and perhaps more on the continent. It is inevitably extremely difficult and is perhaps seldom practiced. We could say this, that it is marginally superior to first method; at least there is eye contact. But there is a very interesting exception to this: You may have heard of Louis Bourdaloue (1632–1704). He was the famous Jesuit orator who preached before the court of Louis XIV in the seventeenth century. Apparently, this famous orator, who wrote his sermons out and then committed them to memory, would often shut his eyes and deliver them in this way. Obviously, there was not a lot of eye contact when Louis Bourdaloue was preaching! The problem here is that the sermon essentially becomes a performance. Thus, there are deep, intrinsic problems in this method. Obviously, this method demands that the sermon first be composed and then memorized. It is an extremely burdensome and demanding type of delivery. But the major problem to my mind is this that it is akin to the work of the actor—the actor who has to learn the lines of a script and deliver them verbatim from memory. Inevitably you have once again this mechanical element which we have already noted in the writing and reading of sermons. Listen to R. L. Dabney: "The mind, painfully occupied with the toil of verbal recollection, cannot realize to itself the subject, or feel the emotions which it should inspire. The air is almost unavoidably constrained, and the utterance artificial."[16] Listen to C. H. Spurgeon: "We do not recommend the plan of learning sermons by heart, and repeating them from memory; that is both a wearisome exercise of an inferior power of the mind and an indolent neglect of other and superior faculties."[17] Listen to Dr. Lloyd-Jones: "To memorize this written sermon is to me almost as bad. . . . My chief reason is that it binds the man, it interferes with the element of freedom.[18] . . . The living element is lessened, and the mechanical element comes in more."[19] So then, that is the second method, namely, that of *writing and memorizing*.

The third method—the method which I wish to advocate here this evening—is that of *extemporizing*. We can call this "the *ex tempore* method." What exactly is that method? It is important that the method should be defined. Negatively, it means this: It is not without premeditation. It does

15. Dabney, *Evangelical Eloquence*, 331.

16. Dabney, *Evangelical Eloquence*, 331.

17. Spurgeon, *Lectures to My Students*, 142.

18. Lloyd-Jones, *Preaching and Preachers*, 239.

19. Lloyd-Jones, *Preaching and Preachers*, 240.

not insist that there be no preparation. The concept is often misunderstood. Broadus says this: "It is utterly unfair to represent the advocates of extemporaneous preaching as meaning that men shall preach without preparation."[20] Preparation is, in fact, central in this whole process. Preparation is pivotal and absolutely essential in extemporaneous preaching. Moreover, extemporaneous preaching does not mean that it is impromptu. We are not saying that there is no study. This is not preaching *ex nihilo*! This is preaching out of very careful preparation and premeditation. But there is something about the delivery, something special, something quite unique that distinguishes it from the other methods. That is the issue here. Preparation is essential as a precursor; but the delivery itself is characterized by freedom.

Moreover, this method is not *memoriter*. Now, let me qualify that by saying that memory, in the extemporaneous method, does play a part; in fact, memory plays a very important part. But the part played by the memory in extemporaneous preaching is that of a servant, not a master. In the *memoriter* method, clearly the memory is the master; memorization is everything. In the extemporaneous method memory is very important; indeed, a man cannot preach well extemporaneously unless he makes use of his memory, and unless he uses it well. So it plays a part, but it is subsidiary. It is not the dominant element. The superior faculties of the mind are much more in control than the memory.

Moreover, this does not mean that it is without all notes. Extemporaneous preachers can use an outline and still preach extemporaneously. Admittedly, there are varieties of extemporaneous preaching. There are those that have no notes at all; and there are those that preach from an outline. But I want to emphasize that, as Broadus puts it, "preaching from notes is fairly called extemporaneous."[21] If you look at Dabney, if you look at Lloyd-Jones, if you consider Al Martin, you will see that the extemporaneous method is compatible with a certain limited use of notes and of an outline.

Let me illustrate this. I am referring to Robert Roberts, one of the great preachers of Wales, who lived from 1762 to 1802. This is what Owen Jones says in his fine work, *Some of the Great Preachers of Wales*:

> He does not appear to have written his sermons carefully out word for word; he wrote them in outline only. He thought out the subject carefully; he meditated upon it; he prayed fervently for the help of God; then wrote an outline of his thoughts, and depended upon the stability of the laws of nature—that those thoughts which glowed so brightly, and made him feel so deeply

20. Broadus, *Preparation and Delivery*, 458.

21. Broadus, *Preparation and Delivery*, 457.

> in meditation, would come again with the same effects before the congregation.[22]

Positively, then, what exactly is this extemporaneous method? What does it mean? Well, the word "extemporaneous" or the verb "to extemporize" comes from the Latin term *ex tempore*, which literally means "out of the time," or we could translate it "out of the moment." The *Oxford English Dictionary* translates it in that way: that which is *at the moment*, that which is *from the moment*, that which arises *out of the moment*. So there is, in the extemporaneous mode of preaching, a certain immediacy, a certain spontaneity. It has been called, I think justifiably, "preaching in the grand manner."

Now, it has to be conceded that there is, in this method, always this element of risk, in a sense; there is always the element of the unknown. I often say to the students that in utilizing this method you never ever know what the middle word is going to be; you never ever know how long the sermon is going to last. But there is also this element of what Dr. Lloyd-Jones calls "the romance of preaching."[23] You never quite know what is going to happen. You never know, when you go into the pulpit, what degree of liberty, power, and authority God might grant you. In other words, there is this tremendous potential in the extemporaneous mode of preaching which is utterly absent, in my judgment, from the first method—that of writing and reading—and from the second method, which is that of writing and delivering from memory.

Listen to W. G. T. Shedd:

> This species of Sacred Eloquence has always existed in the Church, and some of the best periods in the history of Christianity have been characterized by its wide prevalence, and high excellence. The Apostolic age, the missionary periods in Patristic and Medieval history, the age of the Reformation, the revival of evangelical religion in the English Church in the eighteenth century, in connection with the preaching of Wesley and Whitefield, and the "Great Awakening," in this country, were marked by the free utterance of the extemporaneous preacher.[24]

What exactly are the problems, the difficulties, the risks involved in this particular method? It is undeniable that there are some. The first that I have listed is this: *a spirit of fear*. I believe that a spirit of fear is one of the major reasons why men do not utilize this more demanding method of

22. O. Jones, *Great Preachers of Wales*, 144.
23. Lloyd-Jones, *Preaching and Preachers*, 283–303.
24. Shedd, *Homiletics*, 218.

preaching *ex tempore*. The dread of failure, the dread of breaking down, the dread of being humiliated in the pulpit, the danger of making blunders—blunders in grammar, blunders in diction. Let me say this, however. I have often noted that men who read their sermons make blunders too; and the reason why they make blunders, in my opinion, is very interesting: *they are not thinking on their feet*. The whole process, in their case, is somewhat mechanical; and, therefore, there is just as much risk of making blunders in reading one's sermon as there is in delivering the sermon *ex tempore*. Moreover, Broadus makes a very interesting observation about the nature of speaking in general and preaching in particular: "A man not capable of failing, can never be eloquent."[25] That is a very interesting point; and the reason for that is that he is not prepared to take the risks which are required by eloquence. Yes, he avoids the potential humiliation, he avoids the breaking down, he avoids the failure, the slips, and the blemishes; but I would put it this way: he may never know the depths; but he will not know the heights either—the heights that are inevitably attached to and associated with the extemporaneous mode of utterance. He will be settling, in my judgment, for mediocrity in the whole issue of delivery.

Then, second, there is *the temptation to slothfulness*—the temptation on the part of the minister, in time, to laziness, to dilatory, inadequate preparation. In time, he may well find that, having the gift of speech, he is able to get away with certain things using this method. He begins to neglect the sheer hard work that is pivotal, and central, and inherent in this particular method of preaching. Dabney puts it this way: "The great danger which attends the *ex tempore* preacher is that he will, after a time, abuse his facility."[26] Martyn Lloyd-Jones: "The greatest danger confronting him will be to content himself with an inadequate preparation."[27] In other words, the man that adopts this method must recognize that integral to the method is the sheer hard work, wrestling with the text, studying the text, analyzing the text, dissecting the text, dividing the text, producing a skeleton, producing flesh that will cover the bones and muscle that will cover the flesh—that is pivotal and crucial to true preaching; and, of course, it must be done beforehand. It cannot be left to the moment; so that we find in extemporaneous preaching that there is indeed this delivery *ex tempore*—*out of the time, out of the moment*; but that does not mean that it has not been excogitated first. It *has* been excogitated first; and a process of invention or reinvention, a process of creation or recreation, is occurring in the pulpit. Otherwise, the

25. Broadus, *Preparation and Delivery*, 469.

26. Dabney, *Evangelical Eloquence*, 337.

27. Lloyd-Jones, *Preaching and Preachers*, 224.

extemporaneous method will degenerate rapidly into that which is merely impromptu. Spurgeon said this: this is not "a pillow for an idle head";[28] and he went on to say this: "Only thoughtless persons think this to be easy; it is at once the most laborious and the most efficient mode of preaching, and it has virtues of its own."[29]

The third problem, difficulty, or risk, if you like, is *the danger of repetition*; or perhaps I should say, *the danger of being repetitious.* The danger, quite simply, is that of repetition, redundancy, intricacy, complexity. There is the danger of rambling, there is the danger of meandering. In other words, the man that preaches *ex tempore* must keep a very tight rein upon his tongue, as it were; he must beware of undue repetition. There is, of course, a place for an element of repetition in preaching; indeed, I would say that it is pivotal and central to it. But the danger of being repetitious is nevertheless very real. Listen to what Dabney has to say here: "But there are serious obstacles in the way of true success in *extempore* speech. . . . The difficult thing for the *extempore* speaker is to make his words scarce. . . . In a word, the great difficulty in the way of *extempore* eloquence is to avoid verbal redundancy, and to make the style compact, nervous and clear."[30] Dabney goes on to say this: "The simple, brief, compact sentence (which is the proper form for oratory) is exacting. It demands the right phrase by its very directness, and demands it at once. . . . The main obstacle you have to overcome, young gentlemen, in order to speak *extempore,* is redundancy and intricacy."[31] James Waddel Alexander (1804–59), the son of Archibald Alexander, says this: "It has been often observed, that preachers who rely on their extemporaneous powers, are very apt to fall into a great sameness. They repeat the same thoughts and the same trains of thought, and at length almost the same sermons: and this they do without being conscious of it." They "hitch into the old rut."[32]

What, then, is the antidote to this? These problems are real—they have to be faced. We have to acknowledge their reality and their danger. What is the antidote to this danger of repetition, for instance? Well, I would say that, alongside of the sheer hard work involved in preaching the word of God well is the use of the consecutive expository preaching method. When a man is expounding consecutively the word of God, then the word of God itself governs and controls the sermon, provides the matter, the material, the content for that sermon. Thus, although there is, theoretically, and,

28. Spurgeon, *Lectures to My Students*, 143.

29. Spurgeon, *Lectures to My Students*, 142.

30. Dabney, *Evangelical Eloquence*, 335.

31. Dabney, *Evangelical Eloquence*, 336.

32. Alexander, *Thoughts on Preaching*, 11.

in fact, a real danger of repetitiousness, surely the consecutive expository preaching method, undertaken well and assiduously, ought to counteract this problem. A man that adopts this method is able to "bring forth things new and old" from his treasury (Matt 13:52), and to do so week after week. All these disadvantages, and they are real, says Broadus, "can be completely obviated by resolute and judicious effort, while reading and recitation have many inherent disadvantages which . . . can never be removed."[33]

Very well, then—we have considered some of the difficulties, the risks, and the problems of the extemporaneous method. What about the advantages of this method? I believe that they are immeasurable. Dabney again: "The advantages of the *extempore* method are decisive with the man who has a true ideal of oratory."[34] The first advantage that I want to emphasize is this: *the extemporaneous method enhances the concentration of the preacher.* This is a very interesting point. Dabney says this: "The capital advantage is, that the mind is required to perform over again the labour of invention, during the actual delivery of the discourse. It is thus aroused and nerved."[35] There is a very interesting difference between this and the reading of a manuscript. I have noted in myself, sometimes, when reading the Scriptures in the pulpit, that my mind, if distracted or preoccupied with something, can, in fact, be entirely elsewhere. I am undertaking the mechanical activity of reading the words; but my mind is essentially somewhere else. This is not the case in the same way with the extemporaneous method. The very method inevitably requires and infallibly secures a concentration of the mind of the preacher upon the matter in hand. It is aroused; it is nerved; it is ready for battle. It is like the soldier, who, though disciplined, is nevertheless aroused in every single faculty of his being. In other words, as the preacher utilizing this extemporaneous method delivers the sermon, so there is a certain *friction of the truth upon the mind.* There is this labor of invention or reinvention that is occurring—this labor of creation or recreation that is occurring. He is thinking on his feet. That is the issue, and it is a very wonderful thing; and there can be no doubt about it that it is far, far more impressive, far, far more conducive to that eloquence that is desirable in the preaching of the word of God than any other method that we have considered here tonight.

Second, *the extemporaneous method enhances the rapport between the preacher and his hearers.* This rapport, this connection, this relationship between the preacher and his hearers is, of course, always very important; and this is a method that enhances that rapport. Broadus says this: "With the

33. Broadus, *Preparation and Delivery*, 469.

34. Dabney, *Evangelical Eloquence*, 332–33.

35. Dabney, *Evangelical Eloquence*, 333.

masses of the people it is the *popular* method." Thus "we most readily gain the sympathy of our hearers."[36] Moreover, it enhances the concentration of the hearers. We have just noted that it enhances the concentration of the preacher; he is forced to focus, he is forced to concentrate, he is aroused, he is nerved, his whole system is, in a sense, on edge as he delivers the sermon. But it also enhances the concentration of the hearers. They are able to follow him more easily, I believe, than if a sermon is being read or delivered *memoriter.*

I often remind the students that they are in a battle—a battle for the concentration of their hearers; and it behooves them to do all that they can to enhance that concentration. Bad preaching will break it. Good preaching enhances it; it secures it. Thus, this is part of the battle. The point is this: the extemporaneous preacher tends to break his matter up; he tends to break his matter down. He knows how to distribute the bread of life more readily, I believe, whereas the reading preacher is often too demanding. He is often too demanding in the *density of his matter* and also in the *pace of his delivery.*

Moreover, the eye contact that is secured by this method also enhances that rapport between the preacher and his hearers. Eye contact, yes, and heart contact, ideally, as well! The preacher's eye is upon the people. It is not constantly glancing at the manuscript; it is upon the people. Dabney says this: "It institutes a commerce of eye and countenance between the speaker and his hearers."[37] Now, compare that with the man who reads his sermon. There is, at least in a relative sense, a certain air of detachment about such a man. The man is absorbed in his manuscript. He is hunched over it. His whole posture is cramped. His eyes are downwards. Inevitably, he is absorbed in his paper. He is reading it. He might look up from time to time; but essentially, his eyes are downwards. Inevitably, they are on the paper.

You see, the eyes are crucial in the preaching of the word of God. Broadus speaks of "the expressiveness of the eye." Indeed, he speaks of "the marvelous, magical, at times almost superhuman power of an orator's eye."[38] This is not just true of preaching, but of oratory in general. "Now in reading," Broadus adds, "this wonderful expressiveness of the eye is interrupted, grievously diminished in power, reduced to be nothing better than occasional sunbeams, breaking out for a moment among wintry clouds."[39] But with the extemporaneous method, while there are perhaps occasional glances at the manuscript, the man is essentially looking at the people

36. Broadus, *Preparation and Delivery*, 463.

37. Dabney, *Evangelical Eloquence*, 334.

38. Broadus, *Preparation and Delivery*, 445.

39. Broadus, *Preparation and Delivery*, 445.

themselves. I believe that this is conducive to much greater expressiveness and to much greater impressiveness in the act of preaching.

Third, *the extemporaneous method enhances the harmony between word and action.* What I mean by that is this: the preacher, when preaching, in a sense speaks in two different ways. As Dabney puts it, there is the "utterance," and there is the "gesture." There is "the management of the voice" and there is also "the posture of the body and the employment of its limbs and features as aids to expression."[40] The point I am making here is that there is, in this method, much more harmony, much more consonance between tongue and action, between what the preacher says and the action of the rest of the body. There is a kind of integration of the two—a kind of integratedness is achieved. There is a naturalness in the relationship between what is said and the actual delivery—the gesture, the posture, the language of the body itself. Broadus says this: "The ideal of speaking, it has been justly said, cannot be reached in any other way. Only thus will the voice, the action, the eye, be just what nature dictates, and attain their full power."[41]

Then, fourth, *the extemporaneous method enhances liberty.* These things are, of course, all interrelated; but we can, I think, analyze them separately. This method enhances the freedom of the preacher—this freedom, this liberty that is so crucial to the act of preaching in the ideal sense. Listen to Lloyd-Jones again: "The great thing is freedom. I cannot over-emphasize this. It is of the very essence of the act of preaching—this freedom in your own mind and spirit, this being free to the influences of the Spirit upon you."[42] He goes on to say this: "Do not be tied, do not be fettered";[43] and in a remarkable passage with regard to this freedom, he adds this:

> How does one know it? It gives clarity of thought, clarity of speech, ease of utterance, a great sense of authority and confidence as you are preaching, an awareness of power not your own thrilling through the whole of your being, and an indescribable sense of joy. You are a man "possessed," you are taken hold of, and taken up. I like to put it like this—and I know nothing on earth that is comparable to this feeling—that when this happens you have a feeling that you are not actually doing the preaching, you are looking on. You are looking on at yourself in amazement as this is happening. It is not your effort; you are just the instrument, the channel, the vehicle: and the Spirit is using you, and you are looking on in great enjoyment and astonishment. There

40. Dabney, *Evangelical Eloquence*, 303.
41. Broadus, *Preparation and Delivery*, 462.
42. Lloyd-Jones, *Preaching and Preachers*, 229.
43. Lloyd-Jones, *Preaching and Preachers*, 230.

> is nothing that is in any way comparable to this. That is what the preacher himself is aware of.[44]

In other words, Lloyd-Jones is speaking here of a kind of *ekstasis*—a kind of standing outside of oneself, whereby the preacher is enjoying such liberty, such astonishing freedom, that it is almost as if he is standing outside of himself and is looking on at himself as he preaches. This freedom comes, of course, from the Spirit of God himself, who utilizes the man who has sought to prepare diligently for this particular occasion.

Then, fifth, *the extemporaneous method enhances animation.* Cicero speaks of *sermo corporis—the speech of the body, the sermon of the body.* That coheres precisely with what Dabney says: there is the "utterance," and there is the "gesture"; there is the "utterance," and there is the "posture."[45] There is what the man says and there is the way in which he conducts himself in the pulpit, because the body itself has a language. It speaks; there is a certain sermon being preached by it. Demosthenes was once asked what the three crucial elements in oratory were; and his immortal reply was this: "The first thing is *action*! The second thing is *action*! The third thing is *action*!" By "action" he meant "delivery." He did not just mean gesticulation. Gesticulation, in and of itself, can be artificial, and affected, and abhorrent. No, no! This must be a natural, yet spiritual thing. Dabney says this: "The classic masters concur in making it [action], at the least, the half of the orator's power."[46] He goes on to say this: "When the orator can combine it with the spoken language, he acquires thereby exceeding vivacity of expression. Not only his mouth, but his eyes, his features, his fingers, speak. The hearers read the coming sentiment upon his countenance and limbs almost before his voice reaches his ears: they are both spectators and listeners; every sense is absorbed in charmed attention."[47] I like the way Dabney puts it: "They are both spectators and listeners." You see, a sermon is not simply to be listened to; a sermon is to be witnessed. We are to *look* as well as to *listen*; and the action—this *sermo corporis*—is a crucial aspect of the sermon itself.

Now let me illustrate this from one of the greatest preachers that the church has ever seen. I refer to George Whitefield (1714–70). Arnold Dallimore, in his fine biography of Whitefield, says this: "As he preached his whole person became alive in a powerful yet altogether natural dramatism; yet its elements—the movement of body, the expression of his countenance and modulations of his voice—are, of course, entirely lost upon the printed

44. Lloyd-Jones, *Preaching and Preachers*, 324.

45. Dabney, *Evangelical Eloquence*, 303.

46. Dabney, *Evangelical Eloquence*, 303.

47. Dabney, *Evangelical Eloquence*, 323.

page."[48] This reminds me of a very interesting incident in the life of Whitefield. Once he was asked by someone if he would permit the publication of his sermons. This was Whitefield's reply: "Of course you may, if you can put down on the printed page the thunder and the lightning!" You see, the thunder and the lightning and the rainbow are crucial parts of the sermon; and Whitefield realized this. This was a very significant element of that wonderful seraphic power that was manifested in his ministry. The thunder and the lightning that accompanied his preaching!

There is a famous description of a certain preacher whose name appears to be lost—apparently a German reformer. I want to apply this to Whitefield himself: *Vividus vultus, vividi oculi, vividae manus, denique vivida omnia*,[49] which means this: "His face was animated, his eyes were animated, his hands were animated; in short, everything was animated." Animation! That is a crucial element in the preaching of the word of God; and I would insist upon it that the extemporaneous method, when utilized well, *transfigures preaching*. It transfigures the sermon in comparison to the sermon that is read or the sermon that is delivered memoriter.

How, then, does the preacher acquire this ability to preach extempore? Well, first, there must be, in my judgment, *a studious avoidance of the full manuscript*. I am referring to young preachers. Young preachers, once they embark upon this particular method of utilizing a full manuscript, taking it into the pulpit with them, reading it verbatim from beginning to end, have set foot upon an almost fatal path. It becomes very difficult to break that particular method. A habit is introduced, a dependence upon the manuscript is inculcated. Moreover, I believe that the seminaries play a crucial part in this. I understand that there are some seminaries that actually *require* a full manuscript from their students. The students are not permitted to preach without this full manuscript; it is required. My position is this: not only should the seminaries not *require* this full manuscript; they should not even *permit* it! Once this is permitted, the fatal habit and the dependence are introduced and become very, very difficult to break.

Second, there must be a *resolution to break free from the full manuscript*. I refer here to those who already use a full manuscript. We must lay the axe to the root of the problem. This is an inhibiting, cramping system—this full manuscript. At Greenville Seminary we lay the axe to the root of the problem by not permitting the student to come into the pulpit with it. "Reduction!" That's the word I often use. "Reduce your notes! Reduce them! Pare them down! Trim them back! Fix the matter into your heart and mind and soul!

48. Dallimore, *George Whitefield*, 2:526.

49. Cited in O. Jones, *Great Preachers of Wales*, 104.

Don't just have it there on the paper!" That is the problem with a great deal of preaching. The matter is there on the paper, but it is not there sufficiently in the heart and soul and mind. Listen to Al Martin: "The man of God ought to aim at reducing the sermon to a one page skeleton to be carried into the pulpit.[50] . . . The preacher should look at his paper only as much as is absolutely necessary."[51] Al Martin makes the point that the preacher should be "only minimally dependent on the skeleton for his flow of thought."[52] Thus there is a very important connection between this method and the outline. There is a very important connection between extemporaneousness in the pulpit on the one hand and the actual mode of preparation on the other hand. The preacher—let me repeat it—must be very, very carefully prepared. He must be very assiduous, very diligent in this. He should, in my judgment, write, and write a great deal. He is permitted to bring an outline into the pulpit, but the outline itself must not be too full; otherwise, the outline will itself cramp and inhibit. The aim in this is to minimize the eye contact with the paper and to maximize the eye contact with the people. The reading preacher does the reverse: he maximizes the eye contact with the paper and minimizes the eye contact with the people.

Third, there must be *the most thorough preparation*. There is no substitute for the sheer hard work of sermon preparation. This will involve study, and study for many hours. The preacher must wrestle with his text. He must analyze the text. He must dissect the text. He must write a great deal. He must structure his sermon. He must produce a skeleton. He must put flesh on the bones. He must put muscle on the flesh. He must know what he is going to say from beginning to end, although there is always this element of the unknown. He has no idea, in advance, how successful the sermon will be. Nevertheless, that is the method. Study! Writing, and a great deal of it! Crystallizing one's thought! Fixing the thought in one's heart and mind and soul! Dabney makes this observation: "He who labours most on each sermon is usually the best preacher."[53] It is my conviction that one of the reasons for the relatively poor state of preaching throughout the world, even in Reformed and evangelical circles, is that many men do not work sufficiently hard in their sermon preparation. Martyn Lloyd-Jones says this: "Prepare as thoroughly as you can so that you will know in your mind what you want to say from beginning to end. I cannot emphasize this too strongly."[54] The

50. Borgman, *My Heart*, 245.

51. Borgman, *My Heart*, 246.

52. Borgman, *My Heart*, 245.

53. Dabney, *Evangelical Eloquence*, 344.

54. Lloyd-Jones, *Preaching and Preachers*, 226.

aim of this preparation is this: to master one's material! Not only to master one's material, but to be mastered by it! To be gripped by it! Thus, when that time comes, when the man steps into the pulpit, the sermon goes forth with authority, and unction, and blessing, and power.

Now, to this end I recommend that the preacher *live* with his sermon throughout the week. I often say to the students, "You have Monday, Tuesday, Wednesday, Thursday, Friday, Saturday, and a few hours on Sunday morning to prepare something of quality, to deliver it in a manner appropriate to the matter, and to see to it that the people are fed, and fed well." My question, therefore, is this: In view of the fact that men have the truth, in view of the fact that they have the time, why this frequent mediocrity in the sermons within evangelical and Reformed circles? I want to emphasize the crucial importance of rumination in this. This is a vital aspect of living with the sermon throughout the week, or as long as possible. As we walk about, as we drive around, as we take our exercise, and as we lie down at night, the matter of the sermon is turning over in the mind. The preacher is ruminating on the material; he is chewing the cud, he is digesting it, he is assimilating it, it is becoming part of him. Indeed, there is a connection, in my judgment, between rumination on the one hand and animation on the other.

Then, fourth, *constant practice*. The importance of practice! The young preacher, any preacher, must constantly practice the extemporaneous method. He must do so persistently, perseveringly, habitually, patiently, constantly. You see, experience is essential. If we are to rid ourselves of this spirit of fear, experience is essential. Therefore, practice is crucial; and it is this practice and this experience that breed the confidence that enables a man to stand up before the people and deliver the word of God in the way that I am describing. W. G. T. Shedd puts it this way: "The confidence before an audience, and the skill, . . . are the result, not of mere nature, but of habit and practice."[55]

Then, fifth, *a conscious dependence upon the Holy Spirit*. We must never ever forget the ministry of the Third Person of the blessed Godhead in the act of preaching. We must pray for his influences; we must ask for his blessing; we must look to him. Listen to Pierre Charles Marcel: he speaks of "the freedom of the Spirit." Now, that is a very interesting phrase. We often speak of the freedom of the preacher, and, of course, that is connected with this. But Marcel emphasizes the freedom of the Spirit: "We must let the Spirit be free to intervene in the course of preaching." He goes on to say this:

> If the preacher is and remains dependent upon his manuscript or upon his memory, there is not *just one* prisoner—there are

55. Shedd, *Homiletics*, 226.

> two: the preacher and the Spirit, and through the Spirit, Christ. The written or memorized text of the sermon at this moment exercises its dominance. Christ through the Spirit is not free.[56]

Marcel adds: "We must tend to allow the Spirit the widest possible liberty. . . . God forbid that we imprison the Spirit in a rigid scheme!"[57] He speaks of the preacher "abandoning himself to the Spirit" in the act of preaching.[58] So then, there is this obvious dependence—a dependence that we must cultivate—upon the Spirit of God. That does not for one moment preclude the crucial work of preparation; on the contrary, it goes hand in hand with it. It does not for one moment preclude the act of prayer; on the contrary, it goes hand in hand with it. But there is a looking to the Spirit to intervene, to break into the act of preaching itself, to suggest perhaps new ideas, fresh trains of thought, so that things are said, truths are uttered which were not, in fact, premeditated at the time. I like to put it this way: the paper, the outline, the manuscript is like fire—it is a good servant, but a bad master. It serves you well if it is a servant; but don't ever let it become a master!

I want to illustrate these principles via the preaching of Dr. Martyn Lloyd-Jones (1899–1981)—in my judgment unquestionably the greatest preacher of the twentieth century and one of the greatest preachers raised up by God in the history of the Christian church. You come into contact with his books—you think they are wonderful. I did. But then you hear the man himself, and you notice that it is not just the *matter*; it is the *manner*! It is not just the *truth*; it is the *delivery*! The wonderful power, the wonderful passion, the wonderful pathos of this preacher as he preaches in the Spirit!

What was his practice in these things? From 1927 to 1938 he ministered, of course, in Aberavon in South Wales; and his practice at that time, in the early phase of his ministry, was to write out verbatim one sermon per week. Not, notice, that he might take it into the pulpit to read; but rather as a discipline. He was disciplining himself to write out the whole sermon from beginning to end. His practice, prior to preaching, was to read the sermon through some three times; to seek to master the material, to fix it in his heart and mind and soul, and then to reduce it to an outline. He would preach from the outline. The outline, the skeleton, constitutes, of course, the bare bones. It was only in the act of preaching that those bare bones came to life with such energy and power.

56. Marcel, *Relevance of Preaching*, 95.
57. Marcel, *Relevance of Preaching*, 97.
58. See Marcel, *Relevance of Preaching*, 100.

I am fascinated—indeed, enthralled—by Dr. Lloyd-Jones' delivery; and I have sought to analyze certain elements in that delivery. These are my findings: the slow, deliberate way in which he introduces and warms to his subject; the acceleration, the slowing down, the change of pace, the change of pitch, the remarkable hastening of the tempo; the pace, the speed, the pause, the pulse, the pulsation of his sermons; the short, sharp, staccato sentences; his remarkable use of emphasis, the power and range of his voice, the marvelous modulation and expressiveness of his voice; the energy of his soul, the movement, the momentum, the power, the passion, the pathos; the thunder and the lightning, the roaring of the lion, the sheer *explosive* element in the preaching of this man—these are the factors that contribute to the power of his sermons and to his unquestionable greatness as a preacher. Dr. J. I. Packer, who first heard him preach in Westminster Chapel in the late 1940s, said this: "I have never heard another preacher with so much of God about him."[59] Iain Murray comments on "the awesome element in the services at Westminster Chapel."[60] Thus, to my mind, *it is utterly and absolutely inconceivable* that Dr. Martyn Lloyd-Jones could have preached as he did, if he had utilized a manuscript! The manuscript would, from the very beginning to the very end, have cramped him and inhibited him and restricted him. You see, the reading method *flattens* preaching! The extemporaneous method *unleashes* the preacher, sets him free, and enables him to deliver the word of God with power and authority.

In 1885 Owen Jones, in the book that I mentioned earlier, *Some of the Great Preachers of Wales*, made a very interesting comparison between sermons that we can read today—and we bless God for them—and sermons that we actually witness; and this is what he says about sermons as they now appear on the written page: "It matters little how they appear now; the chief element is gone—the man, the body, the soul and spirit are gone."[61] He says:

> We look at the sermon after the preacher is dead, but what we find is not much. The greatest factor in the sermon is the man himself: his spirit, his soul, his body, his face, his eye, his voice, his hands, with all their movements, are essential parts of the sermon. And the effect produced is due much more to these than to that accumulation of ideas and words which we call a "sermon." That is but the dead cannon ball. The real sermon is

59. I. Murray, *Lloyd-Jones*, 2:325.

60. I. Murray, *Lloyd-Jones*, 2:325.

61. O. Jones, *Great Preachers of Wales*, 258.

> the cannon, the powder, the fire, the ball, the momentum, the crash, and catastrophe.[62]

It is not often that I find myself in agreement with Charles II; and doubtless his proclamation to the University of Cambridge in 1674 to the effect that the practice of reading sermons was, as he put it, "a supine and slothful way of preaching" was something of an impertinence on his part. But I have to say it: on *this* occasion and in *this* matter, the king was absolutely correct! Paper is a very poor medium in which to carry fire! Amen.

62. O. Jones, *Great Preachers of Wales*, 278.

# THE NEW AGE MOVEMENT[1]

I WANT to begin this lecture on the New Age movement by taking you, in your mind's eye, into one of the public schools in Los Angeles. Twenty-five first graders are lying quietly on the floor, being guided through a meditation. This is part of the new curriculum. They are being told that they should imagine that the sun is shining down upon them in all its radiance and brightness; not only that, but they are to look into the brightness and the radiance of the sun without fear of being hurt by the sun; and then they are also told by the teacher that they are to try to imagine the sun coming down into them and embracing them with its warmth and power and illumination. These twenty-five first graders are told that they are to imagine that they are doing something perfect and indeed that they are perfect; and they are reminded that they are intelligent and magnificent, and that they contain all the wisdom of the universe within themselves.[2]

Now that gives you some idea as to what is happening in this country, and even within the schools of this country, as a result of the New Age movement which has burgeoned and flourished during the last twenty-five to thirty years. We are dealing here with a remarkable phenomenon—a phenomenon that is, I believe, godless and anti-Christian. But it is very important that we, as God's people, should be aware of it and that we should be aware of the forces of Satan which are accompanying it. There is, I think, something really rather elusive about this particular movement for this reason: it has no particular headquarters; you cannot point to any particular leader; there is no subscription, no uniform. Someone has described it as "a slippery eel."[3] It is decentralized, and therefore you cannot say, "Lo, here!" or "Lo, there!" It is rather part and parcel of the spirit of the age.

1. This lecture was given at Woodruff Road Presbyterian Church, Greenville, SC, Mar. 3, 1996.

2. See Groothuis, *Unmasking the New Age*, 13–14.

3. P. Jones, *Gnostic Empire Strikes Back*, 4.

Let me read to you a quotation from Dr. J. Gordon Melton: "The New Age Movement is an international social movement which emerged in Western society in the late 1960s and which, during the 1980s, has showed itself to be an important new force in the development of the ever-changing Western culture. It can be defined by its primal experience of 'transformation.' While the New Age Movement is a social movement, it is also an inherently religious one, though many New Agers might prefer the label 'spiritual.'"[4] We are dealing here, then, with an international movement, a social phenomenon. New Agers regard it as religious, they regard it as spiritual. Certainly, it poses as a new spirituality, but as we shall see it is radically unspiritual in its whole essence and in its various doctrines and emphases.

Now, according to the New Age movement we have, from an astrological point of view, entered into a new age—the age of Aquarius. The age of Pisces, they say, is now over; the age of Pisces, in which Christianity and the masculine emphasis which has characterized Christianity have predominated, is now superseded by the age of Aquarius with its more feminine emphasis. This New Age is not so much the age of God the Son as the age of the Spirit; and you will notice, I think, as you look at New Age literature that there is this quasi-spirituality about it. New Agers refer to the Spirit. They seem to honor the Spirit. However, they may honor the Spirit with their lips, but their hearts are far from him. There is something powerfully anti-Christian about this whole movement.

Marilyn Ferguson, one of the leading proponents of this movement, describes it in this way: "A leaderless but powerful network is working to bring about radical change in the United States"; and she goes on to speak of "the most rapid cultural realignment in history."[5] There is, then, something quite remarkable and quite phenomenal about this particular movement and it is vital, therefore, that we should be aware of it.

My first point here this evening is this, that according to the New Age movement *all is one.* According to the New Age movement there is a oneness about everything. New Agers speak of "the One." Now, that phrase "the One" is a phrase which is strange to our ears. You and I, as Christians, are not used to hearing about "the One." But you will find that the New Age movement speaks about "the One" time and time again. It is very concerned about the oneness of everything, the interrelatedness of everything, how that everything is interlocking and interpenetrating—one vast system! New Agers have a slogan which goes like this: "Experience the One; believe in

4. Melton, *New Age Encyclopedia*, xiii.

5. Cited in Amano and Geisler, *Infiltration of New Age*, 12.

the One; hope in the One."[6] They are concerned with this "oneness with the One." What exactly do they mean by it? Philosophically this is known as *monism*—the idea of the oneness of everything. Let me explain more carefully what I mean. You and I, as Christians, do not believe in the oneness of everything. You and I, as Christians, believe in a certain dualism, that there are in fact two realities. There is God and there is man. There is the Creator and there are the creatures. There is good and there is evil. There is heaven and there is hell. That is a dualistic worldview. Two realities, if you like. And we, as Christians, do not confuse the Creator with the creature. We do not confuse heaven with hell. We do not confuse right with wrong or good with evil. There is this dualism about the Judeo-Christian worldview. However, when you come to the New Age movement there is this monism. There is this oneness, they say, about everything. Douglas Groothuis has said that monism is "the basic premise of the New Age Movement."[7] I want to emphasize that, therefore, here this evening.

Now, where does this idea come from—this idea of the oneness of all things? Well, you see here the radical and increasing influence of Eastern thinking. Harvey Cox has said, "The West is turning East."[8] It is turning East in its thinking. The West is turning East to Hinduism, to Buddhism, to India, to China, for its philosophy, for its religion, and for its worldview. The West is indeed turning East; and you see here the radical pervasive influence of Eastern thinking. You see, according to Hinduism, God is simply an impersonal energy force. That isn't the God of the Bible, as you and I well know. God is in heaven and we upon earth. It is he that hath made us, and not we ourselves. God is not impersonal, nor is he merely some energy force. But that is the view of Hinduism, and that is the view that is increasingly being adopted by the New Age movement. Dr. Norman Geisler has put it this way: "A widespread network of Eastern-oriented groups make up what is called the New Age Movement."[9]

Now, what are the implications of this idea that all is one—that there is this oneness or unity about everything? Well, one of the major implications of that is this, that all is God! If you say that all is one, then you have to say that all is God; and that is precisely what New Agers do say. Theologically and philosophically, this is *pantheism*. It is monistic and it is pantheistic. In other words, there is no distinction between God and man, between the Creator and the creature. Indeed, New Agers have their own scriptures.

6. Cited in Groothuis, *Unmasking the New Age*, 50.

7. Groothuis, *Unmasking the New Age*, 19.

8. Cited in Amano and Geisler, *Infiltration of New Age*, 11.

9. Amano and Geisler, *Infiltration of New Age*, 12.

They have gone back to the Gnostics and brought forward what they call the Gospel of Thomas where the Lord Jesus Christ allegedly says this: "Split a piece of wood, and I am there. Lift up the stone, and you will find Me there."[10] No distinction, you see, between wood and Christ, between a stone and Christ! The *oneness* of everything! The deity, the divinity of everything!

You see, logically, according to pantheism there is no difference between any of the objects which you see—between the birds of the air, the fishes of the sea, the beasts of the field, man himself and the Lord Jesus Christ. There is this fundamental oneness, according to them. Of course, logically in that case, there is no difference between good and evil, between right and wrong. I want to emphasize that the Bible, the word of God, doesn't teach pantheism. It teaches *theism.* It teaches this, that "In the beginning God created the heaven and the earth" (Gen 1:1). God is in heaven and we upon the earth; it is he that has made us, and not we ourselves. And that is the Christian position; so that this idea that all is one, and this idea that all is God, runs directly counter to the whole word of God itself.

Then, second, according to the New Age movement, *humanity is god*—mankind is god. You and I are god. Now this follows, you will notice, quite logically from the first point. If all is one, then all is god. If all is god, then man is god. Humanity, mankind at large, is divine. And this, too, is one of the great tenets of the New Age movement; it believes in the essential divinity of humanity. Now let me substantiate that by quoting a number of the New Age representatives. Listen to Michael Murphy: "God is not dead; He is in the gut."[11] Listen to L. L. Whyte: "It is time that God be put in His place, that is, *in man*."[12] Listen to Stewart Brand: "We are as gods, and might as well get good at it."[13] Listen to J. Z. Knight: "God is inside each individual, and everyone is divine."[14] Listen to the New Age periodical *Manas*: "Man is no sinful worm, but potential divinity."[15] And then listen to Shirley MacLaine, one of the leading celebrities and New Age figures at the present time: "I am God, because all energy is plugged into the same source. We are all individualized reflections on the God-source. God is us, and we are God. Each soul is its own god. You must never worship anyone or anything other than self. For *you* are god. To love self is to love god."[16]

10. Cited in Groothuis, *Unmasking the New Age*, 28.
11. Cited in Groothuis, *Unmasking the New Age*, 23.
12. Cited in Groothuis, *Unmasking the New Age*, 21.
13. Cited in Groothuis, *Unmasking the New Age*, 22.
14. Cited in Gordon, *Channeling into New Age*, 100.
15. Cited in Groothuis, *Unmasking the New Age*, 52.
16. Cited in Amano and Geisler, *Infiltration of New Age*, 17.

So you see, according to the New Age movement, the *answer* to all our problems lies within us. Now you will be aware, my good friends, that that is the utter and complete opposite of the Christian position. According to the New Age movement the answer lies within us. You can see here, then, this powerful element of arrogance and blasphemy which characterizes the New Age movement. Not only that, but there is this obsession with self. Dr. Norman Geisler has commented that theology is becoming "meology"—there is this profound preoccupation with oneself. Birger Pearson, referring to the connection between ancient Gnosticism and the New Age movement, has put it this way: "The heart and core of the Gnostic religion [is] the consubstantiality of the self with God."[17] Notice the Trinitarian overtones here: "the consubstantiality of the self with God"! My dear friends, the Lord Jesus Christ is consubstantial with the Father—of the same substance with the Father; but you and I, as creatures and sinners, are certainly not consubstantial with God! But that is part and parcel, you see, of the New Age movement. Dr. Norman Geisler has put it this way: "Self-deification is the gospel of the New Age."[18]

You can see, then, I think, how profoundly anti-Christian this movement is in its whole worldview—in its view of man—how it elevates man. Notice its profound humanism. Notice its arrogance. Notice its deification of man. Let me remind you of what the word of God says about man. Man is made in God's image, after God's likeness, in God's similitude; yet we are fallen and sinful creatures. We have left undone those things that we ought to have done, and we have done those things we ought not to have done. We fall short of the glory of God. Yes, there *is* something very wonderful about man. There is a glory about him; and yet there is also a wretchedness and a fallenness about him; and this, my dear friends, is the message of the gospel. According to the gospel, the *problem* lies within—not the *answer*! "From within," says the Lord Jesus Christ, "proceed evil thoughts" (Mark 7:21) and all the corrupt ideas and actions that characterize each one of us and society in general. The problem is this, that the New Age movement has no doctrine of sin whatsoever and would dearly love to eradicate the Christian doctrine of man from off the face of the earth.

Third, the New Age movement is concerned about producing what it calls a *change in consciousness*. In other words, it wants to bring about change and transformation in society at large. It wants to bring about "a new consciousness." There is this emphasis, as we have seen, upon "transformation." Now, Christianity also teaches about change, doesn't it? It also

17. Cited in P. Jones, *Gnostic Empire Strikes Back*, 24.

18. Amano and Geisler, *Infiltration of New Age*, 51.

teaches about transformation. And yet how different are the two emphases! The Lord Jesus Christ says that there must be a change. He says, "Ye must be born again! Nicodemus, you and the Pharisees and the scribes and all men everywhere must be born again! If you are not born again, you cannot see or enter into the kingdom of God" (see John 3:3–7). But the New Age movement believes that we ourselves are able and capable of bringing about this change and this transformation. Listen to Douglas Groothuis with regard to the views of New Agers: "They would all resonate with the idea of releasing human potential by realizing the oneness of all things."[19] Notice that—"by realizing the oneness of all things" and "by releasing the human potential" that is within us. You see, New Agers believe very profoundly in man. They believe in man's potential divinity; they believe in man's evolutionary godhood; they believe that man is advancing and progressing and making astounding progress. According to the New Age movement the problem with man is simply this, that he has been ignorant. Indeed, it would lay the charge of this and the blame for it at the door of Christianity. The problem is man's ignorance; he doesn't know what he is; he doesn't know what he can become. The problem, according to the New Age movement, is simply his "divine amnesia"! And so, what we need, supposedly, is a new awareness, a new consciousness. We need this self-discovery, we need this self-realization, we need this self-actualization. How do New Agers advocate that we achieve this? Well, they say that self-discovery starts like this: "Start liking yourself! Start loving yourself!" Notice the correlation between this and "the gospel of self-esteem" which is so powerful today. It is, contends Dr. Norman Geisler, "a psychology and religion of selfism"[20]—there is this profound preoccupation with self and this elevation of oneself and man in general, this profound degradation of God and of Christ at the same time.

Now, one New Age advertisement reads in this way: "The only way *out* is *in*." Notice again the idea that the answer to our problems lies within ourselves. This is why they have the meditation techniques; this is why there is such an emphasis on self-knowledge and self-realization. Philosophically or theologically, this is mysticism. Pantheism! Mysticism! These two things always go together, and they go together here in the New Age movement. But my dear friends, Christianity isn't mysticism. Christianity is a revealed religion. Christianity is a redemptive religion. It tells us that we are, each one of us, "alienated from the life of God," that we are "dead"—"dead in our trespasses and sins," that we need a Savior. Yes, it emphasizes change and transformation, but one which is very, very different from that of the New

19. Groothuis, *Unmasking the New Age*, 36.

20. Amano and Geisler, *Infiltration of New Age*, 51.

Age movement. The great Founder of Christianity puts it this way: "Ye must be born again!"

My dear friends, I want to ask you this evening: Are you born again? Are you a new creature in Christ Jesus? Do you know the Lord Jesus Christ, and is he your Savior, and are you trusting here tonight in his precious atoning blood? That is the change! That is the transformation! Not this nonsense that we find increasingly in the New Age movement.

But then, fourth, I want to speak about the *cosmic optimism*, so called, of the New Age movement. There is this note of hope, this note of optimism which runs very deeply throughout the New Age movement. New Agers are not pessimistic about the future; indeed, they lay the charge of pessimism at the door of Christianity. No, they are hopeful, and they are optimistic. They sometimes put it this way: "We have had five thousand years of hell. What lies ahead is five thousand years of heaven"—a kind of millennium of light and love and peace. And so, they have this rather naïve confidence concerning the future. They are concerned about transforming the planet; they have this new concept of "planetization"—the oneness, the unity of everything! What we need to do, of course, is simply learn to release our boundless potential. Do you remember those twenty-five first graders in the Los Angeles school imagining that they are embracing the sun in its warmth and its power and bringing the sun down into themselves? Do you remember how they were told that they themselves were perfect beings? We are simply to realize our boundless potential and our infinite capacities.

There is, therefore, not surprisingly, a profound dislike of the whole idea of sin and evil. In fact, with regard to evil they say this, that evil is just "negative energy"; evil is just "energy flying backwards"! Shirley MacLaine has put it this way: the word "evil," spelled backwards, gives you the word "live"! You see, you have here an example of the profound anti-intellectualism and irrationalism of the New Age movement. New Agers are not concerned with thinking or rationality; they are simply concerned to create their own realities, and it is almost a gospel of wishful thinking at many, many points.

There is, then, this note of optimism and confidence; it is very, very powerful in the New Age world. We have, supposedly, entered the age of Aquarius. The age of Pisces is now behind us. Now, it is interesting to note that the New Age movement has in fact adopted a particular theory; it is a theory which goes back a number of centuries, and which is known as "the three ages of history." According to this theory there are three ages: the age of Aries, the age of Pisces, and the age of Aquarius. The age of Aries coincided with the age of Judaism; that, they say, was the age of God the Father. The age of Pisces, recently past, coincided with the age of Christianity; it was the age of God the Son. The New Age is the age of Aquarius and it coincides with the age of the Spirit. Now, theologically, of course, this is a piece of nonsense, but it coheres with their particular worldview. I want to emphasize, therefore, that there is, on the one hand, something profoundly pessimistic about the biblical view of man in this respect, that the biblical view of man does not tell us that we are like gods or that we are gods; the biblical view of man tells us indeed that we are made in God's image, but that we are fallen and sinful and we have evil hearts. But equally there is also something profoundly optimistic about the gospel of the grace of God. It is the power of God unto salvation to everyone that believes it, so that a poor, weak, fallen sinner, lying in the gutters of this world, can be raised up from the dead spiritually by the Lord Jesus Christ and be made into a new creature and can live a truly transformed life. That is the wonderful optimism of the gospel.

My fifth point, then, has to do with *reincarnation*. Now, what exactly is reincarnation? Well, "reincarnation" has been defined as "the belief that the soul, or some power, passes after death into another body." In other words, at death the soul simply lives on in some other body or being. So then, there is in the New Age movement this belief in past lives and in future lives. Listen to Dirk Benedict: "The older I get, the more I sense past lifetimes."[21] Now, you may well be aware that this is indeed one of the leading tenets and beliefs of the New Age movement—this idea of reincarnation. Listen again to Dr. J. Gordon Melton: "Of the most commonly accepted opinions within the New Age Movement, few are held with such passion and even dogmatic certainty as the belief in reincarnation."[22] I dare say that as you move about in society—in business, among friends, among colleagues at work—you have met people, many of you, who believe in this idea of reincarnation—this idea that they are going to live on in some other person or being in the future. What is so startling is this, that in 1982 an opinion poll taken here in the United States of America revealed that about one quarter of the people of the United States believe in some form of reincarnation. That was some fourteen years ago. I suspect that the percentage has increased since then; and this belief in reincarnation is being popularized increasingly by leading celebrities such as Shirley MacLaine, Tina Turner, and Peter Sellers. New Agers will often give you dates as to when they lived. What is so remarkable is that so many of them, apparently, were Napoleon! So many of them were Cleopatra!

Now this idea of reincarnation is basically an Eastern idea. It comes from Eastern religion. Peter Jones, in his fascinating book on the subject of

21. Cited in Groothuis, *Unmasking the New Age*, 25.

22. Melton, *New Age Encyclopedia*, xvi.

the New Age movement, has said this: "The goal of the New Age reincarnation, like that of the ancient Gnostic, is to be finally freed from the illusion of physical existence and the great wheel of *karma* and to be absorbed in the All."[23] Notice then the connection between reincarnation and pantheism. But what do the Scriptures say about this? Well, my dear friends, the word of God has absolutely nothing to say on the subject of reincarnation. The Bible doesn't teach *reincarnation*! The Bible teaches *the* incarnation! The incarnation of the great God of heaven who is none other than "God manifest in the flesh" (1 Tim 3:16)! In the fullness of time the Lord Jesus Christ came out from God, came down from heaven, was born in Bethlehem, grew up, lived a perfect life, and went about among men. This is none other than "God manifest in the flesh." *The* incarnation—not *reincarnation*!

Again, the Bible doesn't teach *reincarnation*! It teaches *regeneration*, which is a very, very different thing; and it tells us that right now, here and now in this life, we must be born again. But if we are not born again, then we shall never see or enter the kingdom of God.

Again, the Bible does not for one moment teach *reincarnation*! It teaches *resurrection*—the resurrection of the dead! There is going to be a last and final judgment when the Lord Jesus Christ comes again, and the dead shall be raised and shall stand before the Son of Man; and I believe that one of the great reasons why this idea of reincarnation is so popular today is that it enables men, who hate God and love their sin, fondly to imagine that they do not have to face that "last enemy," that "king of terrors," death itself, and that there is no such thing as meeting their Maker. "It is appointed unto men once to die," says the word of God, "but after this, the judgment" (Heb 9:27). But it is to escape that idea that men have invented this idea of reincarnation. My dear friends, let me remind you here this evening that it is appointed unto *you* once to die, and after this, the judgment—that you yourselves, you young children and you older ones too, must one day meet God and stand before him, and that none of us is going to be reincarnated. We have one opportunity in this life to get right with God, and that is through the Person and work of the Lord Jesus Christ.

And then, sixth, *astrology*. This, again, is a very powerful component of the New Age movement. Now let me emphasize that by astrology I do not mean astronomy. Astronomy is a wonderful science; I am very interested in it myself. The word of God, in effect, speaks of astronomy. Listen to the psalmist: "When I consider thy heavens, the work of thy fingers, the moon and the stars which thou hast ordained; what is man, that thou art mindful of Him, and the son of man, that thou visitest him?" (Ps 8:3–4). Yes, the

23. P. Jones, *Gnostic Empire Strikes Back*, 47.

works of God's fingers—the sun, the moon, the stars, all the heavenly host that adorns the sky! There is a beauty and a wonder about them! Astrology, however, is something that is quite different. The *New Dictionary of Theology* defines astrology in this way: "Astrology is a form of divination. It has developed into the use of complicated tables of planets and houses which mark out the present and future of clients."[24] Horoscopes come under this category. Let me read to you from the *New Age Encyclopedia*: "Astrology is a divinatory art that uses the placement of the fixed stars and of the sun, moon, and planets to forecast events on Earth. In its classic form, astrology was a type of fortune-telling used to predict the future for people, businesses, and nations. Modern or New Age astrology instead focuses on delineating the individual personality; here the planets are seen as giving the person various strengths and weaknesses that will influence the way in which he or she deals with life in general."[25]

Notice, then, the emphasis upon divination—something that is prohibited by God in his word; but this is becoming increasingly popular in the New Age movement. I want to emphasize, then, that this is an occult practice, and that the occult is a very important aspect and strand of the New Age movement. It is becoming increasingly prevalent, and it has been estimated that there are probably more than ten thousand professional astrologers in the United States and that they have over twenty million clients. Think of all the horoscopes which are burgeoning at the present time.

Now, in March 1992, when I was still in Great Britain, a friend of mine told me that a New Age shop had just opened in Gloucester near to where I lived. I decided that I would pay a visit to this New Age center. There was a man running the shop who probably viewed me as a potential client! He didn't realize that, like Caleb or Joshua, I was going merely to spy out the land! Now I noticed that in what was called the "exhibition room" there was a great deal about astrology. It is one of the leading aspects of the New Age movement. I wrote down these statements which were on the wall of their "exhibition room": "Astrology is the belief that our lives are somehow directed by the movement of the planets." "Astrology can give us psychological insights into ourselves." "Astrology tells us about 'inner space' rather than 'outer space.'" Notice how clever this is. Astronomy—"outer space"! Astrology—"inner space"! Very clever and very pernicious! There was tremendous emphasis on "birth charts." You could get one done for about $25. These complicated "birth charts" would work out the future, your prospects, your problems, your strengths, your weaknesses simply by

24. Ferguson et al., *New Dictionary of Theology*, *s.v.* "Astrology."

25. Melton, *New Age Encyclopedia*, 37.

your giving to them your date of birth and even the exact time of your birth. My dear friends, I want to warn you—I want to warn you young people—to beware of this. The word of God prohibits it and forbids it very, very clearly indeed. Listen to what the word of God says: "Let now the astrologers, the stargazers, the monthly prognosticators, stand up, and save thee from these things that shall come upon thee" (Isa 47:13). In other words, judgment is coming, as it came then. The Lord Jesus Christ, who died for sinners, who was buried, and who rose again the third day and ascended up into heaven, is going to reappear. He is going to come with great power, majesty, and glory, and you and I are going to stand before him. What use then will be the astrologers, and the stargazers, and the monthly prognosticators as man stands before the living God and gives an account of the way in which he has lived? That is the challenge which the word of God gives to those that practice astrology.

My seventh point has to do with *channeling*. What exactly is "channeling"? Well, "channeling" is an exercise undertaken by New Agers. It involves contact with certain "entities," as they are called. These are "ascended masters"—almost godlike figures—or "spirit guides," as they are sometimes called. Let me give you the names of some of them: Ramtha, Seth, Mafu, Lazaris. It is interesting—it is never Burt, or Jo, or Fred, or Doug! It is always Ramtha, or Seth, or Mafu, or Lazaris! Now, a channel, you see, is just another name for a medium; and these mediums, such as J. Z. Knight, "channel" these "entities." "Channeling" has become one of the hallmarks of the New Age movement. Listen again to Dr. J. Gordon Melton writing in his *New Age Encyclopedia*: "Unprecedented numbers of individuals of all walks of life and socio-economic backgrounds are engaging in channeling activities and, by extension, increasingly varied populations are being exposed to the phenomenon through workshops and loosely formed networks that exchange audio and video tapes, newsletters, and periodicals. A number of channels offer channeling classes, claiming that just about anyone can learn to channel."[26]

These gods are strange gods, and these "entities" are nonentities! The Lord Jesus Christ warned us many, many years ago: "Beware of false prophets" (Matt 7:15). "Many false prophets shall rise, and shall deceive many" (Matt 24:11); and this is, my good friends, precisely what is happening at the present time.[27] Many, many people are being deceived by these impostors and by these false prophets in the New Age movement.

26. Melton, *New Age Encyclopedia*, 102.

27. See, e.g, Encyclopedia. "Ramtha."

My eighth point has to do with *Mother Nature*. Have you noticed how that the phrase "Mother Nature" or "Mother Earth" is becoming increasingly popular all around us in society? You see it on stickers, you see it in advertisements. Now, I want to emphasize, of course, that nature is God's creation; nature is fearfully and wonderfully made. We cannot look at the birds of the air, and the fishes of the sea, and all the beasts of the forest and the field, and man himself, without realizing that nature, God's creation, is fearfully and wonderfully made. It is the work of his fingers, and it declares his glory day after day. But what we are seeing at the present time is not an emphasis upon God's creation, but rather an emphasis upon "Mother Earth" and "Mother Nature"; and that is a very significant difference. Have you seen that sticker on the back of cars, "Love your Mother!"? What it means is this: "Love Mother Earth! Love Mother Nature! Take care of her! She is a goddess!" That is the view that is coming increasingly to the fore; and so, in the New Age movement you have a new view of nature. It is new in one sense and yet it is old in another; this is the pantheistic worldview. If all is God and God is all, then there is no distinction between the creature and the Creator. Creation, nature itself, is God, or, as New Agers particularly like to put it today, a goddess. You will notice, I believe, increasingly a kind of goddess spirituality emerging in present-day society. It is already there: it is even invading some of the liberal churches of our land. Now, the Christian position is this—we worship the God of nature. We do not worship nature; we worship the God of nature because of the beauty and the wonder, the harmony and the order, the glory and the majesty of nature itself. But we do not worship nature itself. What these New Agers have espoused is a pantheistic worldview, and they are fond of putting it this way: "Planet Earth isn't just a lump of dead rock: that is the old idea. No, no! Planet Earth is animate. It has life. Even the rocks have life. There are veins, there are arteries in this goddess, this Mother Earth. Man himself is one of the veins, one of the arteries." And so New Agers emphasize what they call the "Gaia hypothesis"—this idea that the Earth is a goddess, that the Earth is divine, and that all living matter is characterized by a oneness—that it is one single living organism. Thus, there is, supposedly, a oneness between human life and the complete biosphere of the Earth. Have you ever wondered why there is, at the present time, such an obsessive interest in ecology and environmentalism? I will tell you why, my good friends. To a significant extent this is part and parcel of the New Age movement. Do not misunderstand me. I do not believe that all their concerns are to be rejected. We are to take care of this planet; but equally we are bidden to subdue it and to make use of it. But this obsessive interest in ecology and environmentalism comes, I believe, from the political agenda of the New Agers. They are concerned about the planet

Earth; they are concerned about "saving the planet." You will have noticed that, I'm sure. And so, you have, of course, the rise of "Green Politics"—the rise of the "Green Movement" in many countries throughout the world. According to New Agers this planet Earth has been dismissed too long as just a lump of dead rock. My dear friends, Christians have never said that anyway! You and I as Christians do not regard the planet as a lump of dead earth or rock. We regard it as the work of God's fingers and the work of God's hands; but we make distinctions—distinctions which are lost upon them because of their monism and their rejection of dualism. Now, according to the New Age worldview the Earth has been desacralized; and it lays the charge and the blame at the door of Christianity very often. The Earth has been desacralized, they say; the element of sanctity and sacredness has been taken out of it. What is needed is a re-sacralization of the Earth; they want to see "the re-enchantment of the world."[28]

Now, I have here a leaflet which I picked up in Great Britain a few years ago. It is called "Dolphin Love: a day-workshop to connect with dolphin energies and open up our creativity and sense of cosmic identity"—classic New Age ideas! What is included? Well, for $30 you get this: a "talk on creation mythology and the dolphin links with Sirius and Isis, a dolphin video 'Oceania,' guided visualizations, meditation for healing the oceans, dolphin music and much, much more"! What is interesting is this, that these people are looking to dolphins as the prophets of the present and the future! They do not want the one great Prophet that has come into the world—the Lord Jesus Christ, who is the Truth and who has the words of eternal life. They want to listen to what the dolphins have to say! The dolphins have a message for man—we need to listen to their vibrations! Dolphin love! Dolphin vibrations! This is one of the ideas that is being proclaimed by the New Age movement. Now, my good friends, you can see, I think, that the Creator is being replaced increasingly by the creature. This is inevitable in a monistic, pantheistic system such as this, and it is reminiscent of what the apostle Paul says in Romans chapter 1. "They worshipped and served the creature more than the Creator" (Rom 1:25). That is what the New Age movement is doing—worshipping and serving the creature more than the Creator. New Agers do not believe in the Creator; they believe in the One.

My ninth point has to do with the *Cosmic Christ*—the New Age doctrine of the Lord Jesus Christ. Now, what exactly does it have to say about him? Well, the Christ of the New Age movement is not the Lord Jesus Christ as revealed in the Scriptures—not the blessed, eternal Son of God who came down from heaven to seek and to save us who were lost. No, no!

28. Cited in Groothuis, *Unmasking the New Age*, 50.

The New Age Christ is a principle and a presence—a cosmic principle and a universal presence. New Agers have an interest in the Lord Jesus Christ for this reason—they believe in evolution; they believe in the evolutionary advancement of man. They believe in releasing the divine potential within us, and that presumably we can eventually become like Christ himself. Listen to what Douglas R. Groothuis says on this matter: "For the New Age in general, the Christ is a universal Presence working within all humanity to raise it to a higher level of evolutionary attainment. Christ is not so much a Person as 'a cosmic principle, a spiritual presence whose quality infuses and appears in various ways in all the religions and philosophies that uplift humanity and seek unity with spirit.'"[29] Listen to Matthew Fox, who is having such a considerable influence for the New Age movement within the Episcopal Church of this land: "We are Cosmic Christs."[30] Notice again the tendency to deification—the divinizing of man.

Now, I want to emphasize this about the New Age movement's attitude towards the Lord Jesus Christ: New Agers may honor Christ with their lips, but their hearts are far from him! They use his name, and yet they reduce him to a mere principle, a mere presence within humanity at large; and because they can make use of him, they are able to buttress their evolutionary theory that man is advancing and progressing to some kind of Christlikeness. I want to emphasize, however, that the New Age movement utterly denies the uniqueness of Jesus Christ. It does not believe that he is the blessed, eternal Son of the living God. The New Age movement utterly denies the atonement of the Lord Jesus Christ; it does not believe that he died for sinners on the tree. The New Age movement denies the resurrection of the Lord Jesus Christ; it will not have a living Christ reigning and ruling over this universe. The New Age movement denies the second coming of the Lord Jesus Christ, and it asserts that New Age centers such as Findhorn in Scotland are the second coming! My dear friends, listen to what the apostle Peter has to say when the Lord Jesus Christ asks the apostles, "Whom do men say that I the Son of Man am?" (Matt 16:13). The apostle Peter says this: "Thou art the Christ, the Son of the living God" (Matt 16:16). My good friends, can you say that? Can you say, "Thou art the Christ, the Son of the living God"? Do you believe him to be the Messiah—God himself, the Second Person of the Trinity, come down from heaven, living here upon this earth, dying for our sins and rising again? "What think ye of Christ? Whose son is he?" (Matt 22:42). What is your view of him, my friends? He is not merely some

29. Groothuis, *Revealing New Age Jesus*, 222.

30. Cited in Groothuis, *Revealing New Age Jesus*, 222.

presence; he is not merely some principle. He is the Lord of glory, the Lord from heaven, and he died for sinners such as you and me.

My tenth and last point is this, that according to the New Age movement *all religions are one.* It is not surprising that New Agers should say this—according to them there is a oneness about everything. All is one! According to them all religions are one. It is not surprising, therefore, to find that New Agers are unashamedly working for world unity or global unity; they speak of this "global village." Have you noticed this kind of terminology? It is New Age thinking. They are emphasizing again the oneness of everything. They want to get rid of national distinctives. My dear friends, this New Age movement is infiltrating our society. It is coming into our schools; it is there in the political agenda. This agenda includes feminism, abortion, and gay rights. The New Age movement is working for world unity—global unity in this "global village"—a new world order, politically, economically, and socially; and the United Nations Organization is infected by this particular movement.

Now, what is so interesting and so significant here is this: there is, I believe, an obvious compatibility between the New Age movement on the one hand and the ecumenical movement on the other hand—between the movement for "world unity" on the one hand and the idea of "one world church" on the other hand. In other words, I anticipate that the New Age movement and the ecumenical movement will increasingly find common ground. "All is one!" Have they not been saying something similar in the churches for a long, long time? "Let's get together! Let's hold a World Congress of Faiths! Let's unite in one great, vast world church"—irrespective of what happens to the truth in the process! My dear friends, I want to emphasize that both these movements are in fact enemies of the gospel of Christ. Let me demonstrate that with regard to the New Age movement: the New Age movement denies all the cardinal doctrines of Christianity. It denies the doctrine of God. It denies the doctrine of creation. It denies the distinction between God and the creature—between the Creator and man. It denies the great doctrine of the Person and the work of the Lord Jesus Christ. It denies that he is the Second Person of the Godhead. It denies his incarnation. It denies his atonement. It denies his resurrection. It denies his ascension. It denies his second advent and the day of judgment. These great truths are discarded and rejected by the New Age movement. Oh yes, they honor him with their lips, but their hearts are far from him! There is, therefore, something very, very pernicious about this New Age movement. Let me remind you, my good friends, that the word of God says this: "There is *one* God, and *one* mediator between God and men, the man Christ Jesus" (1 Tim 2:5; emphasis added). Yes, there is a "oneness" about the Christian faith—but it is the *oneness of uniqueness*. One God! One Mediator! One Lord! One faith! It is the oneness of uniqueness—not the oneness of the New Age movement with its monism and its pantheism.

My dear friends, as I close, I want to ask you this: Have you ever grasped, in your mind and in your heart, the uniqueness of Christianity and the uniqueness of the Lord Jesus Christ? Do you see that there is but one God, and one Mediator between God and men, the man Christ Jesus? Listen to what he says: "I am the way, the truth, and the life: no man cometh unto the Father, but by Me" (John 14:6). Have you ever come to him? Do you love him? Is he your Savior, is he your Lord? Is he the One who deals with your sin and reconciles you unto God? He is not some mere principle, some mere presence! He is the Lord of glory! He is the Lord from heaven! He died for sinners, and he invites us to come to him; and if we come to him, he will not cast us out or turn us away. For he has given us his own promise: "Him that cometh to Me I will in no wise cast out" (John 6:37). Amen.

# THE GLORY OF CREATION[1]

I WOULD like to take as my text the thirty-first verse of the first chapter of Genesis where we read these words: "And God saw every thing that he had made, and, behold, it was very good. And the evening and the morning were the sixth day." Now these words bring to a conclusion Moses' great account of the creation. This account of the creation, of course, dominates exclusively this great first chapter in the word of God; and it is very evident from this particular chapter that the way in which our Maker created the heavens, and the earth, and the sea, and all that is in them, was, in fact, by a series of mighty acts—a series of mighty acts which lasted some six days in all. In other words, he created, as it were, through steps and through stages; there is a progressive element, an element of development here in this account of the creation. And here in the thirty-first verse of this first chapter we come to the end of the sixth day. The creation was now complete—it was now finished. God had made the heavens, and the earth, and the sea; he had made the sun, and the moon, and the stars; he had made the birds of the air, the fishes of the sea, all the beasts of the forest and the field, and he had made man also, who is the crown and the pinnacle of God's creation. And having done so, what the Lord God now does is this: he surveys and he evaluates the work of his hands, and this was his verdict: "And, behold, it was very good."

Now these words here in the thirty-first verse do not simply refer to the work of creation which took place on the sixth day. These words, this verdict, if you like, apply to the totality, to the entirety of God's creation. It was this, in all its entirety, which was "very good," we read. And indeed, this phrase "very good" is an interesting phrase. Let us take the word "good" itself: the word means "pleasing" or "pleasant." It is sometimes used in the

1. This sermon was delivered during the annual spring conference of Greenville Presbyterian Theological Seminary, at Woodruff Road PCA, Simpsonville, SC, Mar. 10, 1999.

Old Testament of a woman. It is used to describe Rebekah. She was a fair woman; there was a beauty about her. There was something very pleasing, something very pleasant about her; this is the term that is translated "good" here; and in fact, this is the seventh time that Moses uses this term "good" here in this first chapter. But the interesting thing about this seventh occasion is that, whereas before we read this: "And God saw that it was good" as he evaluated each step and stage of the great process of creation, here as he surveys the entirety and the totality of the works of his hands, he says this, that it was "very good." There was something remarkably good about it; and therefore, we see God's delight, his approval, his satisfaction in the work of his fingers and of his hands. There is this idea of something superlative here. We could translate this phrase in this way: "And God saw that it was exceedingly good" or "God saw that it was exceedingly pleasant." And so, what we have here is an emphasis by God himself upon the goodness of his creation, upon the essential excellence of his creation, indeed upon the perfection of his creation. There was nothing that was not good in this creation which came from his hand; it was characterized in all its entirety by an absolute perfection.

Now we know, of course, that it was not long before sin entered into the world, and death by sin. As sin entered into the world, so it brought in with it a great train of catastrophic consequences; and we know this from the early chapters of Genesis, that this creation, that God himself pronounced to be "very good," "exceedingly pleasant," and perfect in and of itself, was now marred. "Cursed is the ground for thy sake," says the Lord unto Adam. And from this point onwards there is this reflection of evil upon the creation itself. It was not that the creation itself in its entirety was evil, but rather that the reflection of evil coming down from man, the crown of God's creation, was upon the face of nature and creation itself. That's why we have "Nature, red in tooth and claw."[2] That's why there is this destructive, this ferocious element within creation as well as an essential and remarkable goodness about it. This is why there were "thorns and thistles." This is why there are catastrophes within creation and within nature itself. And the apostle Paul, writing to the Romans, seizes upon this point. He says that "the creature was subjected to vanity;" that is to say, the entire creation was subjected to futility. There is now this "bondage of corruption." Death has invaded because sin has invaded the universe. And therefore, that which was originally "exceedingly good" is now marred and spoiled and is not characterized by the perfection which it had as it came from the hand of God. Nevertheless, I believe it to be true to say that in spite of this intrusion

2. "In Memoriam A.H.H.," under "Quotations," canto 55.

of sin, in spite of the cursing of the ground by its Maker, there was and there is still a fundamental goodness about the creation which God has made. Listen again to what verse 31 says: "And God saw every thing that he had made, and, behold, it was very good." Yes, it is now spoiled, it is now marred, and that perfection has gone; but nevertheless, though man has fallen from a great height, there is still an essential goodness—not a perfection—but a remarkable goodness that characterizes the whole of creation itself. This evening I want to consider the various aspects of God's creation and to see the essential goodness and excellence that still pertains in these realms. What was it, then, to which God was referring? What was it to which Moses was referring when we read in verse 31: "And God saw everything that he had made, and, behold, it was very good"?

Well, obviously one of the first things is *the creation of space, matter, and time*. And this, then, is my first point. I want us to consider the fact that God, when he created the heavens, and the earth, and the sea, created initially space, and matter, and time. Look at the first verse of this great chapter: "In the beginning God created the heaven and the earth." You have here, I believe, the creation of space and matter. In other words, you have here the creation of the raw material out of which God was to fashion the entire cosmos during the space of six days—the raw matter, the raw material out of which he was to make all things. Now notice, however, the condition of the earth at this early stage. It is there in the first part of verse 2: "And the earth was without form, and void; and darkness was upon the face of the deep." We can see that what we have here is not, at this stage, a cosmos. There in verse 31 it is a cosmos—a wonderful, well-ordered cosmos, characterized by perfection, order, design—a most wonderful contrivance. But here, in the second verse, in the early stages of the week, we read that "the earth was without form, and void; and darkness was upon the face of the deep." What does that mean? It means this, that there was, if you like, an emptiness; there was a desolation; there was a darkness which characterized the whole of the creation at this stage. It was not a cosmos; it was still a chaos. It was not habitable; it was utterly uninhabitable. But what was to happen in the remainder of this week of creation was this, that a wonderful shaping process would occur. God would take this chaos that he made at the beginning, and he would mold it, and make it, and fashion it into a wonderful cosmos throughout the course of six days. Notice, then, the various steps and stages in this shaping process that God undertook.

The first is the creation of light. Notice that light was created on the first day. God said, "Let there be light." He gave his *fiat*, and it was so. He created the light. So the creation of light was absolutely essential for the shaping process, for the making of the cosmos, upon which man himself was to dwell. And then the second thing that we notice is the creation of the firmament, this expanse. What exactly was it? It was probably the sky, the heavens, and probably included the atmosphere. It was this that God created on the second day. Then on the third day, you will notice, there is this separation of the dry land from the waters that had dominated this chaos from the beginning. "Let the dry land appear." And so you have the appearance, through the mighty *fiat* of God, of the great land masses and the great continents. And so what God is doing here is this—he is molding and making, fashioning and shaping what he had made in the beginning.

But it is not, you notice, until the fourth day that you have the creation of the heavenly bodies themselves. Notice verse 16: "And God made two great lights; the greater light to rule the day, and the lesser light to rule the night: he made the stars also." You have here, of course, the creation of the sun, and the moon, and the stars. You now have a solar system in place. You have with this the regulation of time which was created on the first day. So we see then in the first place that we have the creation of space, and matter, and time during the first four days of this creation week.

Now then, my good friends, I want to ask you: Do you ever reflect upon the wonder of this solar system which God has made? Do you ever reflect upon the wonder of the sun—that "greater light" that rules the day, upon the wonder of the moon—that "lesser light" that rules the night? This sun is the very center of the solar system, situated at a distance of some ninety-three million miles; it is the gravitational center of the solar system. It is around this that the planets revolve. It is around this that planet Earth revolves. What a wonderful thing it is! How utterly indispensable to life it is—this source of heat, this source of light! And the planet Earth, as scientists will tell you, is situated in the "temperate zone" of this solar system. If it were much closer, if it were any further away, life, as we know it, would be impossible. Yes, he made this "greater light" to rule the day—the sun. But he also made this "lesser light" to rule the night; he made the moon—our nearest satellite some 232,000 miles away. And what a wonderful thing it is, and how we tend to take these things for granted! The waning, the waxing moon, which gives us light during the night; what an amazing phenomenon it is, and it accompanies us continually. As we revolve around the sun, so it revolves around the earth. And do you ever consider the mighty, mighty mechanisms which God put and placed here in this solar system? Once every twenty-four hours planet Earth rotates upon its own axis, tilted slightly at an angle of twenty-three and one third degrees, and revolves around the sun once every 365 days. These are things which man takes for granted. He gets up in the morning; he knows the sun will rise. He goes to bed at night; he knows the sun will set. But men take for granted the work of God's fingers. But these are, my good friends, mighty, mighty mechanisms which God has put there and placed there through the laws of his own hand.

Now the prophet Jeremiah speaks very interestingly and wonderfully of these mechanisms. He speaks in fact of the "ordinances" of God. He speaks of "the ordinances of the moon and of the stars" (Jer 31:35). God himself speaks of "my covenant of the day, and my covenant of the night" (Jer 33:20). Do you ever think of that—the wonderful reliability of this mechanism which God has made? The reliability, the dependability, the predictability is such that we know we can predict precisely when the sun will rise in the morning, when the sun will set at night. It is God's covenant—his covenant of the day, and his covenant of the night. And here too we see his essential goodness, that though the creation is marred and spoilt, it is still characterized by a wonderful goodness on the part of God and shares some of his own goodness.

But notice, also, the reference to the stars. I love this reference to the stars! There in verse 16 we read, "And God made two great lights; the greater light to rule the day, and the lesser light to rule the night: he made the stars also." It is almost presented as an aside. It is almost presented as a fact of little significance. But when we consider the billions and billions of stars which God in fact made and brought into being, we realize the stupendous import of this particular statement. Did you know, for instance, that within our galaxy, the Milky Way, there are some one hundred thousand million stars? And did you know that God has created at least one thousand million galaxies? The vastness of it all! The staggering immensity of God's creation! It is truly phenomenal. "The heavens declare the glory of God," says the word of God, "and the firmament sheweth his handywork. Day unto day uttereth speech, and night unto night sheweth knowledge" (Ps 19:1–2). My good friends, we live in a universe that is most fearfully and wonderfully made! And it declares the glory of God. The glory of creation is none other than the glory of the Creator himself. Space, matter, and time, and the energy of light.

But second, I want us to consider *the creation of plant life*. It is there in verse 12: "And the earth brought forth grass, and herb yielding seed after his kind, and the tree yielding fruit, whose seed was in itself, after his kind: and God saw that it was good." Now this occurred, of course, on the third day. The Lord had already said, "Let the dry land appear." It was crucial, fundamental, that there should be dry land in order for the appearance of vegetation. So what the Creator now does is this: He now adorns this dry land that was created on the third day. He adorns this dry land with plants and with trees—plants that contain seeds, trees that contain fruits. Now notice those words—it is a very important phrase—"whose seed was in itself." Why is that significant? It is significant for this reason, that God is not merely creating; he is providing for the continuation of this creation; he is providing for its preservation. And one of the wonderful things about creation, and you see this not only in plant life, but also in animal life, and also in human life, is the marvelous successfulness of it all! This has never ever fizzled out and it never will, because it comes from the hand of God, and it is most "fearfully and wonderfully made." "Whose seed was in itself."

But let me tell you something about the astonishing variety of God's creation. We have a God who loves variety! We have a God who loves diversity! He loves beauty! He hasn't created a dull, monotonous cosmos. He has decked it and adorned it with great beauty and diversity. It is teeming with life, teeming with interest, full of color. Let me tell you how many different kinds of plants they tell us exist: approximately half a million! This almost inconceivable number of different kinds of plants, each one of them inevitably an idea in the mind of God from eternity!

Now why did God create such diversity? Why did he create such variety? Well, he was providing for the needs, for the necessities of his creatures. He was providing for the animal creation that was shortly to come. He was providing for the human creation that shortly was to come—providing for your needs and for my needs. Do you ever think of the whole issue of food? No doubt, like me, you give thanks for your daily bread, but in addition to giving thanks for your daily bread, do you ever think and reflect and meditate upon your daily bread, that this is a wonderful provision, an ongoing, constant provision which comes from the hand of your Creator? There are approximately six billion people in the world today. That is a phenomenal number. But you see, such is the fertility of this planet, such the fecundity and fruitfulness of this planet, that it is easily able to sustain the enormous amount of food which the whole cosmos devours each and every day. This is truly a most remarkable thing, but it is part of the wonder of God's creation; and so he was therefore providing for the needs and the necessities of his creation; he was providing for our daily bread.

But in addition to that, and this also is a very wonderful thing, he was providing, I believe, for our enjoyment. Do you ever think of this, my good friends? Look at verse 9 in chapter 2: "And out of the ground made the Lord God to grow every tree that is pleasant to the sight, and good for food." He was providing for our enjoyment, for our pleasure, for our recreation. Do you ever reflect upon the wonder of flavor? Do you ever reflect upon the wonder of taste? You see, God is a Spirit. He is not physical, he is not corporeal, he doesn't have a body as you and I have. And yet with that wonderful omniscience, he knows precisely what the flavor, what the savor, of each fruit and vegetable is going to be. With unerring skill he makes it and fashions it and decks the earth with it all so that you and I may not only have our necessities provided for, but we might also actually enjoy those things that we need. Just think of the great variety, again, which God has created in this area—the great variety of vegetables. The potato, the carrot, the bean, the pea, the cabbage, the cauliflower, the lettuce. We could go on and on. Each and every one of them, an idea in the mind of God from eternity, and he made it! "He spake, and it was done!"

Or take the wonderful variety of fruits which God has made. Do you ever think of this?—the apple, the banana, the orange, the lemon, the grapefruit, the lime, the peach, the pear, the plum, the blackberry, the raspberry, the strawberry, and many, many others which I don't have time to mention? This wonderful variety, this amazing, astonishing diversity, which comes from the hand of our Maker.

Now it is very interesting that there is, in fact, no mention of the eating of meat here; and this I believe to be very significant. There was, I believe, no meat eaten at this particular stage, for the eating of meat implies the death of the animal. But this stage was prior to the entrance of sin and, therefore, prior to the entrance of death. Thus both the animal creation and the human creation are shut up, as it were, unto the provision which God has made in the plant realm. But even here we see the wonderful foresight, the wonderful forethought, and the wonderful provision of God. Now we eat meat, and what a wonderful flavor it has! Again, we see the wonderful skill and wisdom of the Creator in knowing precisely what the flavor, the attractiveness of the savor, would be unto man who has a body such as we ourselves.

And then take, my good friends, the whole issue of beauty. You see, it wasn't merely "good for food;" it was "pleasant to the sight." There is a wonderful beauty still about God's creation even though it is marred, even though it is spoilt; even though it has lost its original perfection, there is still a wonderful beauty about it. Do you ever thank God for the beautiful blueness of the sky? Do you ever thank God for the beautiful greenness of nature? The greens, the browns, within nature, the whiteness of the clouds, the beautiful blueness of the heavens? Or have you ever stopped to examine a rose? Where I come from, namely England, there are many beautiful roses. Do you ever stop to consider the beauty of its fragrance, the beauty of its form, the texture of its petals? It is most fearfully and wonderfully made, and it declares the glory of its Maker. Why, man cannot even make a blade of grass! But the great God of heaven has decked the whole planet with wonderful plants, with wonderful vegetables, with trees and with flowers, to adorn it and to beautify it. These things are "pleasant to the sight," says the word of God; and that is why the Lord Jesus Christ says, "Consider the lilies of the field." "Consider the lilies of the field, how they grow; . . . and yet I say unto you, that even Solomon in all his glory was not arrayed like one of these" (Matt 6:28–29). We see, in the delicate flowers that God has made, the glory of creation and the glory of the great Creator.

But then third, we come now to *the creation of animal life*. Look at verse 21: "And God created great whales, and every living creature that moveth, which the waters brought forth abundantly, after their kind, and every winged fowl after his kind: and God saw that it was good." We have now reached the fifth day. There is this element of advance, progression, and development. There are steps, there are stages throughout this week. On the fifth day you have the creation of the birds of the air and of the fishes of the sea. And then look at verse 25. In verse 25 we read this: "And God made the beast of the earth after his kind, and cattle after their kind, and every thing that creepeth upon the earth after his kind: and God saw that it was good." God has just filled the earth, he has just filled the planet with vegetation, with plant life. Now he brings in this next step—animal life.

Now notice what the word of God says here: that each was made "after his kind." Now that is a very important phrase in this first chapter of Genesis. It occurs some ten times—"after his kind," "after its kind." Well, this is sometimes referred to as the doctrine of the stability of kinds. What it means is this, that there is a genetic stability about what God made. Like begets like. You don't have cats begetting dogs! You don't have horses begetting porpoises! No, no, there is this stability of kinds. It is not a chaos, it is a cosmos; and it is most fearfully and wonderfully ordered. Each is "after its own kind"; and science has, in fact, shown that it is via the exceedingly complex DNA molecule, this double helix, that God has given this blueprint, this code of life, this genetic information program. It is via this DNA molecule, which in itself is so wonderfully structured. It is in this way that God has created, and in this way that he has ensured the stability of kinds. Each "after its own kind."

But then consider the astonishing variety of animal life. If the plant realm shows some half a million different kinds of vegetation which God has made, it is interesting to note that the animal world shows some two million different kinds of species. Again, it shows us God's love for variety, his love for diversity. Now let me just select a few of those. Take the horse. Have you ever looked carefully at a horse, my good friends? How fearfully and wonderfully made the horse is! How crucial for man, especially prior to this twentieth century! Its exceeding strength, its agility, its speed, its marvelous footwork, its tameableness! God was providing for man, providing for man's travel and his travel needs. Or think of the cow. What a wonderful creature the cow is! So docile, essentially; yielding milk day after day in tremendous profusion, milk which will feed man himself and nourish him. Or take the dog, sometimes described as "man's best friend." Where does that friendliness come from? (I speak of certain dogs!) Where does that affability come from? Where does that loyalty come from—that loyalty that becomes an aggressiveness at times? You see, God has put and placed in each of these animals these instincts, these characteristics, these traits which mark each one out. Each is "after its own kind."

Then consider some of the marvelous instincts which God has put in certain animals. I was reading just recently of the salmon. Did you know that the salmon, after hatching in a stream or a river, then goes out to sea, generally the Pacific Ocean, and spends some five years at sea? But then after some five years, it has this unerring instinct to return to its very birthplace in order to lay its eggs, and it finds with unerring skill the very river, the very stream where it was hatched. Back it goes, jumping over rocks, ascending even waterfalls in order to find that birthplace. Why is it so? It is because God made it so, and it is most fearfully and wonderfully made!

Or take the grunion fish, which I understand visits the shores of California each year. The grunion fish is a most remarkable fish for this reason—the way in which its eggs hatch. What happens is this, with this amazing instinct, the grunion fish knows about the tides and it comes in on one of the two high tides each month, lays its eggs in the sand, and then retreats back into the sea. Some two weeks later another high tide comes—just in time for the eggs to hatch and to swim back out into the sea. How do they know how to do this? My good friends, it is the instincts that God put in them; and they are, therefore, most fearfully and wonderfully made.

Or take the golden plover. The golden plover is a very interesting bird. It nests in northern Alaska, and having brought its young into the world, it then decides to fly some two and half thousand miles due south, straight to the Hawaiian Islands, leaving its young behind! However, you need not fear because, before long, the young birds follow! The parents have gone on ahead, the young birds follow; they go unerringly straight to the Hawaiian Islands. Man cannot fathom this; God's ways are past finding out! But these are some of the instincts which God has put into his creation. These are not rational creatures; this is not even the highest form of God's creation. But nevertheless, they have these wonderful instincts; there is this wild wisdom about them, because God put it there.

Now, my good friends, do you begin to see something of the wonder of God's creation? How we all tend to take it for granted! How we tend to go through life preoccupied with our own business, forgetting the work of God's fingers, forgetting the work of God's hands. But you see something of the wonder of what he has made, something of the glory of creation, something of the glory of the Creator. It is here; it is there between the lines in this first chapter of Genesis.

But look fourth at *the creation of human life.* Look at verse 26: "And God said, Let us make man in our image, after our likeness: and let them have dominion over the fish of the sea, and over the fowl of the air, and over the cattle, and over all the earth, and over every creeping thing that creepeth upon the earth." Notice that man was created last of all. And this, of course, is highly significant. Man is the most important, the most significant of God's creation. There is a sense in which all that preceded this point was a preparation for man himself. Everything else was preparatory for this point, and for man himself. And what the Creator was doing, therefore, for you and for me, was this: he was creating a home, he was creating a habitat for us. He was taking this chaos that we find in the second verse and turning it into a wonderful cosmos. He was taking away the chaotic, unstructured, disorganized elements and molding them and fashioning them. He made it, he fashioned it, and he furnished it; and he did so for man himself essentially.

Now let me illustrate briefly, by way of contrast, the remarkable suitability of this planet. Think of the moon, this near satellite of ours. You will know that back in 1969 man landed on the moon. Man had this wonderful opportunity of actually walking on the moon. Ah, yes, but man could not live upon the moon. It isn't a home for man; it isn't a habitat for man. Let me tell you why. There's no water there; there is no atmosphere there. There's no vegetation there. There are no animals there. There is no food there whatsoever. The force of gravity is not adjusted to man's structure; it is far too weak. The sky itself would not be blue precisely because there's no atmosphere; the sky would be black even during the daytime. Man went to the moon, he walked upon the moon, but he could not live there. It is no habitat for man; and that shows us, by way of contrast, the wonderful provision which God has made on that planet upon which those men were able to look down—this living planet, the third planet from the sun—planet Earth, the planet that stands out from all the other planets.

Now then, what exactly were the characteristics of this man that God had made? Well, let me deal briefly with his body. Man's body, my good friends, is a divine masterpiece! The eye alone is a divine masterpiece. The human ear is a divine masterpiece. The human hand a divine masterpiece. The human heart, which never stops beating until death, is a divine masterpiece. Man's body alone is fearfully and wonderfully made. Ah, yes, but that isn't all. The most important thing about man is this—that he is made in God's image, after God's likeness, made in God's similitude. What does that mean? Notice verse 26: "And God said, Let us make man in our image, after our likeness: and let them have dominion over the fish of the sea, and over the fowl of the air." It is this dominion. This dominion is part of the image of God. Man is God's vice-regent here upon earth. He is the lord of creation under God himself. He has dominion over the animal creation; and one of the reasons why he has this dominion is this, because he is characterized by rationality. The mind of man, man's intellect, man's intelligence! It is this that sets him apart from the animal world, fearfully and wonderfully made though that is. Listen to the great Blaise Pascal. He once said this: "Man is but a reed and the weakest in all nature, but he is a reed that *thinks*."[3] He is able to think. He has this power of thought. He has this capacity for language. He is able to speak. He is able to learn languages. Ah, yes, but not only able to speak with one another, able to speak to his Maker also. He is made with a rational soul.

Another aspect of this image of God surely is the creativity of man, the sheer inventiveness of man. Now compare and contrast man again with the animal world at this point. I often point out to the students that cows never ever build a civilization! They are fearfully and wonderfully made. I love the beef; I love the milk; I am grateful for the leather. They are fearfully and wonderfully made and structured, but they are not rational creatures. They have no creativity. It is the same bovine stupidity year after year! Emil Brunner reputedly once spoke of "the changeless beehive." The beehive never ever changes. It is always the same. But with man there is this inventiveness, this capacity to advance and to grow, and to produce a civilization. There is, you see, this godlikeness, this God-relatedness about man. He is made "a little lower than the angels." He is the crown and the pinnacle of God's creation; and that is why man has this mandate to subdue the earth; and in the advance of civilization, marred though it is by sin, that is what you see. You see man subduing the earth. The problem is, my friends, that though he subdues the earth, he cannot subdue himself! He cannot subdue his own heart. He cannot subdue his own passions and lusts and drives. He can subdue the earth; he can split the atom; he can go to the moon. But he cannot control himself because he is a sinner in rebellion against God; and so once again we see that this image of God is marred. Nevertheless, there is still a remarkable dignity about man; there is still a remarkable nobility about man. He is still the highest of God's creatures; and that image can be restored in Christ. Listen to the way in which the great William Shakespeare described man himself. He said this: "What a piece of work is a man! How noble in reason! How infinite in faculty! In form, in moving, how express and admirable! In action how like an angel! In apprehension how like a god!

3 See quote 13 at https://www.oxfordreference.com/display/10.1093/acref/9780191843730.001.0001/q-oro-ed5-00008181 for an alternate translation: "Man is only a reed, the weakest thing in nature; but he is a thinking reed."

The beauty of the world!"[4] My dear friends, man is both the glory and the scandal of the universe! Made in God's image, fallen into sin, a rebel against his Maker.

Now then, one of the interesting features about this particular passage, this first chapter, is, in my view, the sobriety of the account. There is in the account here a remarkable restraint, a remarkable reserve, and a note of understatement rather than overstatement. I am tempted almost to speak of the modesty of God as he describes this creation of his! Just think, as we have done in part, of the astonishing detail that lies here between the lines—the astonishing variety of the plant world, the astonishing variety of the animal kingdom, the amazing profusion, the amazing proliferation of human life. You see, there is this glorious fullness about God's creation, this wonderful lavishness, this wonderful profusion, this wonderful extravagance on the part of God; and in a sense what you have in the creation of the universe is a *divine extravaganza* which comes from the hand of God! And that's why the psalmist, thinking of this, says, "O Lord, how manifold are thy works! In wisdom hast thou made them all: the earth is full of thy riches" (Ps 104:24); and that's why the great John Calvin says, "Man was rich before he was born,"[5] because of the wonderful care and provision, foresight and forethought which God has shown in his creation. My dear friends, do you see what a great Mind lies at the back of the universe? Do you see that he is glorious in wisdom, glorious in power, fearful in praises, and doing wonders? These mechanisms he has made, these organisms that he has created and which he sustains! Do you not see what a great Intellect he is, what a glorious Being he must be, so glorious in wisdom, goodness, and power? Let me put it this way: What a marvelous Astronomer God is! What a marvelous Physicist God is! What a marvelous Chemist God is! What a marvelous Meteorologist God is! What a marvelous Geologist God is! What a marvelous Agriculturist God is! What a marvelous Botanist he is! What a marvelous Zoologist he is! What a marvelous Biologist he is! And the whole earth is full of his glory, and it is most fearfully and wonderfully made; and all that man does, in his pursuit of science and knowledge, rightly so called, is to "think God's thoughts after him."

But let me emphasize the role of Christ in this. The word of God tells us this: "All things were made by him; and without him was not anything made that was made" (John 1:3). In other words, this same Jesus who came down from heaven, this same Jesus who was born there in Bethlehem, this same Jesus who was laid in a manger, the carpenter's son and who labored as

4. Shakespeare, *Hamlet*, act 2, scene 2, lines 294–97.

5. Calvin, "Commentary on Genesis," Gen 1:26.

a carpenter himself, this same Jesus is none other than the mighty Maker of the universe! "By him," we read, "by him were all things created" (Col 1:16)! Yes, and "by him do all things consist" (Col 1:17), and cohere, and hold together. He is the Maker, he is the Sustainer of the universe! Just think of his ministry. What displays of omniscience, what displays of omnipotence he manifested continually throughout those three years or so! It is this same Jesus, this same blessed Second Person of the Godhead who made it, who fashioned it, who furnished it, and who sustains it.

But let me ask the question: Why did God create the universe? I have no hesitation in saying that the great reason why he did so was that he might display his perfections, that he might display his attributes, that he might display his excellencies, that he might display his wisdom, display his power, display his goodness, that he might manifest unto other creatures what kind of being he himself was. You see, as the great Jonathan Edwards once put it in a remarkable treatise of his, if God had not created the universe, then there is a sense in which these wonderful attributes of his, these wonderful excellencies and perfections of his, would have lain forever dormant, unexerted, unexercised, unable to be acknowledged by any creature outside of God himself; and so God spake and it was done, he gave the commandment and it came forth. He made the heavens, and the earth, and the sea, and all that in them is. Why? That he might display his perfections, that he might display his glory. And there's also another reason why he did it. He wanted, he desired to display his perfections in a way that was even more wonderful than that of creation itself, namely through redemption—through the redemption of man who, though made in God's image, was going to fall into sin.[6]

My dear friends, do you not see something of the glory of creation? As you think of the creation of matter, of space, and of time, of the sun, and the moon, and the stars, and all the heavenly host, as you think of the creation of the plant realm, as you think of the creation of the animal realm, as you think of the creation of man, and as you think of the fact that it was "very good," do you not see something of the glory, and the majesty, and the magnificence of God's creation? And do you not see something of the glory of redemption also, in that in the fullness of time God sent forth his Son to save sinners—to save those, who though they could subdue the earth, could not subdue themselves and their own sinful hearts? My good friends, let me encourage you to open your eyes, and to open your hearts, and to open

6. "The End for Which God Created the World," in Edwards, *Works* (Hickman), 1:94–121.

your mouths about the great fact of creation, to speak much more than we do about our Creator and about our Maker, and to say with the hymn writer:

> Oh Lord my God, when I in awesome wonder
> Consider all the works Thy hands have made,
> I see the stars, I hear the mighty thunder,
> Thy power throughout the universe displayed!
> Then sings my soul, my Saviour God, to Thee;
> How great Thou art, how great Thou art!
> Then sings my soul, my Saviour God, to Thee;
> How great Thou art! How great thou art![7]

7. Hine, "How Great Thou Art."

# THE EXCLUSIVENESS OF CHRIST[1]

If I were to ask you here this evening, "Which is the highest mountain in the world?" you would, all of you, I'm sure, without any hesitation respond that it is Mount Everest; and you would, of course, be correct. Mount Everest is part of the great Himalayan range of mountains often referred to as "the roof of the world." Mount Everest itself, situated on the borders of Tibet and Nepal, rises some 29,028 feet into the air, that is, five and a half miles above the level of the sea. Now, this, you will realize immediately, is not some matter of opinion. It is an established fact that Mount Everest is the highest mountain in the world. Moreover, we live in a world in which there are many such objective facts. It is an objective fact that the Battle of Hastings was fought in 1066; it is an objective fact that Tony Blair is the prime minister of Great Britain; it is an objective fact that water boils at 212 degrees Fahrenheit at sea level; and it is an objective fact that Mount Everest is the highest mountain in the world. Thus, you never hear people arguing, "Well, there are several highest mountains in the world." You never hear them say, "Well, Mount Everest might be the highest mountain in the world for *you*, but not for *me*." There is an objectivity about the height of Mount Everest and about its supremacy as the highest mountain that God has created.

It is very important to note that Christianity deals with objective facts. We are not dealing here with mere ideas, or opinions, or ideals, or aspirations. We are dealing with objective facts precisely because Christianity is a historical religion. Jesus of Nazareth was born under the reign of Caesar Augustus; he suffered under Pontius Pilate; he lived for some thirty-three years upon this earth. Christianity is a historical religion; and because it is a historical religion it deals with objective facts—objective facts which are given by revelation, and which are to be received by faith. We see the

1. This lecture was given during the annual spring conference of Greenville Presbyterian Theological Seminary, Taylors, SC, Mar. 14, 2007.

importance of objective facts in the text that I have chosen here this evening, the twelfth verse of the fourth chapter of the Acts of the Apostles. There we read this: "Neither is there salvation in any other: for there is none other name under heaven given among men, whereby we must be saved" (Acts 4:12). These words are spoken by the apostle Peter in Jerusalem. It is not long after the day of Pentecost. The Son of God incarnate has gone to the cross at Jerusalem, has laid down his life for the sins of his people there, has been buried, and has risen again; and after showing himself alive by many infallible proofs, he has ascended to the right hand of God the Father on high. Shortly after his ascension the Spirit of God is poured out, empowering these otherwise weakened and enfeebled apostles.

The context of this text is interesting. It is that of "a notable miracle" (Acts 4:16)—the healing of a man who had been "lame from his mother's womb." This poor man, who had been crippled for over forty years, was carried daily by friends, or perhaps by his family, to the Beautiful Gate of the temple, where they laid him. There he begged his living day after day after day. On this particular occasion this poor man sees Peter and John approaching the Beautiful Gate of the temple and he asks them for alms. Peter's reply is this: "Silver and gold have I none; but such as I have give I thee: In the name of Jesus Christ of Nazareth rise up and walk" (Acts 3:6). So Peter takes this man by the right hand and raises him up; and this man, who had never ever been able to walk before, goes into the temple with Peter and John, walking and leaping and praising God. Not surprisingly, the people are "filled with wonder and amazement" (Acts 3:10). They knew this man and now they see him for what he is—a new creature physically.

But the apostle Peter utilizes this opportunity to preach the gospel. This whole incident isn't merely about a miracle of healing; it is also about the preaching of the gospel of the Lord Jesus Christ. The Jewish authorities, on hearing the preaching of the gospel, are grieved. They are grieved that Peter is preaching Jesus and the resurrection from the dead. Thus, Annas and Caiaphas, the high priests, ask, "By what power, or by what name, have ye done this?" (Acts 4:7). The answer that the apostle Peter gives is this: "By the name of Jesus Christ of Nazareth" (Acts 3:10). It is in his name, it is through his power, that this poor cripple has been raised up. The apostle Peter, in verse 12, goes on to say this: "Neither is there salvation in any other: for there is none other name under heaven given among men, whereby we must be saved" (Acts 4:12).

We see, then, from this text the absolute exclusiveness of Christ and the absolute exclusiveness of Christianity. My first point, then, is this: *no other religion provides salvation.* This is a fundamental tenet, a fundamental corollary, of the Christian position. Listen again to what the apostle Peter said: "Neither is there salvation in any other: for there is none other name under heaven given among men, whereby we must be saved" (Acts 4:12). We have here a very important negative truth; and negative truths are very important. It is part of the spirit of the age, tragically, that it dislikes negative truths. The great cry today is: "We must be positive! We must not be negative!" Negations are, therefore, not common in theological circles and they are not popular. But they are very necessary. I want to underline the fact that the apostle Peter uses a powerful negation here: "Neither is there salvation in any other" (Acts 4:12).

Now, why is this particular negation so important at the present time? Well, it is important for this reason: We live in a multicultural, pluralistic world. There are five great world religions, so called. There is not only Christianity; there is also Judaism; there is Islam; there is Buddhism; and there is Hinduism. In addition to these there is a plethora of other religions. The twentieth century has witnessed the phenomenon of the ecumenical movement—an ecumenical movement which has degenerated increasingly into a movement which is prepared to sacrifice truth on the altar of unity as the churches obsessively come together. It is interesting to note that side by side with this ecumenical movement has grown what is known as the interfaith movement. Thus, in the twentieth century and in the twenty-first century you have not only this tendency for *churches* to come together; you have also the tendency for the *world religions* to come together and to merge their differences.

The first World Congress of Faiths was held in 1936. This particular movement has gathered significant momentum in the last forty years or so. It is an interesting fact that in Westminster Abbey in London every year an interfaith service is held at which all the great world religions, so called, are represented and at which the Queen is often in attendance. The great emphasis in such circles is upon dialogue; it is upon mutual understanding; it is upon esteem; it is upon respect. It is upon the idea that we must learn to tolerate one another. We must not be exclusive; we must not exclude anyone. No one religion rises above any other religion. No, no! All the great world faiths are equally valid and they all, ultimately, lead unto God. That, fundamentally, is their position.

This is known as the *pluralist* position. As the word suggests, this position holds to a plurality of religions. The idea here is that many world religions are saving. All the great world religions are supposedly saving, and you will find salvation through them. Therefore, it is not only Christianity that is saving; Judaism is also saving. So, too, is Islam; so, too, Buddhism; so, too, Hinduism. The question as to whether Satanism is saving is unanswered! The question as to whether the Jim Jones cult is saving is, again, left unanswered! But this is the great cry, you see, that all the great world faiths are saving. According to John Hick—perhaps the doyen of the pluralist movement—all these great world faiths are essentially saying the same thing. He sums this up as "salvation-liberation."[2] If you look at all the great world faiths, he says, they are saying the same thing. In other words, it is salvation or liberation from self-centeredness and transformation from that self-centeredness into what he calls "reality-centeredness."[3] To demonstrate how significant the inroads of this pluralist movement are I want to quote Dr. Robert Runcie. Dr. Runcie was the Archbishop of Canterbury in the 1980s—he was the leader of the Anglican Communion. In 1986, on the fiftieth anniversary of the World Congress of Faiths, this is what he said: "Other faiths than our own are genuine mansions of the Spirit."[4] In 1992, Pope John Paul II, during a visit to the continent of Africa, said this: "Christians and Muslims worship the same God."[5] So this is the cry: "All the great faiths are fundamentally the same; they are all saying the same thing; they all lead to God; and it doesn't really matter which one you adopt. You will find salvation and liberation and transformation through any one of them."

Let us examine, then, this idea that all the great faiths are saying the same thing. Why, on the very surface it is preposterous! Are Judaism and Islam saying the same thing? Are Christianity and Islam saying the same thing? Are Christianity and Judaism saying the same thing? And if they *are* saying the same thing, why is it that Judaism and Islam have persistently persecuted Christianity? It is manifestly absurd; it is palpably preposterous to assert that all the great faiths are saying the same thing! You might just as well say that all sports are the same! You might just as well say that American football and cricket are the same, that golf and tennis are the same, that soccer and basketball are the same! Or you might just as well assert that there is no real difference between the Democratic Party on the one hand and the Republican Party on the other, or between the Socialist Party on the one hand and the Conservative Party on the other. No self-respecting sportsman, or politician, or religionist, surely, would utter such nonsense if they really considered what they were saying.

Let us look for a moment, then, at the differences between Christianity and Islam. We are being told by the pope—the Second Vatican Council laid a foundation for this—that these two religions worship essentially the same God. Well, do they? Look at Islam; the Five Pillars of Islam are as follows:

2. John Hick, in Gundry et al., *Four Views*, 44.

3. John Hick, in Gundry et al., *Four Views*, 127.

4. Cited in Pollitt, *Inter-Faith Movement*, 78.

5. See Wells, *Revolution in Rome*, 80.

first, the acknowledgment of Allah as the one true God and of Mohammed as his prophet; second, prayer five times a day; third, the giving of alms; fourth, fasting in the month of Ramadan; and, fifth, at least one pilgrimage to Mecca during one's lifetime. It is obvious, surely, that we have here in Islam a religion of works righteousness; it is a religion of self-salvation; it is a legalistic religion; it is a religion characterized, in my judgment, by the most appalling bondage; and it is in utter contrast to that wonderful religion of grace founded by Jesus Christ of Nazareth some two thousand years ago. What we find in pluralism, then, is the great liberal tendency to collapse and conflate different phenomena into the same phenomenon. There are, in fact, colossal, monumental differences between the world faiths; and it lies upon the very surface that that is so.

How, then, does the pluralist refer to God? Well, John Hick—we will take him as our representative—likes to refer to God as "the Real," "the Ultimate," "the Transcendent," or "the Transcendent Real." But he can't decide what gender to use in describing this God, whether to use "he," "she" or "it"! There is this terrible air of unreality about "the Real" that he posits! One is tempted to say that pluralists such as John Hick ought really to erect an altar to "the unknown god" and entitle it "The Real." I would remind you that the Bible speaks of "other gods"—"other gods" that are "strange gods," "other gods" that are "false gods," "other gods" that are "no gods," "other gods" that are utter nonentities—the concoctions of men's minds and the imaginations of their hearts! That is what we have, frankly, in pluralism. Pluralists bypass and reject the one true and living God, and they invent gods of their own in this ecumenical, interfaith enterprise.

What, then, does the pluralist do with Christ? Well, this is very interesting. You see, Christ is a great problem for the pluralist. The problem with Christ for the pluralist is this: he pins men down; he puts men on the spot; he demands an answer; he requires a commitment. Jesus Christ is a totalitarian master, a totalitarian Lord; and this is the reason why Jesus Christ is a problem as far as the pluralist is concerned. Now, I say that he is a problem for this reason: In the 1970s John Hick proposed what he called a Copernican revolution in this whole matter. He said that hitherto Christ has been the great sun or the great center around which Christianity and all the world religions revolve. He said, in effect, "We need to do away with that. Let's move Christ aside. Let's have God at the center; let God be the sun; let him be the epicenter around which all the great world religions revolve."[6] The reason why he says this, of course, is that some notion of God is, more or less, present in all of these great world faiths. But Jesus Christ is a problem

6. "The Copernican Revolution in Theology," in Hick, *God and the Universe*, 120–32.

to the pluralist; he is an embarrassment to the pluralist. The pluralist wishes to get rid of him. He reduces Christ in classic liberal fashion to "our revered leader, inspiration, and model." There is this reduction of the divine Christ to simply a great teacher of mankind.

But, you see, the problem of Christ remains precisely because He makes the most monumental claims for himself. Listen to some of them: "I am the bread of life" (John 6:35). "I am the light of the world" (John 8:12). "The Son of Man hath power on earth to forgive sins" (Matt 9:6). "Heaven and earth shall pass away, but my words shall not pass away" (Matt 24:35). The great Augustine reputedly said, "Jesus Christ is either God or he is not a good man." You cannot have it both ways. He makes these colossal, monumental claims. He is an embarrassment to the pluralist; he is a problem to the pluralist agenda. That is why they are seeking to brush him aside. But he cannot be brushed aside precisely because he is himself God the Son, the Second Person of the Godhead. Listen, again, to what our text says: "Neither is there salvation in any other: for there is none other name under heaven given among men, whereby we must be saved" (Acts 4:12).

But in addition to the problem of the pluralist, there is another problem. It is the problem of what is known as the *inclusivist*. What, exactly, is this position? The pluralist believes there are many, many religions, equally valid, all of them saving. The inclusivist, however, takes a somewhat different stance. He maintains the priority, the primacy, and the preeminence of Christianity; but he does not wish to exclude these other religions such as Judaism and Islam, Buddhism and Hinduism, et cetera. Indeed, following the Second Vatican Council the inclusivist says this: these other religions are (and I quote) "a preparation for the gospel"[7]—they are a preparation for Christ. I want to emphasize here this evening the colossal significance of the Second Vatican Council. It met from 1962 to 1965. It involved, in a sense, an opening up of the windows of Catholicism. A new breath of fresh air came through, supposedly. There is this modernization that has occurred and it has resulted in what has been called a "new Catholicism." In particular, what has resulted is a new attitude towards the world religions. The position of the council is this: that our attitude, indeed God's attitude, towards the world religions can be likened to a series of concentric circles. At the center is Christ; in the inner circle are the Roman Catholic faithful; in the next circle you have non-Catholic Christians such as ourselves; in the next circle you have non-Christian religions such as Judaism, Islam, Buddhism, et cetera; and in the outer circle you have, supposedly, atheists. All of these, whether Roman Catholics or Protestants, Jews, Muslims, or even atheists—all of these are

7. Flannery, *Vatican Council II*, 22.

somehow related to Jesus Christ; all of them benefit from his saving work, according to the Second Vatican Council. Thus, you have the concept of what Karl Rahner has called the "anonymous Christian"; a man can, supposedly, be a Christian anonymously.[8] He can, supposedly, be a Christian without even knowing it; he can be a Christian even though he rejects the Lord Jesus Christ. Even an atheist can, supposedly, be a Christian. This is the position of the Church of Rome, as the Second Vatican Council documents demonstrate.

But how does the Church of Rome justify this position? It justifies this position largely on the basis of its view of the incarnation. We need to understand that Roman Catholic theology is, essentially, an incarnational theology. It emphasizes the incarnation of Christ. Let me quote from the Second Vatican Council. "By his Incarnation, he, the Son of God, has in a certain way united himself with each man."[9] Thus we are being told by the Second Vatican Council in the 1960s that, essentially, the incarnation of Christ saves. The image that illustrates this is as follows: just as dye, when cast into a pond, will eventually suffuse and permeate the whole, so, too, supposedly the incarnation of Christ in this world has, with time, suffused and permeated the whole. The whole of life is sacralized, the whole of life is divinized, the whole of life is leavened by the coming of the Son of God into the world. That is the official position of the Second Vatican Council in the 1960s. You find exactly the same doctrine in the teaching of Pope John Paul II. Early on in his significant pontificate in 1979 he said this in an encyclical: "Man—every man without any exception whatever—has been redeemed by Christ."[10]

These are staggering assertions. We have here the most blatant and astonishing universalism. The Church of Rome used to say that outside of the church—meaning itself—there is no salvation; now it is saying that there is salvation for all men everywhere, not only for Roman Catholics, but even for the "separated brethren" such as you and me, also for non-Christian religions, also for the atheist. They, too, can find salvation through Christ. Now, this is clearly an abuse of the doctrine of the incarnation of Christ. The incarnation of Christ is a great and a wonderful doctrine. This incursion of the Son of God into time, this intrusion of the Second Person of the Godhead into this world—it is a great and a glorious doctrine, and we cherish it in a manner that is second to none. But we insist that the incarnation does not save men; the incarnation, in and of itself, is not saving. The incarnation

8. Cited in Wells, *Revolution in Rome*, 80.

9. John Paul II, *Redemptor Hominis*, 39.

10. John Paul II, *Redemptor Hominis*, 39.

is always *unto* the atonement. The birth of Christ always looks forward to the death of Christ; Bethlehem always looks forward unto Calvary.

So we have here a bypassing of the doctrine of the cross of Christ. The cross of Christ, William Cunningham insisted in the nineteenth century, is thrown into the background in Roman Catholic theology.[11] Roman crosses are everywhere in the foreground; yes, but the actual doctrine of "Jesus Christ and him crucified" is thrown into the background. You find exactly the same thing today. The incarnation is supposedly that which saves us. "Jesus Christ and him crucified" has been forgotten and neglected. But listen to what the word of God says—indeed, the Church of Rome ought to listen to the man that it regards as the first bishop of Rome, because this is what he said some two thousand years ago! "Neither is there salvation in any other: for there is none other name under heaven given among men, whereby we must be saved" (Acts 4:12).

But the problem today is that men are listening to the Church of Rome. The impact of the Second Vatican Council has been colossal, and you see it in the ministry of a man such as Clark Pinnock. You may well be aware that Clark Pinnock's theological journey has been somewhat strange. He began in Calvinism, moved into Arminianism, and has recently espoused the "openness of God" theology, which blasphemously asserts that God does not know what the future is! Clark Pinnock is an inclusivist. He believes in the primacy of Christianity; but he also believes that you can come to Christ via these other religions. This is what he says: "Everyone must eventually pass through Jesus to reach the Father. But there is more than one path for arriving at that place."[12] In other words, he is saying that Christ is essential; he is not formally denying the centrality of Christ. But he is saying you can come to Christ through these other religions; they are, as the Second Vatican Council puts it, "a preparation for the gospel."

You have here, then, the idea that the Spirit of God is active and present and redemptively at work among other religions. The question, however, is this: How is this supposed to occur? Well, there is a real vagueness at this point; indeed, there is a real difficulty at this point. Men such as Clark Pinnock have to postulate the idea that this possibly occurs after death through some sort of postmortem encounter. In other words, a man can live as a Muslim, or a Buddhist, or a Hindu, but these things are a preparation for Christ; and, perhaps, after death he will come to Christ, be received by Christ, and be saved by him at that particular point. But the word of God holds out no hope whatsoever for any kind of postmortem encounter, some kind of

11. See Cunningham, *Historical Theology*.

12. Clark H. Pinnock, "An Inclusivist View," in Gundry et al., *Four Views*, 119.

second opportunity after death. The word of God is abundantly clear: "It is appointed unto men once to die, but after this the judgment" (Heb 9:27). You see, this inclusivist idea is, in the final analysis, simply wishful thinking. Men are prophesying out of their own hearts rather than listening to the word of God. Their position is, in many ways, reminiscent of the Samaritans in the Old Testament Scriptures—the Samaritans who "feared the Lord and served their own gods after the manner of the nations" (2 Kgs 17:33).

Moreover, this idea that the Spirit of God is active and latent and present in all the world religions must also be examined. I would remind you that the Spirit of God is the Spirit of truth. His concern is to take the things of Jesus Christ, to testify to him, to glorify him, to convince men of sin and of righteousness and of judgment to come, to bring the sinner to "Jesus Christ, and Him crucified" (1 Cor 2:2). It is a blasphemy to say that the Spirit of God is latently present and active in these other religions. The Spirit of God is the Spirit of truth. He honors the truth, not error. He is not the Spirit of error; he is the one who, in the word of God, regards such religions as manifestations of darkness and ignorance and delusion, not some sort of "preparation for the gospel." Listen again, then, to what the word of God has to say. "Neither is there salvation in any other: for there is none other name under heaven given among men, whereby we must be saved" (Acts 4:12).

But there is, interestingly, another spirit at work today—it is the spirit of the age. I am referring, in particular, to postmodernism. You may have heard of postmodernism and, perhaps, have wondered what it is. It is a difficult, somewhat complex and elusive concept; nevertheless I will explain briefly what it involves. It is very significant and powerfully present in our society at the present time. Postmodernism arose, essentially, in France in the 1970s. Its roots go back to Friedrich Nietzsche; but it was in the 1970s in France that an intellectual revolt occurred against the Enlightenment. The Enlightenment, of course, had its roots very much in France, as well as in Germany and in Great Britain. There is this revolt that has occurred against the use of reason, against the cult of reason, against an overemphasis upon reason.

Now, in some respects that is good; in other respects, it is bad for this reason: reason is a gift of God; reason is "the candle of the Lord." Rationality is part of man's being made in the image of God; it is essentially a good thing, provided it is under revelation, provided it is under God himself. The Enlightenment, however, exaggerated reason. So, there has been this turning away from the whole concept of reason and the emphasis is put, now, upon feelings, upon subjectivism. Postmodernism tends to be very negative, very critical; it tends to be iconoclastic; it tends to promote skepticism; it promotes subjectivism; it promotes relativism so that, for instance, a postmodernist might say, "Well, Jesus Christ might be a Savior for you, but not for me." Or he might say, "Well, Jesus Christ is a Savior for me, but not for you." Or he might say, "Well, Jesus Christ is a Savior if you are European, but not for an Asian." You see the relativism that is rampant there; that is the spirit of postmodernism.

Colin E. Gunton, in his 1992 Bampton Lectures, said this: "What is new in Postmodernism is the loss of the commitment to objective truth."[13] Remember, we live in a world characterized by many, many objective truths. But the modern man and the modern mind don't like objective truth; they love subjectivism; we live in an age of feelings. "Well, that may be true for you, but not for me. It's true for me, but not for you." So, there is this loss of grip upon the concept of objective and absolute truth. The postmodernist doesn't discover truth as men did in the past; he creates his own truth. "Truth is whatever you want it to be." That is the modern idea. Thus, postmodernism reinforces pluralism; it reinforces this idea of relativism; it reinforces the idea that there are many gods, many saviors, and many different paths to redemption.

My good friends, you see, perhaps, the significance of the times in which we live: pluralism on the one hand, inclusivism on the other hand, and then postmodernism—all of them encroaching upon the church, many of them peddled by the church. These things are undermining this whole idea found in our text of the exclusiveness of the Lord Jesus Christ as the Savior of sinners. It must be evident that there is a massive collision here between what Christianity says and what pluralism says, between what inclusivism says, and what postmodernism says. I emphasize afresh, therefore, the biblical position. These other religions are, in the final analysis, not some "preparation for the gospel of Christ," but rather manifestations of the blindness and the darkness and the strong delusion to which men are subject as natural men; that is how we should regard them; they are demonstrations of man's ignorance, demonstrations of man's rebellion against God. "And this is the condemnation," says our Lord, "that light is come into the world, and men loved darkness rather than light, because their deeds were evil" (John 3:19). They love the darkness; they hate the light. They love their error; they reject the truth.

I want to emphasize here this evening that there is a fundamental intolerance on the part of Christianity with regard to other religions. It is what I call *an ideological intolerance.* It is not a personal intolerance; we are not personally intolerant of the Jew, or the Muslim, or the Buddhist, or the Hindu. On the contrary, we seek to love them, to come alongside of them,

13. Gunton, *One, Three and Many*, 67.

and to win them for the Lord Jesus Christ. There is nothing personal about it; it is an ideological intolerance. We are utterly intolerant of their ideology; we have no hesitation whatsoever in saying that it is wrong on the basis of the word of God. This is precisely what our text is saying: "Neither is there salvation in any other: for there is none other name under heaven given among men, whereby we must be saved."

But then, my second point is this: *Christianity alone provides salvation.* Listen again to our text: "Neither is there salvation in any other: for there is none other name under heaven given among men, whereby we must be saved." We have here, of course, a very important, positive truth. Yes, it is cast in the negative; it must be cast in the negative. Negatives are essential; but they essentially capture a great positive truth. Negatives imply positives; and that is what you have here: a great positive affirmation of the uniqueness and the exclusiveness of Jesus Christ of Nazareth. This position is taught throughout the New Testament Scriptures. Listen to what the apostle Paul has to say. "For there is one God, and one mediator between God and men, the man Christ Jesus" (1 Tim 2:5). The uniqueness, the exclusiveness of Jesus Christ, the God-Man!

Then listen to the God-Man himself: "I am the way, the truth, and the life: no man cometh unto the Father, but by me" (John 14:6). Our Lord is making there a most momentous claim. He is taking the name of Jehovah, I am, *ego eimi*. He is taking that name, and through a remarkable allusion to the situation there in the Old Testament at the burning bush, our Lord is taking the very name of Jehovah upon his own lips. There are these overtones of deity in the claim itself: "I am!" Thus, it is evident that the New Testament itself insists upon the uniqueness of Jesus Christ, upon the exclusiveness of Jesus Christ; and that this insistence upon the uniqueness and the exclusiveness of Jesus Christ is, in fact, the classic, traditional Protestant position.

But the situation is changing, and it is changing rapidly. Voices are being heard insistently and insidiously that Jesus Christ is not the only way. You see, it comes in various forms: the pluralist takes one position; the inclusivist takes another position. There are even Evangelicals today who are saying it is not necessary to hear of Jesus Christ in order to be saved. It is an astonishing fact that a survey of the American people taken in November 2001 revealed that 75 percent of Americans believe that many religions lead to eternal life. Now, given the high percentage of churchgoing in this country, this must mean that a very significant number of those interviewed attend church, perhaps evangelical churches, and yet believe that there are many different ways to reach eternal life.

I want to emphasize, therefore—and I do so on the basis of this text—that this name of Jesus Christ of Nazareth is "given." Listen again to the word: "Neither is there salvation in any other: for there is none other name under heaven given among men." It is given by God; there is a givenness about it. This is part of the revelation which God himself has given to us. I want to emphasize, therefore, that Christianity, unlike these other religions, is a revealed religion. "God, who at sundry times and in divers manners spake in time past unto the fathers by the prophets, hath in these last days spoken unto us by his Son" (Heb 1:1–2). It is a revealed religion! This name has been given to us. But it is also a redemptive religion. Notice the word "salvation" there in this text. "Neither is there salvation in any other." It brings salvation; it has a Savior; it has a Redeemer. The sinner is "not redeemed with corruptible things, as silver and gold . . . ; but with the precious blood of Christ, as of a lamb without blemish and without spot" (1 Pet 1:18–19). Unique, exclusive, towering above all others! It is a revealed religion, a redemptive religion. It is a dogmatic religion; it is an exclusive religion; there is none other name!

I want to insist, therefore, that this exclusiveness in Christianity is rooted and grounded in the uniqueness of Jesus Christ of Nazareth. It is rooted and grounded in the fact that he himself is utterly and absolutely unique. Let me demonstrate this: Christ's *origin* is unique. He is not from below; he is from above. The word speaks of his preexistence. "In the beginning was the Word, and the Word was with God, and the Word was God" (John 1:1). The preexistence of Christ! He is from above and he is above all; and though he begins his life as the God-Man at Bethlehem, that was not the beginning of his existence. He is a heavenly being; he comes out from God, he comes forth from the Father, he comes down from heaven, he is born in this world. The utter absolute uniqueness of Jesus Christ of Nazareth! His origin is utterly unique.

But so, too, is his *birth*. He was born of a virgin, born of the Virgin Mary. The Holy Spirit came upon this young woman. The power of the Highest overshadowed her, and that holy thing that was born of her was called the Son of God. He was born "without the means of man." His mother is Mary; Joseph is not his father. There is this unique birth, this supernatural conception which, again, marks him out as utterly unique.

But then look at his *life*. Christ's life is also unique. "Which of you convinceth me of sin?" (John 8:46), he was able to say; and how they would have loved to do so! But he flings down the gauntlet to the Jewish leaders: "Which of you convinceth me of sin?" He is without original sin; he is without actual sin. He knew no sin; he did no sin; there is no unrighteousness in him. He lived a perfect, matchless, impeccable life such as has never been lived before and will never be lived again upon the face of the earth. His life is unique.

But so, too, are his *works*. His works are gloriously unique. Think of the miracles, the signs, and the wonders that he performed. Think of the wonderful things that he did. My good friend, show me another man who can turn water into wine! Show me another man who can walk upon the water! Show me another man who can rebuke the wind and the waves and the sea and say, "Peace, be still," and there is "a great calm" (Mark 4:39)! Show me another man who can touch the eyes of the blind, restoring the sight, who can give hearing to those that are deaf, who can loosen the string of the tongue of those that are dumb! These works of Christ are glorious works; they mark him out as utterly and absolutely unique. He shows himself thereby to be the God of nature, the God of all creation, to have the very command of the universe at his fingertips. My good friends, Jesus Christ is the wonder of the ages! He is the great phenomenon of all time! There is none like unto him! Who can be likened to this God-Man who performs such great and wonderful and mighty deeds?

But Christ's *death* is also unique. It was no ordinary death. He died for our sins; he bore our sins in his body on the tree; he is a sacrifice for sins; he is a substitute for sinners. It is an atoning death; he is expiating sin; he is propitiating God. It is a transaction between the Father and the Son. His death is utterly and absolutely unique.

But so, too, is his *resurrection*. He that raised others from the dead—Lazarus, the widow of Nain's son, Jairus' daughter, and probably many others—he himself rose from the dead. "He . . . saw no corruption" (Acts 13:37); there was no decomposition of his body. He lay there in the tomb for three days and three nights; but God raised him up, as Peter himself reminds us here in this very sermon. "I am the resurrection, and the life," says the Lord Jesus Christ (John 11:25). It was not possible that the One who is the resurrection and the life should be held by death. He showed himself alive unto his disciples "by many infallible proofs" (Acts 1:3).

My good friends, do you not see something of the glory of this Jesus Christ of Nazareth? Do you not see that he is, in fact, utterly unique? His origin is unique! His birth is unique! His life is unique! His works are unique! His death is unique! His resurrection is unique! He himself is utterly and absolutely unique! There is a glory and a majesty about Jesus Christ of Nazareth which he shares with none other.

There is a very interesting and important difference between the founders of these other religions and the Founder of Christianity. The difference is this: The founders of other religions such as Buddha, Confucius, and Mohammed, point the way to God. But Jesus Christ presents himself as the way; He is the way to God. Buddha, Confucius, and Mohammed were the first confessors of the religions that they founded; and you could dispense with them more or less and still have the religion. But you cannot dispense with Jesus Christ. He himself is Christianity! He himself is the way! He is the rock, the foundation upon which the superstructure is built. That's the difference between them and him.

But this very exclusiveness is an affront to the modern man; he doesn't like it; it is an insult to him! He regards it as narrow, bigoted, dogmatic, intolerant, imperialistic, and chauvinistic! That is his attitude; and he will have none of it! No, no! All the churches must come together! Religious convergence is the order of the day! But more than that, all the faiths must come together! No one religion must stand supreme; no one religion must regard itself as exclusive! We live—and I warn you about this—in a climate of political correctness. The concept of political correctness is moving into the churches. We have now the concept of religious correctness in this sort of area; and the ethic of civility, which must not criticize or say that such and such a thing is wrong, rules the day.

But what saith the Scripture? The Scripture says this: "Neither is there salvation in any other: for there is none other name under heaven given among men, whereby we must be saved." I remind you, again, that the word of God speaks of "other gods" and prohibits and forbids "other gods." We live, as you well know, in a post–September 11 world. I want to insist upon it in this context that Allah is a false god, that Mohammed is a false prophet, and that Islam is a false religion! I say so on the authority of the word of God itself that insists upon the uniqueness and the exclusiveness of the Christian faith.

"Ah," says someone, "you mustn't say things like that. If you say things like that, you will be a threat to world peace!" They might be right. There is an element of truth in it. Islam is on the march; Islam is taking aggressive strides throughout the earth. It may be a threat to world peace. But our business is not to consider that. Our business is to preach the word, to preach the truth, to preach the uniqueness and the exclusiveness of Jesus Christ and to leave consequences to God himself. The Son of God said this: "Suppose ye that I am come to give peace on earth? I tell you, Nay; but rather division" (Luke 12:51). The Son of God came to bring division, fire, and a sword. He divides families; he divides friends; little wonder if he also divides nations. But we can leave those consequences to God himself; our business is to preach the truth and the exclusiveness of his blessed name.

We are living in days when Christ is being marginalized; he is being pushed to the periphery by the pluralists, by the inclusivists, and by the postmodernists. Men today are busy touting other names; and these are the names that they tout: Socrates, Buddha, Confucius, Mohammed, Gandhi, Lenin, Krishna, the Dalai Lama! But it is an insult to the Lord Jesus Christ to range or to rank anyone with him. These men honor Christ with their lips, but their hearts are far from him. For if their hearts were with him, they would insist—as I do tonight—upon his uniqueness, upon his exclusiveness; and they would not be ashamed of the dogmatism of the Christian faith. To rank anyone with Christ, to range any other master or savior with him is ultimately to deny him; it is to betray him. I remind you that Jesus Christ is a totalitarian master; He is a totalitarian Lord. He demands and expects obedience and submission and commitment unto him on the part of those that are his followers.

Do you see the importance of this verse? Do you see the importance of this truth? We are living in days when this position is under attack. I want to insist upon it, therefore, that there is no other religion that brings salvation, and that Christianity alone brings salvation; Jesus Christ is the only Savior. This verse is, therefore, an excellent litmus test for our position and, indeed, our condition. Test yourself by it! Is this your position? Do you believe here tonight that there is no salvation in any other, that there is none other name given under heaven among men whereby we must be saved? Is that your position? Is it your church's position? Is it your denomination's position? Is this the position you espouse? This is the biblical position. The apostle Peter says so; the apostle Paul says so; the Lord Jesus Christ says so. The whole of the word of God insists upon it—this utter, absolute uniqueness of Jesus Christ of Nazareth. Is he your Savior? Is he your Lord? Are you saved by him here this evening? Do you realize that you are a sinner? Do you realize that you have left undone those things that you ought to have done, that you have done those things you ought not to have done, and that, by nature, there is no health within you whatsoever? You are in desperate need of the great Physician, the only Savior of sinners that God has provided. Is this your position? Is this your Savior, and are you clinging to him?

This truth is so important that it constitutes the mainspring of evangelistic and missionary activity. If you deny this, you might just as well abandon evangelistic activity. You might just as well say, "Well, they'll come to Christ anyway. It might even be worse if we preach Christ to them; they will be more responsible; they will have more light. We will leave them in their darkness." This truth is the mainspring of evangelistic and missionary activity, and that is why we must defend it. We defend it precisely because the church is drifting; it has been drifting for some forty years or so away from its moorings and its foundation in this respect. You and I must contend earnestly for this faith once delivered unto the saints. It is a precious treasure; we must defend it and guard it; and we must proclaim it.

You see, the word of God knows nothing of "an unknown Christ." The word of God knows nothing of "a cosmic Christ." It knows nothing of "the

Christ principle." That is what they love to speak of today. What it knows is this: Jesus Christ of Nazareth, the carpenter's son, as was supposed—the man who went about among men doing good, healing the sick, raising the dead, teaching the people, uttering things kept hidden from the foundation of the world. This is the One they know; and this is the One we preach, the Christ revealed in the Scriptures. We have to defend it; we have to proclaim it.

The Great Commission requires this proclamation. Listen to what the Savior said: "Go ye into all the world, and preach the gospel to every creature" (Mark 16:15). "Go ye therefore, and teach all nations, baptizing them in the name of the Father, and of the Son, and of the Holy Ghost" (Matt 28:19). In order to implement the Great Commission we have to go to every creature, that means to every religion. Yes, we take the gospel to the Jew and the Muslim and the Buddhist and the Hindu and whatever religion men may hold, or none at all. The gospel is to go out and it is to go forth unto all; the Great Commission of Christ requires it.

You see, the great emphasis today is upon dialogue and not upon proclamation. But God is a God of proclamation, not of dialogue. He does not sit down and discuss these things; he announces his word; he gives it categorically: "Neither is there salvation in any other: for there is none other name under heaven given among men, whereby we must be saved" (Acts 4:12).

There are a number of mountains in the great Himalayan range which nearly approach to Mount Everest. K2 and Kangchenjunga approach to within approximately one thousand feet of the summit of the highest mountain in the world. Mount Everest has its rivals. But with Jesus Christ it is not so; with Jesus Christ it is utterly different. He has no rivals; he towers above them all; and he stands, like Mount Everest, unrivaled, unchallenged, and supreme in the midst of a range of tiny, little, insignificant hills. Amen.

# Bibliography

Alexander, James W. *Thoughts on Preaching: Being Contributions to Homiletics*. Edinburgh: Banner of Truth, 1975.

Amano, J. Yutaka, and Norman L. Geisler. *The Infiltration of the New Age*. Cambridge: Tyndale, 1989.

Anglican-Roman Catholic International Commission. *The Final Report*. London: CTS/SPCK, 1982.

Blaikie, William G. *The Preachers of Scotland: From the Sixth to the Nineteenth Century*. Edinburgh: Banner of Truth, 2001.

Blake, William. *Blake: Complete Writings with Variant Readings*. Edited by Geoffrey Keynes. 2nd ed. Oxford: Oxford University Press, 1966.

Borgman, Brian. *My Heart for Thy Cause: Albert N. Martin's Theology of Preaching*. Fearn, Scot.: Christian Focus, 2002.

Broadus, John A. *On the Preparation and Delivery of Sermons*. San Francisco: HarperOne, 1979.

Buchanan, Colin, ed. *Anglo-Catholic Worship: An Evangelical Appreciation after 150 Years*. Bramcote, Eng.: Grove, 1983.

Buchanan, Colin, et al. *Growing into Union: Proposals for Forming a United Church in England*. London: SPCK, 1970.

Buchanan, James. *The Doctrine of Justification: An Outline of Its History in the Church and of Its Exposition from Scripture*. Edinburgh: Banner of Truth, 1961.

Cady, Edwin H. "The Artistry of Jonathan Edwards." *New England Quarterly* 22 (1949): 61–72.

Calvin, John. "Commentary on Genesis: Vol. 1." CCEL, n.d. https://ccel.org/ccel/calvin/calcom01/calcom01.vii.i.html.

Carrick, John. *The Preaching of Jonathan Edwards*. Edinburgh: Banner of Truth Trust, 2008.

Chadwick, Owen. *The Mind of the Oxford Movement*. Stanford, CA: Stanford University Press, 1960.

———. *Newman*. Past Masters. Oxford: Oxford University Press, 1983.

———. *The Secularization of the European Mind in the 19th Century*. New York: Cambridge University Press, 1997.

———. *The Victorian Church*. 2 vols. London: A&C Black, 1971.

Charley, Julian. *Rome, Canterbury, and the Future*. Bramcote, Eng.: Grove, 1982.

Coulson, John, and A. M. Allchin, eds. *The Rediscovery of Newman: An Oxford Symposium*. London: Sheed & Ward, 1967.

Cunningham, William. *Discussions on Church Principles: Popish, Erastian, and Presbyterian*. Edmonton: Still Waters Revival, 1991.

———. *Historical Theology*. 2 vols. Edinburgh: Banner of Truth, 1979.

———. *The Reformers and the Theology of the Reformation*. London: Banner of Truth, 1967.

D'Aubigné, J. H. Merle de. *Geneva and Oxford*. London: Dalton, 1843.

Dabney, Robert Lewis. *Evangelical Eloquence*. Edinburgh: Banner of Truth, 1999.

Dallimore, Arnold A. *George Whitefield: The Life and Times of the Great Evangelist of the Eighteenth-Century Revival*. 2 vols. Edinburgh: Banner of Truth, 1970.

Dennison, Charles G. "Some Thoughts on Preaching." *Kerux* 11 (Dec. 1996) 3–9.

Dennison, James T., Jr. "Paul on the Damascus Road." *Kerux* 2 (Sept. 1987) 21–28.

———. "John 2: Structure and Biblical Theology." *Kerux* 11. (May 1996) 3–13.

———. "What Is Biblical Theology? Reflections on the Inaugural Address of Geerhardus Vos." *Kerux* 2 (May 1987) 33–41.

———. "Geerhardus Vos, Biblical Theology and Preaching." *Kerux* 24 (2009) 17–25. Mar. 2, 1998. https://kerux.com/doc/2401A3.asp.

Dessain, C. S. "The Sources of Newman's Power." In *The Rediscovery of Newman: An Oxford Symposium*, edited by John Coulson and A. M. Allchin, 100–143. London: Sheed & Ward, 1967.

Douma, J. *The Ten Commandments: Manual for the Christian Life*. Translated by Nelson D. Kloosterman. Phillipsburg, NJ: P&R, 1996.

Dudley-Smith, Timothy, and John Stott. "Foreword." In *Evangelical Anglicans and the ARCIC Final Report: An Assessment and Critique*, by John Stott, 2. Bramcote, Eng.: Grove, 1982.

Edwards, Jonathan. *The Great Awakening*. Edited by C. C. Goen. The Works of Jonathan Edwards 4. New Haven, CT: Yale University Press, 1972.

———. *Letters and Personal Writings*. Edited by George S. Claghorn. The Works of Jonathan Edwards 16. New Haven, CT: Yale University Press, 1998.

———. *Original Sin*. Edited by Clyde A. Holbrook. The Works of Jonathan Edwards 3. New Haven, CT: Yale University Press, 1970.

———. *Sermons and Discourses, 1720–1723*. Edited by Wilson H. Kimnach. The Works of Jonathan Edwards 10. New Haven, CT: Yale University Press, 1992.

———. *Sermons and Discourses, 1734–1738*. Edited by M. X. Lesser. The Works of Jonathan Edwards 19. New Haven, CT: Yale University Press, 2001.

———. *Sermons and Discourses, 1739–1742*. Edited by Harry S. Stout et al. The Works of Jonathan Edwards 22. New Haven, CT: Yale University Press, 2003.

———. *Sermons and Discourses, 1743–1758*. Edited by Wilson H. Kimnach. The Works of Jonathan Edwards 25. New Haven, CT: Yale University Press, 2006.

———. *Treatise on Grace and Other Posthumously Published Writings*. Edited by Paul Helm. Rev. ed. London: Clarke, 1988.

———. *The Works of Jonathan Edwards*. 2 vols. Edited by Edward Hickman. Edinburgh: Banner of Truth, 1974. First published 1834.

Elwood, Douglas J. *The Philosophical Theology of Jonathan Edwards*. New York: Columbia University Press, 1960.

Encyclopedia. "Ramtha." Encyclopedia, n.d. From *Encyclopedia of Occultism and Parapsychology*. https://www.encyclopedia.com/science/encyclopedias-almanacs-transcripts-and-maps/ramtha.

Evans, Eifion. *Revival Comes to Wales: The Story of the 1859 Revival in Wales.* Bridgend, Wales: Evangelical Press of Wales, 1979.

Ferguson, Sinclair B. "Exegesis." In *The Preacher and Preaching: Reviving the Art in the Twentieth Century*, edited by Samuel T. Logan Jr., 192–211. Phillipsburg, NJ: P&R, 1986.

Ferguson, Sinclair B., et al., eds. *New Dictionary of Theology.* Downers Grove, IL: InterVarsity, 1988.

Fiering, Norman. *Jonathan Edwards's Moral Thought and Its British Context.* Jonathan Edwards Classic Studies. Chapel Hill: University of North Carolina Press, 1981.

Finney, Charles G. *Revivals of Religion.* London: Oliphants, 1943.

———. *Systematic Theology.* London: Tegg, 1851.

Flannery, Austin, OP, ed. *Vatican Council II: The Basic Sixteen Documents; Constitutions, Decrees, Declaration; A Completely Revised Translation in Inclusive Language.* Northport, NY: Costello, 1996.

Frame, John M. "Ethics, Preaching, and Biblical Theology." *IIIM Magazine Online* 1 (May 10–16, 1999). https://thirdmill.org/magazine/article.asp/link/joh_frame^PT.Frame.Ethics_Preaching_BT.html/at/Ethics,%20Preaching,%20and%20Biblical%20Theology.

Gaffin, Richard. B., Jr. *Reformed Hermeneutics.* Lecture series, Home Missions Training Conference (OPC), Camp Geneva, Holland, MI, May 16–19, 1998. 3 cassettes. Available from the OPC Committee on Home Missions and Church Extension, 607 N. Easton Rd., Bldg. E, Box P, Willow Grove, PA 19090-0920.

Gordon, Henry. *Channeling into the New Age: The "Teachings" of Shirley MacLaine and Other Such Gurus.* Detroit: Prometheus, 1988.

Green, John Richard. *A Short History of the English People.* London: Folio, 1874.

Greidanus, Sidney. *Sola Scriptura: Problems and Principles in Preaching Historical Texts.* Eugene, OR: Wipf & Stock, 2001.

Groothuis, Douglas R. *Revealing the New Age Jesus: Challenges to Orthodox Views of Christ.* Westmont, IL: InterVarsity, 1990.

———. *Unmasking the New Age.* Special ed. Westmont, IL: InterVarsity, 1986.

Gundry, Stanley N., et al. *Four Views on Salvation in a Pluralistic World.* Grand Rapids: Zondervan Academic, 1996.

Gunton, Colin E. *The One, the Three and the Many: God, Creation and the Culture of Modernity; The 1992 Bampton Lectures.* Cambridge: Cambridge University Press, 1993.

Gura, Philip F. "Lost and Found: Recovering Edwards for American Literature." In *Jonathan Edwards at 300: Essays on the Tercentenary of His Birth*, edited by Harry S. Stout et al., 86–97. Oxford: University Press of America, 2005.

Halévy, Elie. *A History of the English People, 1830–1841.* Translated by E. I. Watkin. London: Fisher Owen, 1927.

Herbert, Edward. *De Veritate, prout distinguitur a revelatione, a verisimili, a possibili, et a falso* [On truth, as distinguished from revelation, probability, possibility, and falsehood]. Paris: N.p., 1624.

Hick, John. *God and the Universe of Faiths.* London: Macmillan, 1973.

Hine, Stuart K. "How Great Thou Art." In *Trinity Hymnal*, #44. Suwanee, GA: Great Commission, 1990.

"In Memoriam A.H.H." Wikipedia, last updated Mar. 18, 2024. https://en.wikipedia.org/wiki/In_Memoriam_A.H.H.

Irons, Lee. "Redemptive-Historical Preaching." *Kerux* 16 (Sept. 2001) 40–45.

John Paul II, Pope. *Redemptor Hominis*. Washington, DC: United States Catholic Conference, 1979.

Jones, Owen. *Some of the Great Preachers of Wales*. London: Passmore & Alabaster, 1886.

Jones, Peter. *The Gnostic Empire Strikes Back: An Old Heresy for the New Age*. Phillipsburg, NJ: P&R, 1992.

Keats, John. "Ode on a Grecian Urn." Poetry Foundation, n.d. https://www.poetryfoundation.org/poems/44477/ode-on-a-grecian-urn.

Keble, John. *National Apostasy*. London: Mowbray & Co., 1833.

Krabbendam, Hendrik. "Hermeneutics and Preaching." In *The Preacher and Preaching: Reviving the Art in the Twentieth Century*, edited by Samuel T. Logan Jr., 212–45. Phillipsburg, NJ: P&R, 1986.

Lemay, J. A. Leo. "Rhetorical Strategies in 'Sinners in the Hands of an Angry God' and 'Narrative of the Late Massacres in Lancaster County.'" In *Benjamin Franklin, Jonathan Edwards, and the Representation of American Culture*, edited by Barbara B. Oberg and Harry S. Stout, 186–203. New York: Oxford University Press, 1993.

Lloyd-Jones, D. Martyn. *Preaching and Preachers*. 40th anniv. ed. Grand Rapids: Zondervan, 2012.

———. *The Puritans: Their Origins and Their Successors; Addresses Delivered at the Puritan Studies and Westminster Conferences, 1959–1978*. Edinburgh: Banner of Truth, 2014.

———. *Revival*. Wheaton, IL: Crossway, 1987.

Machen, Gresham. *Christianity and Liberalism*. New York: Macmillan, 1923.

Marcel, Pierre. *The Relevance of Preaching*. Grand Rapids: Baker, 1963.

Marsden, George M. *Jonathan Edwards: A Life*. New Haven, CT: Yale University Press, 2003.

McClymond, Michael J. *Encounters with God: An Approach to the Theology of Jonathan Edwards*. Religion in America. New York: Oxford University Press, 1998.

Melton, J. Gordon. *New Age Encyclopedia*. Detroit: Gale, 1990.

Miller, Perry. *Jonathan Edwards*. New York: Sloane, 1949.

———. *The New England Mind: The Seventeenth Century*. Cambridge, MA: Harvard University Press, 1983.

Murray, Iain H. *D. Martyn Lloyd-Jones*. 2 vols. Edinburgh: Banner of Truth, 1990.

———. *Revival and Revivalism: The Making and Marring of American Evangelicalism, 1750–1858*. Edinburgh: Banner of Truth, 1994.

Murray, John. *Collected Writings*. 4 vols. Edinburgh: Banner of Truth, 1983.

Newman, John Henry. *Apologia pro Vita Sua*. London: Sheed and Ward, 1945.

———. *The Development of Christian Doctrine*. London: Sheed and Ward, 1960.

———. "Remarks on Certain Passages in the Thirty-Nine Articles." Anglican History, n.d. Tract 90. http://anglicanhistory.org/tracts/tract90/introduction.html.

Newsome, David. *Two Classes of Men: Platonism and English Romantic Thought*. London: Murray, 1974.

———. *The Parting of Friends: A Study of the Wilberforces and Henry Manning*. Cambridge, MA: Belknap, 1966.

Orr, J. Edwin. *The Light of the Nations: Evangelical Renewal and Advance in the Nineteenth Century*. Advance of Christianity through the Centuries. Eugene, OR: Wipf & Stock, 2006.

Owen, John. *Hebrews: The Epistle of Warning*. Grand Rapids: Kregel, 1977.

Packer, J. I., ed. *1960–1962*. Vol. 2 of *Puritan Papers*. Phillipsburg, NJ: P&R, 2001.

Pelikan, Jaroslav. *The Emergence of the Catholic Tradition (100–600)*. Vol. 1 of *The Christian Tradition: A History of the Development of Christian Doctrine*. Chicago: University of Chicago Press, 1975.

Pollitt, Herbert J. *The Inter-Faith Movement: New Age Enters the Church*. Edinburgh: Banner of Truth, 1996.

Protestant Episcopal Church in the United States of America. "Articles of Religion." Anglicans Online, 1801; last updated May 23, 2017. http://anglicansonline.org/basics/thirty-nine_articles.html.

Reardon, Bernard. *Religious Thought in the Reformation*. London: Longman, 1981.

———. *Religious Thought in the Victorian Age*. London: Longman, 1980.

Ridderbos, Herman. *Paul: An Outline of His Theology*. Translated by John Richard de Witt. Grand Rapids: Eerdmans, 1975.

Ryle, J. C. *Five English Reformers*. Edinburgh: Banner of Truth, 1960.

Shakespeare, William. *Hamlet, Prince of Denmark*. Shakespeare Online, Feb. 20, 2010. https://shakespeare-online.com/plays/hamlet_2_2.html.

Shedd, W. G. T. *A History of Christian Doctrine*. 2 vols. Minneapolis: Klock and Klock, 1978.

———. *Homiletics and Pastoral Theology*. New York: Scribner & Co., 1867.

Smeaton, George. *The Doctrine of the Holy Spirit*. Edinburgh: Banner of Truth, 1974.

Spurgeon, Charles Haddon. *Lectures to My Students*. New York: Carter and Brothers, 1890.

Stonehouse, Ned B. *J. Gresham Machen: A Biographical Memoir*. Edinburgh: Banner of Truth, 2019.

Stott, John. *Evangelical Anglicans and the ARCIC Final Report: An Assessment and Critique*. Bramcote, Eng.: Grove, 1982.

———. *The Preacher's Portrait: Some New Testament Word Studies*. Grand Rapids: Eerdmans, 2016.

Taylor, John. *The Scripture Doctrine of Original Sin Proposed to Free and Candid Examination*. London: Wilson, 1740.

Taylor, Justin. "The Holy Spirit's Hidden Floodlight Ministry." Gospel Coalition, Sept. 21, 2010. https://www.thegospelcoalition.org/blogs/justin-taylor/the-holy-spirits-hidden-floodlight-ministry/.

Thomas, Geoffrey. "Powerful Preaching." In *The Preacher and Preaching: Reviving the Art in the Twentieth Century*, edited by Samuel T. Logan Jr., 369–96. Phillipsburg, NJ: P&R, 1986.

Tillotson, John. *The Works of Dr. John Tillotson, Late Archbishop of Canterbury*. Edited by M. A. Birch. 10 vols. London: Dove, 1820.

Toon, Peter. *Evangelical Theology, 1833–1856: A Response to Tractarianism*. London: Marshall, Morgan & Scott, 1979.

Townsend, Harvey G. *The Philosophy of Jonathan Edwards: From His Private Notebooks* Eugene, OR: University of Oregon Press, 1955.

Tracy, Patrick. *The Great Awakening: A History of the Revival of Religion in the Time of Whitefield and Edwards*. Edinburgh: Banner of Truth, 1976.

Trimp, C. *Preaching and the History of Salvation: Continuing an Unfinished Discussion*. Translated by Nelson D. Kloosterman. Scarsdale, NY: Westminster, 1996.

Vidler, Alec R. *The Church in an Age of Revolution: 1789 to the Present Day.* Harmondsworth, Eng.: Penguin, 1962.

Vos, Geerhardus. "The Idea of Biblical Theology as a Science and as a Theological Discipline." Biblical Studies Ministries International, May 8, 1894. http://www.bsmi.org/download/vos/BiblicalTheology.pdf.

———. *The Pauline Eschatology.* Eastford, CT: Martino, 2023.

Wells, David F. *Revolution in Rome.* London: Tyndale, 1973.

Wordsworth, William. "The Tables Turned." Poetry Foundation, n.d. https://www.poetryfoundation.org/poems/45557/the-tables-turned.

www.ingramcontent.com/pod-product-compliance
Lightning Source LLC
Chambersburg PA
CBHW060339100426
42812CB00003B/1047
* 9 7 8 1 6 6 6 7 7 6 2 9 4 *